AIR BATTLE FOR
MOSCOW
1941–1942

AIR BATTLE FOR
MOSCOW
1941–1942

DMITRY DEGTEV AND DMITRY ZUBOV

AIR WORLD

AIR WORLD

AIR BATTLE FOR MOSCOW, 1941–1942

First published in Great Britain in 2021 by
Air World
An imprint of
Pen & Sword Books Ltd
Yorkshire – Philadelphia

ISBN 978 1 52677 446 0

A CIP catalogue record for this book is available from the British Library.

Typeset by SJmagic DESIGN SERVICES, India.
Printed and bound in the UK by CPI Group (UK) Ltd, Croydon, CR0 4YY.

Pen & Sword Books Limited incorporates the imprints of Atlas, Archaeology,
Aviation, Discovery, Family History, Fiction, History, Maritime, Military, Military
Classics, Politics, Select, Transport, True Crime, Air World, Frontline Publishing, Leo
Cooper, Remember When, Seaforth Publishing, The Praetorian Press, Wharncliffe
Local History, Wharncliffe Transport, Wharncliffe True Crime and White Owl.

For a complete list of Pen & Sword titles please contact

PEN & SWORD BOOKS LIMITED
47 Church Street, Barnsley, South Yorkshire, S70 2AS, England
E-mail: enquiries@pen-and-sword.co.uk
Website: www.pen-and-sword.co.uk

Or
PEN AND SWORD BOOKS
1950 Lawrence Rd, Havertown, PA 19083, USA
E-mail: Uspen-and-sword@casematepublishers.com
Website: www.penandswordbooks.com

Contents

Preface

Air Battle for Moscow is the first detailed description of an unknown air battle of the Second World War. In it Hitler's Luftwaffe opposed 'Stalin's Falcons' – the elite 6th Air Defence Fighter Corps (IAK PVO).

The battle began with flights of long-range reconnaissance aircraft, which photographed Moscow and the Kremlin – the residence of the 'Red Dictator' Stalin. On 22 July 1941, by orders of the Führer, Operation 'Clara Zetkin' – air attacks on Moscow – began. Known for their devastating air raids on Warsaw, Rotterdam, Belgrade, Athens, London, Coventry and other British cities, the battle-hardened Luftwaffe received a new target – 'the capital of Bolshevism'.

In October 1941, Operation 'Typhoon' and the battle for Moscow began. According to Hitler's plan, it was to be the 'last offensive', after which the Nazi dictator intended to complete the seizure of the Mediterranean, Britain and finally the whole world. The book presents new facts about this major battle and describes in detail the actions of aviation on both sides. The authors are not limited to air battles: they describe the lives of people during the war, anti-Soviet riots in Moscow, and the bloodthirsty and inhuman details of Stalin's regime. The book tells of the tragic fate of German pilots in Russian captivity, and the adventures of those who were able to survive and escape from their executioners. The confrontation between the two totalitarian regimes in the context of the air war is one of the subjects of this book.

The authors debunk typical Russian myths such as: over Moscow the power of the German bomber force was broken; 'Russian fighter pilots were the best'; and the anti-aircraft defence of Moscow was 'the most powerful in the world' and better than that of London.

However, the narrative is also a documentary chronicle. It contains a complete and accurate chronology of the air raids on Moscow, a detailed account of the operations of Russian aviation during the German offensive on Moscow, the counter-offensive of the Russian troops in the winter of 1941/42 and the first battle for Rzhev. The authors have also collected complete information about the losses of the Luftwaffe in the Moscow area.

In addition, the book is produced in a style traditional for the authors, reflecting their 20 years of writing experience. The text focuses not only on documents and 'dry' facts. The book is based on a bright, emotional, exciting description of the events that took place on the ground and in the air, the experience of the war through the eyes of many of its participants. Therefore this book is designed not only for professionals and aviation enthusiasts, but will also be of interest an unlimited number of other readers. This is both a documentary chronicle of action and drama.

The book provides unique details of the battle of Moscow, based on archival documents, scientific research, eyewitness accounts and other sources that the authors have collected for many years. The authors would like to express their gratitude for the help and assistance provided by the military historian Sergey Bogatyrev.

Chapter 1

Operation 'Clara Zetkin': Strategic Operation or Adventurism?

According to the plan of Operation 'Barbarossa', the capital of the Soviet Union, Moscow, was one of the main objectives. However, it was located far from the border, so initially only the Luftwaffe could reach it.

As early as 22 June 1941 a Ju 88 D reconnaissance aircraft of the 1st *Staffel* Aufkl.Gr.Ob.d.L. (also known as 'Group Rowehl') flew to this huge city and from an altitude of 10,000m (33,000ft) took the first aerial photographs. As the weather was clear and the sun was shining brightly, the Russians didn't even notice the small shiny point in the sky.

At this time, the 24th Air Defence Fighter Division (24th IAD PVO), which was tasked with the defence of Moscow, had 278 fighters. Most of them were old I-16s, which German pilots had first encountered in 1936 in the sky over Madrid. New Yak-1s, MiG-3s and LaGG-3s had only just been adopted, while the quality of this equipment was bad. However, in the future, fighter aircraft on the defence of Moscow was rapidly strengthened. The 24th IAD PVO was reorganized into the 6th Air Defence Fighter Corps (6th IAK PVO), which immediately added a few regiments. The city was the home of the Soviet government and Joseph Stalin, so its protection was given great importance.

The 24th IAD PVO, 22 June 1941

Regiment	Airfield	Aircraft	Numbers
11th IAP	Kubinka	Yak-1	38
16th IAP	Lyubertsy	I-16	51
		MiG-3	16
		Yak-1	10
24th IAP	Inyutino	I-16	25
		LaGG-3	13
27th IAP	Klyn	I-16	29
		MiG-3	7

Regiment	Airfield	Aircraft	Numbers
34th IAP	Lipitsy	I-16	25
		MiG-3	18
120th IAP	Alferovo	I-153	46
		Total	278

On 26 June a Ju 88 D-1 of 4.(F)/Ob.d.L. (pilot Oberleutenant Cornelius Noel, navigator Oberleutenant Josef Bisping), made a second reconnaissance flight over Moscow. The sky was again clear that day, and the crew could clearly see all areas of the huge city. On the central streets and squares, Noel and Bisping could even make out the trolleybuses and trams travelling along them. The Kremlin and Red Square were also clearly visible. They photographed several districts of Moscow, as well as anti-aircraft batteries around the city. The pilots saw Soviet fighters take off, but none of them was able to gain enough altitude.

On 2 July Ju 88 D-2 W. Nr. 0857 'F6+NH' of 1st *Staffel* Aufkl.Gr.122 (1.(F)/122) did not return from its flight to Moscow, though its crew managed to cross the front line and reach German units.

On 7 July the Ju 88 D-1 of Oberleutenants Noel and Bisping of 4.(F)/ Ob.d.L. conducted a second survey of Moscow, taking high-quality images of the whole city, including Red Square and the Kremlin. Subsequently, these photos were used to prepare the first massive raids.

On 15 July, Russian fighters were sent to patrol along the Moscow– Kalinin, Moscow–Rzhev and Moscow–Vyazma railway lines. At 13.00 Ju 88 D '6M+DM' (Unteroffizier Richard Läver) of 4.(F)/11 passed over the centre of the city three times at 6,500m (21,000ft). At 14.23 an LaGG-3 element of the 233rd IAP (Captain Kopytin, Lieutenants Prohaev and Belov) took off to intercept. Only Belov was able to attack the target 25km (15.5 miles) south-west of Serpukhov. However, after two attempts, he lost the enemy. Kopytin and Prohaev never returned to base. Russian observers on the ground saw the fighters pursue the Ju 88, but then they mysteriously disappeared.

By 18 July aerial photographs of Moscow taken by reconnaissance aircraft were on the table of the Chief of the General Staff of the German Army Generaloberst Franz Halder. They showed 'very large enterprises with wide access roads'. The pilots reported strong anti-aircraft defences and a large number of barrage balloons.

On 19 July, Adolf Hitler signed Directive OKH No. 33, which, among other things, provided for an air attack on Moscow. The first raid on the Soviet capital was scheduled for 21 July. It was the first major strategic operation on the Eastern Front, codenamed 'Clara Zetkin', after a founder of the German Communist Party. The Nazi leadership believed that the bombing of Moscow would become a 'people's disaster' and 'accelerate the catastrophe of the Russians'.

Note that the main supporter of the raids on the capital of the USSR was the commander of VIII *Fliegerkorps* General Wolfram von Richthofen. He had a cruel and oppressive character and had a lust for the destruction of cities. Since the Spanish Civil War, Richthofen had considered such methods to be extremely effective. Massive air attacks on Warsaw, Rotterdam and Belgrade really demoralized the government and 'accelerated the collapse' of Poland, Holland and Yugoslavia. The sight of burning ruins and thousands of corpses gave Richthofen extraordinary pleasure, as he repeatedly wrote in his diary. Reichsmarschall Göring supported the idea more for reasons of 'prestige': 'By itself, the attack on the capital of Bolshevism will be a symbolic act.' Another point of view was that of the commander of *Luftflotte* 2, Generalfeldmarschall Albert Kesselring. He did not want to risk the crews, whose fate if a plane was shot down over Russian territory would be a cause serious concern. And the Luftwaffe at that time simply did not have the strength to carry out large raids on such a large target.

By the time of the attack on the Soviet Union, 673 twin-engined bombers were concentrated in the East (411 Ju 88s, 215 He 111s and 47 Do 17s). In France and the Mediterranean at that time there were only twelve *Luftgruppen*. During the first month of the operation, the bombers mainly carried out tactical tasks to support the offensive, attacking bridges, railways, columns of troops and artillery batteries. At the same time, many *Staffelen* suffered serious losses, with some aircraft being lost for technical reasons. It was not possible to use the aircraft from the northern and especially the southern parts of the front, where there were constant fierce battles.

Since there were no available reserves, elite and specialized air groups were brought to the airfields in East Prussia and Eastern Poland:

- KG 4 'General Wever' (fifty-eight He 111s, forty-five operational), which specialized in attacks on particularly important, distant point targets, as well as the laying of sea mines;
- III./KG 26 (twenty-nine He 111s, twenty-one operational), which specialized in attacks on naval bases and ships;
- KGr. 100 'Wiking' (twelve He 111s, ten operational), a 'pathfinder' group;
- I./KG 28 (twenty He 111, fourteen operational), based at Bardufoss airfield in Norway, the first land-based torpedo-bomber group.

The Luftwaffe had no airfields for twin-engined bombers near the front lines. Air raids on Moscow had to be launched from airfields located in East Prussia and Western Belarus, 800–1,000km (500–620 miles) from the target, at the limit of range of the bombers. The aircraft could only carry a minimal bomb load, and in the old Do 17Zs of III./KG 3 no more than 500kg (1,100lbs). Operation 'Clara Zetkin' was more adventure and hooliganism than serious activity.

On 20 July, Kesselring held a briefing with his commanders for the upcoming 'historical' air strike. Feldwebel Ludwig Hawighorst of I./KG 28, recalled:

> On the eve of the attack on the Russian capital at the Terespol airfield, where there were two of our squadrons, Generalfeldmarschall Kesselring arrived. He addressed the crews:
>
> 'My aviators! You managed to bomb England, where you had to overcome heavy anti-aircraft fire, rows of barrage balloons, and repel fighter attacks. And you did a great job. Now your target is Moscow. It will be much easier. If the Russians have anti-aircraft guns, the few they have will not give you trouble, as well as few searchlights. They do not have barrage balloons and do not have night fighter aircraft.'

However, some pilots recalled Kesselring's address differently. In particular, according to the memories of the crews of KG 53 'Legion Condor', at the briefing they were told that the Russians would desperately defend their capital and strong air defences were to be expected.

At 10.00 on 21 July, the commander of II *Fliegerkorps*, General Bruno Lorzer, briefed the commanders of *Kampfgeschwaderen*, identifying the main objectives of the first attack, as well as the number of aircraft, departure times and flight routes. After that, briefing of *Staffeln* commanders and navigators began.

The pilots of KG 53 'Legion Condor', who were to make the 'big attack' on Moscow, were to be found in tents near the airfield, where they were sheltering from the unusual heat and Russian mosquitoes under mosquito nets. The commander of the 1st *Staffel*, Oberfeldwebel Willy Haug, recalled:

> It was the afternoon of Sunday. The crews were in their tents. The sun literally burned us here, on the Russian land. This was July 21, 1941 at our air base Minsk-Dubinskaya. All day in our

tent city solemn silence reigned. We listen to the concert on demand on the radio, which reminds us of home.

At noon, we were visited by the group commander Oberstleutnant Kaufmann, who announced to us that something important would begin today . . .

'Readiness No. 3' was announced, which meant that the flight would follow in a few hours. After that, the pilots began to prepare for the flight: putting on their bombers' parachutes, headsets and a supply of water. Haug began to study the maps and the flight route. Meanwhile, flight engineer Hannes Dunfelder cooked roasted potatoes for the whole crew. This idyllic picture: naked pilots dining on the grass and bombers peacefully standing on the airfield was a strong contrast with what was soon to be happen.

Willy Haug and his crew were having dinner, the signal 'Readiness No. 2' sounded at the airfield, which meant that the raid would start in about half an hour. The pilot continued his story:

As soon as we had had dinner, the squadron commander Hauptmann Allmendinger came and announced that we were going to have a night attack as part of a large raid on Moscow (Clara Zetkin) . . . Soon we are running to the airfield. Unteroffizier Retchek reports that the plane is ready to go. My crew and I have been flying since the beginning of the war (Poland, France) and have become a friendly team. We can rely on each other 100 per cent. We are the first to taxi to the start. We glance at the clock and begin. The engines roar and our He 111 'A1+AB' rolls on the runway.

The operation began at 18.00 Berlin time (20.00 Moscow time), with 195 bombers taking part. Willy Haug continued his story:

Smolensk is behind us. We're flying along the highway that leads to Moscow. Fly via Vyazma. Our He 111 shapes its course to the east over the wide Russian plains . . .Our military experience gives us some degree of confidence, however we are always attentive and carefully perform our work. With both eyes we look around the sky in search of enemy fighters. But so far we only see a beautiful sunset.

Other crews had similar experiences. Ludwig Hawighorst recalled: 'Our He 111 '1T+IK' went to Hellman's *Staffel*. The burning Smolensk was a good navigation reference point. The Smolensk–Moscow road could be seen as a clear white streak.'

At 21.58, around sunset, Moscow air defence headquarters received a report of a large group of planes approaching Moscow. Readiness 'No. 1' was declared. At 22.10, targets approached the searchlight zone, and an air-raid warning was sounded in the Red capital. The night was clear and the air temperature was 15–20°C.

At that time, there were 1,044 anti-aircraft guns, 336 machine-gun positions, 618 searchlights and 124 barrage balloons for the defence of Moscow. The basis of the Russian anti-aircraft artillery was the Model 1931 76mm gun and the '52-K' 85mm gun. The first anti-aircraft gun fired shells weighing 6.5kg (14.3lbs) to a height of up to 9,000m (29,500ft). For the second anti-aircraft gun, seven types of shells were developed, but for shooting at aircraft mainly anti-aircraft fragmentation shell weighing 9.5kg (21lbs) with a remote T-5 fuse. The explosive charge of the projectile

37mm anti-aircraft gun on the roof of a high-rise building in the centre of Moscow

MiG-3 fighters on a dirt airfield

consisted of 660–740g (145–163lbs) of TNT. In addition, it was equipped with a special device, which created a bright light flash and a thick brown smoke cloud when it exploded. For shooting at low-flying and diving planes there was the automatic 37mm '61-K' cannon with a rate of fire of about sixty rounds per minute. It fired fragmentation-tracer shells weighing 0.7kg (1.87lbs). In 1940 the 25mm '72-K' cannon was adopted. There were also many anti-aircraft guns dating back to the First World War, as well as Finnish Bofors and Oerlikons captured during the 'Winter War' of 1939–40.

In the 6th IAK PVO, there were nearly 500 fighters, including 170 I-16s, 127 MiG-3s, 91 Yak-1s, 70 I-153s and 37 LaGG-3s. However, it was better equipped to deal with daylight raids, as there were few night fighters.

'In front of us in the dark stretched Moscow'

First to appear over the city were the 'pathfinder' He 111s of KGr. 100, which dropped photoflash bombs and incendiary bombs on it, marking the target for the subsequent bombers. The facilities and sectors of the capital were divided between the *Geschwaderen*. KG 55 'Greif' was to bomb the Kremlin, the Central Office of the Communist Party and the Moscow hydroelectric power station; KG 53 'Legion Condor' was to attack the Belorussky railway station, one of the aircraft factories, the central airfield and the 'Clara Zetkin' factory; while KG 4 'General Wever' was to strike military targets in the western and northern sectors of the capital. The bombers were flying over the city at an altitude of 2,000–4,000m (6,500–13,000ft) and below. Many of them were illuminated by searchlights, and then fired on by flak and attacked by fighters. The surprise was a lot of barrage balloons. Willy Haug described what happened:

> In front of us in the dark stretched Moscow. Altimeter shows a height of 1200m. The defence proved weaker than we expected. The first searchlights on the outskirts of Moscow. They're like fingers through a dark night. However, the beams of the searchlights didn't affect us . . . I counted somewhere between 50 and 100 lights. This is not what we expected, and what we were told about at the briefing before the flight, but I still hate this crowd of beams . . . And what is in this front of us? Searchlights brightly illuminate some aircraft. Several beams caught a plane. Taking the binoculars, I see that it is an He 111 with our comrades on board. He makes wild evasive manoeuvres to escape the clutches of the 'lamps'. But in vain.
>
> Meanwhile, we climbed to 1700m and reached the outskirts of Moscow. Below we see terrible fires and anti-aircraft fire of all calibres. Here one searchlight touches us, but soon loses us. Anti-aircraft guns are firing at us. Front, left and right anti-aircraft shells explode very close.

The Russian anti-aircraft gunners were only firing barrages, not aiming at individual illuminated aircraft, just firing into one or other sector of the sky. The huge number of shell bursts at different altitudes made a strong impression, particularly on inexperienced pilots and on those watching the 'fireworks' from the ground. V.P. Pronin, in 1941 the chairman of the Moscow Soviet of People's Deputies, recalled:

> From the observation post, located on one of the towers of the city centre, we could see how a solid wall of fire blocked the path of enemy aircraft. They rushed, leaving the zone of defeat part

8

to the north, and part to the south, but there, it would seem, in total darkness in front of them instantly there was a flurry of fire.

Like all the aircraft of the group, the underside of Willy Haug's He 111 'A1+AB' had been painted black before the raid on Moscow. Haug believed that it was because of this that the searchlights could not catch him. When dropping bombs on the target, the pilot increased speed and put the plane into a dive. The speed increased to 500km/h (310mph), and the engines began to literally 'whine'. Dropping to 300m (984ft), the bomber flew directly over the roofs of the Moscow houses. After five minutes of such manoeuvres, the experienced Haug turned the plane around and headed west.

'Soon we saw 10 to 20 searchlights creating a light field,' recalled Ludwig Hawighorst.

> Attempts to get around it failed: there were a lot of lights on the left and right. I ordered to increase altitude to 4500m and the crew to put on oxygen masks. Suddenly Russian anti-aircraft artillery opened fire on our plane. Fortunately, they were shooting inaccurately, but the density of shell bursts was high.
>
> When our plane flew close to Moscow, we saw a Ju 88 of another unit – he was preparing to dive on the city. We were going to get rid of our bomb cargo. At this time there was the excited voice of the radio operator:
>
> 'Attention, balloons!'
>
> I ordered the bombs to be dropped, and as soon as we turned back, the radio operator reported the approach of an enemy fighter. A Russian night fighter (which should not have existed) attacked us from above on the left. The radio operator opened fire, and the mechanic immediately joined him. Then the fighter was hit, caught fire and went into a dive. It was the first fighter to be shot down by our crew.

Despite the fact that the raid did not go quite according to plan, most of the German crews completed the mission. During the bombing of Moscow 1,166 fires were started, including more than 100 at military facilities. Aircraft plant No. 1, the 'Serp i molt' (Hammer and Sickle) metallurgical factory, the 'Dynamo' factory and the 'Tryokhgornaya' manufactory were damaged and the Ugreshskaya chemical plant, the 'Moscow ruberoid' plant and railway depots and workshops were completely destroyed.

Despite heavy anti-aircraft fire, Major Ernst Kuhl's II./KG 55 hit the Kremlin. One SC500 bomb hit the Grand Kremlin Palace, broke through the ceiling in the St. George Hall (used today by the Russian president to host guests), buried itself in the floor and did not explode. A second bomb fell in the Taynitsky garden, while B-1E incendiary bombs fell in different parts of the Kremlin.

Another important target was the Moscow hydroelectric power station (MOGES) which was also damaged. Water, gas and electric lines were destroyed in the city. There were huge fires at the Belorussky railway

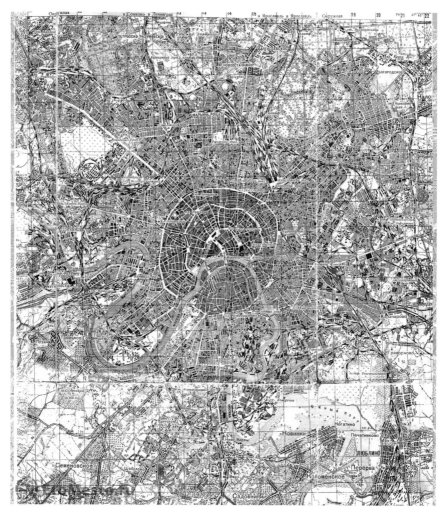

Map of Moscow in 1940

station, with wagons loaded with shells and fuel tanks exploding. 'We sigh with relief when we cross the front line,' Willy Haug wrote, completing his account of the first Moscow raid. 'After almost five hours of flight, we end up safely landing back at Minsk-Dubinskaya.'

A total of 104 tons of high-explosive bombs were dropped during the first raid on Moscow, including the latest SC 2500, as well as 46,000 incendiary bombs. According to Russian data, 150 people were killed and 650 wounded. 'Air raid on Moscow', Generaloberst Halder wrote in his diary. 'There were 200 planes. The latest 2.5-ton bombs were used in the bombing.'

The Russian anti-aircraft artillery fired 29,000 shells of all calibres, and claimed six aircraft shot down. The 6th IAK PVO carried out 173 sorties and claimed 12 aircraft shot down. Officially, the pilots were credited with only eight shared and individual victories.

- Junior Lieutenant Chulkov of the 41st IAP shot down an He 111 in the Istra district;
- Lieutenant Kukharenko shot down an He 111 near Golitsyno;
- Captain Konstantin Titenkov and Junior Lieutenants Bocach and Lapochkin of the 11th IAP shared two He 111s;
- Lieutenants Chensky and Chuikin of the 27th IAP shot down two Ju 88s in the Khimki district;
- Junior Lieutenant Lukyanchikov hit a Ju 88 in the Borovsk district.

There were other claims for downed aircraft. Britenkov's unit claimed a 'twin-engined bomber'. Politruk (Political Advisor) Kuznetsov reported that the aircraft was shot at near Istra, but he did not see where it fell.

The Russians claimed fourteen aircraft shot down, and the 'Soviet Information Bureau' (the main organ of propaganda in the Soviet Union) declared to the population that twenty-two aircraft had been shot down. In fact, the Luftwaffe lost only two bombers over Russian territory:

- The He 111 H-6 of Oberleutnant Harms, commander of 4./KG 55 'Greif', was hit by the MiG-3 test pilot Baicalov, then finished off by flak and fell on Moscow;
- The Do 17 Z-2 W. Nr. 3367 '5K+ET' of Leutnant K. Kuhn of 9./KG 3 was damaged by the test pilot Mark Gallay of the 2nd Separate Fighter Squadron. Kuhn was able to fly as far as Vitebsk, but was forced to land on Soviet territory. All four crew were captured.

Several aircraft were damaged, but were able to reach German-controlled territory. An He 111 H-5 of III./KG 26 crashed, and all four of pilot Leutnant Horst Ludwig's crew were killed, while Ju 88 A-5 W. Nr. 5282 of 6./KG 3 crashed at Boyary airport (near Minsk), all four of Ludwig Bricksus's crew being severely injured. The Russians' own losses were four fighters, but all of these were due to technical problems.

Preparing for the next raid on Moscow, the Luftwaffe changed its tactics. Flight altitude was increased so the bombers passed over the barrage balloons and at the limit of the searchlights, in order to reduce their effectiveness. In the second raid on the evening of 22 July, 115 aircraft participated. Usual Luftwaffe strategy was to use maximum force in the first strike, to exploit the element of surprise to cause maximum damage to the target, then use smaller numbers of aircraft to finish it off. But in this case, 'maximum damage' was impossible, given the size of the target and the number of bombers. '21.55. Enemy planes come from the west,' recorded the duty staff of the Russian air defences. 'Sectors are put at readiness No. 1. 22.05. The enemy approaches the border of the searchlight fields. The city declared "air alarm". The second raid by the enemy on Moscow.'

Raid on Moscow. Photo from *Life* magazine

Fires in Moscow after the bomb attack by Luftwaffe

This time, 98 tons of high-explosive bombs and 34,000 incendiaries were dropped on the city. Russian anti-aircraft fire was not as heavy as the previous night (only 6,340 rounds fired), so it was not much of a hindrance to the Germans. All the bombers passed over the city in formation and hit most of their targets. Sixty-three plants and factories and ninety-six houses were damaged by explosions and fires. The 'Sverdlov' factory, the Presnensky engineering work and the Gazoapparat plant, among others, suffered massive destruction. Damage to hydroelectric power station No. 1 stopped the Moscow tram system and disabled other important facilities. A high-explosive bomb penetrated the roof the engine room and hit the top of the dismantled turbine. Two others struck the overlap of the subway tunnel on the stretch 'Smolenskaya'–'Arbatskaya' and the overpass of the metro bridge. II./KG 55 again attacked the residence of Joseph Stalin – the Kremlin. The bombs hit in Red Square, one exploding in front of the Soviets' main shrine – Lenin's mausoleum. In fact the 'dweller' in the building was gone: in early July his preserved remains had been taken to Siberia. Seventy-six incendiary bombs fell in the grounds of the Kremlin. Casualties in the second raid were greater than in the previous one: 213 Moscow residents were killed and 353 seriously injured.

Russian anti-aircraft artillery reported three downed aircraft. Fighters of the 6th IAK PVO carried out 202 sorties and claimed four downed bombers. Russian pilots said they saw and attacked four-engined 'FW 200' aircraft over Moscow!

In fact Luftwaffe lost only He-111 H-5 W. Nr. 3800 of 2./KG 28. It was damaged by anti-aircraft fire, but reached German territory and made an emergency landing near Baranovichy. The aircraft was completely wrecked, but the crew was unharmed.

'Fascist aims accurately'

On 23 July, the third air raid on Moscow took place. At 18.43, when surveys of damage and searches for bodies were still going on, the air-raid warning was again sounded in the city. But it was only a reconnaissance aircraft which photographed the results of the previous raid. At 20.05 the alert was cancelled, and the residents of Moscow began to go home. But at 21.30 it was reported that a group of German bombers had passed the city of Vyazma bearing 90° and heading for Moscow.

According to Soviet data, 180 aircraft took part in the third raid, some of which were identified by Russian observers on the ground as 'Do 215s'. In fact, 125 aircraft dropped 140 tons of bombs. Important military objectives were hit: aircraft factory No. 1, machine-building plant No. 4, plant No. 28, etc., and civilian targets were also damaged: the 'Vakhtangov' Theatre, the 'Mosfilm' film studio, the Univermag department store on Red Square and the Kremlin hospital.

The attack took place in heavy cloud cover, because of which the searchlights could not illuminate the aircraft, so the anti-aircraft artillery fired blindly. Over 20,000 shells were expended. Russian night fighters made 182 sorties and claimed four victories for the loss of five fighters. Russian pilots had problems flying at night. There were frequent accidents on landing, and some pilots could not find the airfield and were forced to bail out. The Luftwaffe suffered minimal losses. A single He 111 H-3 W. Nr. 6873 of the Stab./KG 53 'Legion Condor' suffered 70 per cent damage in an emergency landing at Orsha.

On 24 July, the staff of the 6th IAK PVO reported: 'The enemy lowered the intensity of raids due to the weariness of its personnel, large losses during raids and at home airfields.' At that time, when the Red Army was suffering defeats and disasters everywhere, Russian commanders constantly lied to

Destroyed houses on Arbat square. July 1941

Aerial photography of Kremlin, after decoding by German specialists. The photo shows that the Russians have made great efforts to change the appearance of the most important buildings. In order to make it difficult to identify these significant targets from the air, they even built several 'false' buildings. However, all the efforts of the Russians were in vain. The Germans easily identified and unmistakably marked all the targets they needed on the territory of the Kremlin on the aerial photograph.

Stalin and the people that 'things are going well' and 'victory is close'. In truth, the air defence of Moscow was weak. The Luftwaffe was able to cause major damage to the Red capital with only small forces while suffering minimal losses themselves.

Fighter Yak-1. The Soviets had high hopes for this plane, but they did not come true

6th IAK PVO pilots before night flight

16

In late July, the Wehrmacht launched an offensive on a huge front from the Baltic to the Black Sea, driving deeply into Russian territory. Panzer divisions everywhere required the support of the Luftwaffe. In this situation, most of the bombers switched to such missions, and it was decided to continue the air attacks on Moscow with only small groups and individual aircraft.

Here is how the war diary of the 1st Air Defence Corps described the fourth Luftwaffe raid on Moscow on the night of 25 July 25:

> 1.40. The troops are ordered to move to status No. 1. Enemy aircraft are heading 90°.
>
> 1.45. The city declared an air-alarm. The enemy aircraft approach the searchlight field.
>
> 3.30. Units to status No. 2. City cancels air-alarm. The fourth raid of the enemy repulsed.
>
> Fighter aircraft carried out 259 sorties for combat and patrols. Shot down five enemy aircraft type Ju 88, of which two were found, one burned all together with the crew, and of the remaining two captured three enemy air crew and all documentation. An I-16 of 34th IAP was shot down by our anti-aircraft artillery, Lieutenant Kabashov seriously injured. The plane crashed. 24th IAP: the LaGG-3 of Lieutenant Terentiev went into a tailspin and crashed.

During this raid on Moscow seven high-explosive bombs were dropped, and as a result house No. 24 on Bolshaya Kommunisticheskaya street was destroyed. The crew of He 111 H-5 W. Nr. 4250 'A1+HH' of 1./KG 53 'Legion Condor', which had been reported missing, were taken prisoner. On this day KG 53 lost another two bombers. He 111 H-5 W. Nr. 5592 of 9./KG 53 was shot down by anti-aircraft fire, but the crew was able to cross the front line. He 111 H-6 W. Nr. 4105 of 4./KG 53 crash-landed on the airfield at Orsha. All four of the crew (pilot Unteroffizier Ludwig Baron) were killed. But the exact circumstances of these losses have not been established.

On 25 July, the Red capital suffered its first daytime raid, during which 22 high-explosive and 100 incendiary bombs were dropped on the city. The tracks and platforms at the Moscow railway marshalling yards were destroyed, and a warehouse at a roofing material plant was burned down. The casualties were thirteen dead and twenty-six wounded. 'But we were in

hell – the fascist accurately aimed his bombs at the trains standing there,'
recalled V.R. Katkov, in 1941 the chief of the Moscow marshalling yard.

> At that moment Sasha Zharinov brought the train in from
> Lyubertsy, and I had to send him urgently to move damaged
> trains. There were human losses. Our deputy Dima Dmitriev, a
> young machinist, and machinists Osipov and Bulaev were killed.
> In the nearest houses the blast wave killed the inhabitants but
> the enemy's calculation to intimidate the Soviet people wasn't
> justified: not fear, but hatred rose up in us at this bloody terror.

During the day, the 6th IAK PVO carried out a record number of sorties –
507 – and claimed three downed aircraft. I./KG 28 and II./KG 3 'Blitz'
participated in the raid. A Ju 88 A-5 of 5./KG 3 sustained serious damage
from close bursts of anti-aircraft shells. The pilot Wilhelm Bender was
wounded by shrapnel in the back and left shoulder. The navigator and the
radio-operator panicked and bailed out of the damaged aircraft. However,
Bender was able to fly the plane alone and, having travelled a considerable
distance, made a belly landing at Orsha-zyud.

In a manner peculiar to Communists, the Russian air defence units
greatly exaggerated the scale of the raid and their own successes. The Soviet

Combustion German incendiary bomb

ЗАЖИГАТЕЛЬНУЮ БОМБУ ОПУСКАЙ В БОЧКУ С ВОДОЙ

Poster showing the way to extinguish an incendiary bomb

summary reported that the raid was made up of 120 aircraft in eight waves, but only six to eight of them managed to 'break through' to the city. This was the standard Russian procedure of lies and false reporting to Stalin, in order not to incur the wrath of the brutal dictator.

On 25 July two reconnaissance aircraft failed to return from flights over Moscow:

- Ju 88 A-5(F)[1] W. Nr. 0453 'F6+AO' flown by Feldwebel Martin of *Erganzungstaffel* Aufkl.Gr.122 crashed and exploded near Dorokhovo station;
- Ju 88 A-5(F) W. Nr. 0285 'F6+AK' flown by Leutnant Stukmann of 2.(F)/122 made an emergency landing in a forest clearing near Istra. Five days later, the plane was taken to Moscow and put on public display in the city centre.

---

1. The first mention in German documents of the modified Ju 88 D-1.

German aircraft Ju 88 A-5(F) W.Nr. 0285 'F6+AK' of 2.(F)/122 at Teatralnaya square in Moscow. The Russians found it in the forest and took it to the centre of Moscow for public display

Near Istra, these reconnaissance aircraft were intercepted and shot down by Russian fighters. The victories were gained by Lieutenant Kuzmenko and Lieutenant Mikhailov of the 41th IAP, and Captain Loginov and Lieutenant Vasilyev of the 11th IAP. Vasilyev's Yak-1 was shot down by rear-gun fire from the German aircraft, but the pilot bailed out safely. On the same day, He 111 H-6 'A1+KL' of 3./KG 53 was also lost in the Moscow area was also lost, probably shot down by I-153 pilots Lieutenants Shevchuk and Shtuchkin of the 120th IAP.

On the night of 26/27 July, sixty-five bombers made another raid on Moscow, as a result of which many plants and factories were hit: a shoe factory, the 'Dynamo' plant, factories No. 93 and No. 239 and ten houses. Thirty-one people were killed, and almost 300 injured or concussed. A direct hit completely destroyed the newly-built school building on the Zemskaya line. Three hundred people who were in the shelter in its basement were buried in the rubble. Despite the fire, the Russian rescue service (MPVO) personnel were able to quickly clear the rubble and save most of the people.

Soviet anti-aircraft artillery fired 34,000 rounds. Night fighters carried out eighty-nine sorties and claimed six victories, including four Ju 88s. Victories were recorded for Lieutenants Lepilin and Korovchenko of the 41st IAP, as well as Lieutenant Borovsky of the 120st IAP. Lepilin's fighter returned to base with numerous bullet holes in it. Russian pilots again used their aircraft 'one-time'. Three pilots were unable to land in the dark and bailed out. According to German data, during the raid only He 111 H-5 of III./KG 26 was lost.

At 22.13 on 28 July Russian ground observation posts (VNOS) again reported a group of German aircraft bearing 90° towards Moscow. Three minutes later sirens howled in the capital once again and the people rushed into the shelters and subway stations. This time 14 high-explosive and about 1,500 incendiary bombs were dropped on Moscow. Because of the cloudy weather, the crews dropped bombs without aiming accurately, so mostly houses were damaged. Explosions and fires destroyed nineteen houses, two shops and a printing works of the Moszhilstroy plant. Five people were killed, and seventy-nine were injured.

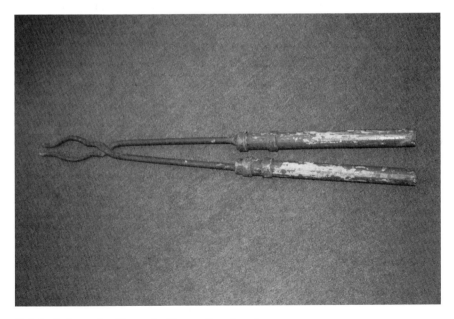

Original clamp for disposal of incendiary bombs

Fire trucks PMG-1 (brand GAZ)

Anti-aircraft artillery put up a powerful barrage, firing 33,000 rounds. Russian night fighters were active again and performed 131 sorties. The pilots claimed four aircraft shot down. According to German data, on this night only He 111 H-5 W. Nr. 4115 '1H+HS' of 8./KG 26 was hit, which crashed near the village of Golovino in the Istra district. Analysis of archival data suggests that most likely at 01.26 the bomber was rammed by the MiG-3 of Lieutenant Peter Eremeev of the 27th IAP. One of the crew members, flight engineer A. Zerabeck, bailed out and survived. The Russian pilot also bailed out and was awarded the highest Soviet decoration – Hero of the Soviet Union. But Eremeev never received it, since on 2 October he was reported missing over German territory . . .

For Russian and German pilots the most terrible fate was to be captured. When a plane was shot down over the UK, the Luftwaffe crew were doomed to stay in a PoW camp until the end of the war, but they were sure that they would survive. The same thing happened to the British and Americans when they were shot down over the Third Reich. However, on the Eastern Front everything was different. Red propaganda sought to inspire in soldiers 'devotion to the Motherland', and getting captured was considered shameful and a betrayal. By order of Stalin, the families of those who were captured were repressed and deprived of food. The mortality rate in German PoW camps was also very high. So for Russian pilots being captured was often worse than death.

Hitler's propaganda also taught soldiers that 'Russians were animals'. And in many ways it was true. Often German aircrew who had bailed out or made an emergency landing were immediately killed by local residents or angry Red Army soldiers. If the pilots made it to a prison camp, horrors and hardship were waiting for them there. In general, in the East, where there was a 'war to the death', the pilots had no guarantee that they would survive! Therefore, once in enemy territory, they first fled the landing site and hid, and then tried to get to the front line and reach their own troops. And many succeeded. Many areas of Russia were sparsely populated, and there were many forests and swamps to hide in. Zerabeck of 8./KG 26 was one of those who were lucky. He managed to escape, hide, and then reach German lines.

On the night of 31 July/1 August, in heavy cloud a small group of German aircraft carried out another air raid as part of Operation 'Clara Zetkin'. This time, the approach to the target was carried out from the south-east. An air-alarm was declared in the Russian capital at 22.43, but neither the searchlights nor the two scrambled night fighters were able to locate the bombers. The target of the attack was the state ball-bearing plant (GPZ-1), located in the south-east of Moscow. It was the main manufacturer of ball-bearings for the Russian aviation and tank industry.

The director of the plant A.A. Gromov recalled:

> In one of the last nights of July enemy aircraft dropped heavy high-explosive bombs on the plant. One of them fell somewhere near the main building. A deafening explosion followed, and all around was enveloped in acrid smoke. The blast destroyed one of the walls. A stream of water gushed out of the broken water pipes. We rushed to the site of the explosion. Under my feet crunched broken glass. A lifeless woman lay nearby. She was the first victim of the Nazi bombing. In those days we all became soldiers on the same front . . .

The workers' barracks and vegetable store located near the plant were also damaged by fires. One person was killed and twenty-nine others injured.

The Composition of the 6th IAK PVO, 31 July 1941

Regiment	Airfield	Aircraft	Numbers
11th IAP	Kubinka Jerschy	Yak-1	55
12th IAP	Vatulino	Yak-1	17
16th IAP	Lyubertsy Bykovo	I-16 MiG-3	21 42
24th IAP	Inyutina Spas-Lucchino	LaGG-3	27
27th IAP	Klin Kalinin	MiG-3 I-16	25 31
34th IAP	Vnukovo	MiG-3 I-16	27 30
120th IAP	Alferovo Kaluga	I-153	63
121th IAP	Chertanovo	Yak-1	19
176th IAP	Stepihino	I-16 I-153	15 5
177th IAP	Dubrovitsy	I-16	51
233th IAP	Tushino	MiG-3 LaGG-3 I-16	18 10 18
1 OAE[2]	Central Airfield of Moscow	MiG-3	9
2 OAE	Ramenskoye	MiG-3 I-153 I-16	6 4 2
		Total	495

During July, Russian fighters defending Moscow performed 8,052 sorties, including 1,015 at night, and claimed fifty-nine victories (forty-six Ju 88s, ten He 111s and three Do 215s). Russian pilots greatly exaggerated their success. Their own losses for the month were heavy: thirty-six fighters, seven pilots killed and fifteen wounded.

At 22.50 on 1 August once again an air alarm was declared in Moscow, which lasted until 02.00. Two high explosive and about 1,000 incendiary

---

2. OAE – Independent Air Squadron (Russian – ОАЭ).

bombs were dropped on the Molotovsky and Kalininsky districts of the city, which caused twenty-seven fires, and a direct hit destroyed a house. The anti-aircraft artillery fired 10,500 rounds, and night fighters made eighty-three sorties. No fighter pilot was able to establish visual contact with the bombers.

The next night in poor visibility a single aircraft reappeared in the Moscow area, but could not find the target. According to the Soviet side, bombs were not dropped on the city. During the night Russian fighters carried out ninety-nine sorties and reported two victories with one fighter lost. Over searchlight area No. 5 (north of Naro-Fominsk), pilots Alexandrov and Scherbina of the 34th IAP intercepted and attacked He 111 H-5 W. Nr. 4044 of 2./KG 53 'Legion Condor'. The bomber received heavy damage, but still limped back across the front line and crashed while attempting an emergency landing near the village of Dubinskaya (Minsk region). All five ofthe crew were killed.

On the night of 4 August, the Luftwaffe made its eleventh attack on Moscow, carried out by nine bombers. The air-raid alarm was sounded at 23:30 and lasted until 01.40. Thirty high-explosive and 1,000 incendiary bombs were dropped on the city. Fires broke out at eleven factories and

The destroyed Vakhtangov theatre in the centre of Moscow

MiG-3 fighters fly over the Kremlin

nine homes. According to the MPVO, twenty-three people were killed and ninety-seven injured.[3] As always, the command of the Russian 1st Air Defence Corps announced that the attack had been repelled. 'This, like all previous ones, was unsuccessful for the enemy,' reported the war diary. But the 6th IAK PVO had a really bad night. After performing fifty sorties, Russian pilots destroyed five of their own fighters. Lieutenant Aleksandrov of the 34th IAP and Lieutenant Kalyanov of the 419th IAP 'broke' their aircraft during landing, Lieutenant Bardin of the 34th IAP made a forced belly landing, and Lieutenant Gridin was killed when his engine failed and he crashed in a forest. Lieutenant Pavlov of the 420th IAP forgot to lower the undercarriage when landing. There were no interceptions of the enemy.

---

3. Soviet reports did not reflect the exact number of victims. They were compiled in a hurry, and then were not corrected later. There was no 'missing persons' column in them. Only the bodies found after the raid were taken into account.

OPERATION 'CLARA ZETKIN'

'We need to find the Red headquarters'

KG 53 'Legion Condor', which was based at Orsha, more often than others continued to carry out attacks on Moscow. On 4 August its bombers attacked a '*Sonderziel*' (special target), which was the aircraft factory No. 1 'Osoaviakhim'. All the incendiary bombs dropped by them fell in the grounds of the aircraft factory No. 32 located next to it, which produced aircraft weapons, and on the surrounding residential areas. The fire at the plant (in the boiler room and warehouses) burned until noon the next day, and was photographed by a Ju 88 D reconnaissance aircraft, flying over Moscow at 13.00.

According to Soviet data, this raid was 'successfully repulsed', although neither the anti-aircraft gunners, who fired 21,514 rounds, nor the night fighters claimed any victories. Only Lieutenant Seldyakov of the 34th IAP reported at 00.50 that he saw and attacked an unidentified aircraft in the area of Naro-Fominsk that dived away. The 6th IAK PVO suffered further losses due to accidents: three fighters from the 34th and 120th IAPs were destroyed.

On the night of 5/6 August He 111s of KG 53 carried out the thirteenth attack on Moscow, dropping six high explosive and 200 incendiary bombs. This time these experienced pilots missed, only two 'stone buildings' burned down, and there were no casualties among the population. Russian artillery put up a powerful barrage, firing off 21,084 rounds, and the 6th IAK PVO completed twenty-six sorties. Captain Nenashev of the 27th IAP in an I-16 twice attacked a bomber in the searchlight field, and Second Lieutenant Viktor Talalikhin of the 177th IAP, also flying an I-16, fired at enemy aircraft in the area of Vnukovo. However, none of the German bombers was damaged that night.

On the evening of 6 August, a group of KG 55 'Greif' crews received orders to carry out another air raid on Moscow. Alfred Strobel, who flew He 111 '1G+CC', was told that the target of the attack would be the central part of the city and the Kremlin, and he needed to fly to the target in the first wave of bombers. In addition, among the targets of the attack were military and administrative elements of the 'political centre of the Soviet Union'.

The flight over the river Berezina and Smolensk took place in dense cloud, and the German pilots even doubted that they would be able to find their objective. However, as soon as the He 111s approached Moscow, the clouds suddenly lifted and the Germans clearly saw the huge city.

'Our meteorologist was again pretty accurate in his predictions, predicting good visibility over the target,' recalled Alfred Strobel.

> We are flying over the dark silhouette of Moscow. We need to find a Red headquarters in a network of blocks and streets. Red gunners put before us an iron curtain of shells. Doesn't matter! We hit it!
>
> Now we are on the outskirts of the city. We are flying in the first wave. Three heavy incendiary bombs, which we are now going to drop, have a very great effect. They contain only a small amount of explosives to spray flammable liquid. Two major highways in Moscow lead from the western outskirts to the city centre and are good reference points. We know where the Kremlin is, we'll find the target that's designated in the mission. Even if we are over the boiling pot, and around the 'stream of vomit' [as German pilots called the tracer fire from light anti-aircraft weapons] and the beams of the searchlights.

Soon in front, right above the centre of Moscow between the barrage balloons, flashed the flares dropped by the pathfinders. 'Right now our planes dropped high-explosive bombs of a heavy calibre immediately followed by incendiary bombs for further damage,' Strobel wrote in his report. 'We turn around home, changing course, but we still have to go through the anti-aircraft barrage fire, which is meant for the next wave of German bombers.'

Strobel's *Staffel* managed to hit the Kremlin. Sixty-seven incendiary bombs fell within its grounds. In Moscow four factories and fifteen houses were damaged.

The weather that night was not the best: there was a heavy overcast, fog and haze, the visibility was 1–6km. The anti-aircraft artillery fired 18,153 rounds, a quarter of which were 37mm. They shot at the bombers approaching the Kremlin from the ground and from the roofs of tall buildings in the city centre: the 'Tchaikovsky' concert hall, the 'Moscow' hotel and houses on Gorky Street. Maxim anti-aircraft machine guns fired a total of 17,500 rounds of ammunition.

The 6th IAK that night performed 104 sorties and claimed seven victories. Russian pilots themselves damaged four of their own fighters in accidents, three of which were from the 27th IAP.

OPERATION 'CLARA ZETKIN'

Among the many pilots who took off that night was Lieutenant Victor Talalikhin of the 177th IAP, flying an I-16. Talalikhin was a typical 'Stalin's Falcon', as Russian pilots were called. At first he worked at a Moscow meat processing plant, then decided to become a pilot. In that era, it was a common thing. Thousands of boys and teenagers saw planes in the sky and dreamed of being in their cockpits. In the 1930s it was the pilots who were the heroes to follow. Young people in Soviet Russia had a choice: work without rest and leave in factories or hard work on collective farms. The factory workers received only a small salary, and collective farm workers did not receive any cash payment. The best way out of Stalin's slavery was to become a pilot. Pilots loved Stalin as they were paid a lot of money. Songs were sung about the pilots, and propaganda praised them. In 1937 Talalikhin entered the Borisoglebskaya Military Aviation School. During the Soviet-Finnish war of 1939–40, he made forty-seven flights and shot down a group of four Finnish aircraft. For this Talalikhin was awarded the Order of the Red Star.

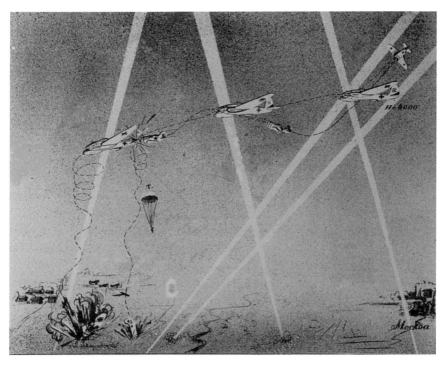

The original scheme of attack by Lieutenant Victor Talalikhin against He 111 H-5 '1H+PR' of 7./KG 26

29

The wreckage of He 111 H-5 '1H+PR' of 7./KG 26

More wreckage of He 111 H-5 '1H+PR' of 7./KG 26

When war with the Third Reich broke out Talalikhin was with the 177th IAP, defending Moscow. When the Luftwaffe raids began, he took off many times but each time returned without success. On Russian 'night fighters' there was no radar or even radio sets. Pilots had only good eyesight, moonlight and the searchlights to help them. When Talalikhin saw a bomber ahead of him on the night of 6/7 August, he was afraid to miss the chance and decided to ram it at 23.28. In the morning the wreckage was found near the village of Kuznechiki (Podolsk district). It was He 111 H-5 '1H+PR' of 7./KG 26. Of the crew, only the pilot, Feldwebel Rudolf Schik, survived to be captured by the Russians. Talalikhin's fighter crashed into the forest near the village of Mansurovo, and the pilot landed by parachute in the river to the north. The next day he was awarded the title of Hero of the Soviet Union.

Soviet propaganda highly praised Talalikhin. 'The fascist vulture was slain by Stalin's Falcon,' the press announced. The journalist Elena Kononenko wrote:

> During the inspection of the corpses at the crash site of the Heinkel it was found that the crew was led by a *podpolkovnik* [lieutenant colonel], who had the Iron Cross . . .: 'Filled with a deadly cargo, the bomber floated ominously across the sky. Sleek Hitler's *podpolkovnik*, crew commander, experienced fascist wolf, viciously anticipated how he would bomb the capital of the Soviet Union . . . Covered with hot flames and smoke, the 'Heinkel' fell down . . . Victor strains all will, all forces and is thrown out with a parachute. Lands in a small lake. He lives. He is full of happiness, love for his native land, Moscow, Soviet people. Here they run straight to the shore, right to him. Native hands embrace him, native lips kiss his wet, dirty cheek . . .

At the beginning of the war, the Russian government did not encourage ramming, believing it to be a waste of military equipment. Propaganda claimed that Stalin's aviation was 'the best' and 'the strongest in the world', so why ram the 'weak' and not shoot them down with machine guns? Therefore, the rammings carried out in June–July 1941 were not rewarded or publicized. But in August, after Stalin's aircraft had suffered huge losses, the slogan 'shoot down the enemy by any means' appeared. This happened in early August, so Talalikhin was immediately declared a hero.

During August, the fighters of the 6th IAK PVO periodically hunted for German reconnaissance aircraft. For example, on 7 August, they attacked three Do 215s in different locations. These aircraft were operated by Aufkl. Gr.Ob.d.L. and flew deep behind Russian lines. The Do 215s photographed railway lines and stations, airfields and field fortifications. These flights over enemy territory, 1,000km (over 600 miles) from base, were very dangerous. In many cases, the reconnaissance aircraft was on its own with groups of Russian fighters. In such situations, everything depended on the skill of the pilot and the gunners. Usually the crews of reconnaissance aircrafts tried to spot the hunters in advance and change course. When this failed, they had to fight.

At 13.25 near Dorokhovo station a Yak-1 element of Politruk Vikhrov, Lieutenant Obukhov and Grachev of the 12th IAP intercepted the first Do 215 at an altitude of 2,000m (6,500ft) and attacked immediately. However, Grachev's Yak-1 was damaged by return fire and made an emergency belly landing. The two remaining hunters continued their pursuit. After a long firefight, Politruk Vikhrov went in to ram. But no sooner had the hunter got closer to the Do 215, than he was hit by machine-gun fire. His Yak-1 caught fire, and Vikhrov bailed out. Left alone, Obukhov continued to chase the Do 215 to Vyazma, but could not bring down the reconnaissance aircraft.

At 13.30 near Gzhatsk another Yak-1 element of the 11th IAP, consisting of Lieutenants Verblyudov and Alekseyev, encountered a Do 215, which was flying to the east. After the third attack, Verblyudov's oil tank was hit, and he was forced to make an emergency landing east of Mozhaisk. Alekseyev could not catch up with the reconnaissance aircraft.

That same day, Do 215 B-1 W. Nr. 0018 'L2+HS' of 1.(F)/Ob.d.L, made a belly landing due to engine damage at Orsha. The aircraft had suffered 70 per cent damage and was disposed of. The cause of this is unknown, but the aircraft may have been damaged in battle with Russian fighters.

Another plane of this *Staffel* – Do 215 B-2 W. Nr. 0069 'T5+BC' – was shot down near Tula by the MiG-3 of Captain Kruglov of the 124th IAP. The commander of this aviation regiment, Major S. Polunin, wrote in his report:

> On August 7, 1941 at 17.10, having received a message at the command post of Tula airfield about the flight to the city of Sukhinichi of an unidentified aircraft at high altitude, my deputy Captain Kruglov took off in a MiG-3 to intercept. He reached 7,000m and was patrolling around Mashkovo. At 17.30 at an altitude of 8,000m he noticed traces of condensation of exhaust fumes. At this time on the radio: 'The enemy above'. But Kruglov found nobody there. Some time later, the pilot saw an approaching point 200–300m above. The dot grew rapidly in size, and at a range of 3,000–4,000m Kruglov identified an enemy aircraft. At a distance of 300–500m, he went into a frontal attack, releasing two bursts with pitching and climb. The MiG-3 dived to the left and passed 100–150m from

the enemy. Probably the Germans did not notice the fighter, because the crew did not fire back. Captain Kruglov levelled out, gained altitude and repeated the attack from the right and below. Two long bursts struck the right engine of the enemy aircraft, which began smoking. Lower gunner opened fire in response. Kruglov began to manoeuvre vigorously, but he was still able to get off two more bursts at the enemy at 200–300m. The enemy tried to escape into a thundercloud. Then the Soviet pilot decided to finish off the enemy at close range; after two short bursts, he hit the second engine. Despite this, the enemy plane disappeared into the cloud. Attempts to find him failed. Kruglov descended to 2,000m could find no trace of his opponent. Then he resumed course and safely set down at Tula.

As a result of this attack, Do 215 B-2 'T5+BC' (pilot Feldwebel Ferdinand Schihgaller, navigator Leutnant Joachim Babik) suffered serious damage. The Germans had no choice but to make an emergency belly landing. The reconnaissance aircraft came down near Maloyaroslavez, and all the crew were arrested by the NKVD. This Do 215 was the first total loss of 1.(F)/Ob.d.L. on the Eastern Front. The crew suffered a sad fate in Stalin's camps. Only the radio operator returned home in 1949, the rest having died in captivity.

Four days later 1.(F)/Ob.d.L. suffered another serious loss. On the morning of 11 August, over the important Kalinin–Toropez stretch of railway, Do 215 B-2 W. Nr. 0075 'T5+LC' (pilot Unteroffizier Rudolf Liebling, navigator Leutnant Rudolf Roder) was shot down. At an altitude of 8,000m (26,250ft) it was rammed by the MiG-3 flown by Lieutenant Alexei Katrich of the 27th IAP, smashing its tail with its propeller and then landing safely back at base. The reconnaissance aircraft crashed in the village of Stariza (45km [28 miles] north-east of Rzhev). Although the battle took place far from Moscow, Russian propaganda announced that Katrich made 'the first high-altitude ram in Moscow air space'.

On the clear night of 9/10 August the Luftwaffe made its fifteenth attack on Moscow. The main target was the 'Serp and Molot' steel plant, which was located in the south-east of the city. Thirty high-explosive and about 1,000 incendiary bombs were dropped on the target. The rolling shop was badly damaged, and thirteen houses near the plant were destroyed. The loss of life was forty-eight dead and eighty-three wounded. The raid was successful, but the Luftwaffe suffered heavy losses.

Russian anti-aircraft artillery expended 11,528 rounds, claiming about six aircraft shot down. In fact, only one – He 111 H-5 W. Nr. 4520 'A1+HH' of Unteroffizier Oswald Schlimann from 1./KG 53 'Legion Condor'– was shot down by anti-aircraft fire. The entire crew disappeared without trace. The 6th IAK PVO carried out 106 sorties. Pilots Lieutenants Kiselev and Ledovsky of the 34th IAP reported that over searchlight field No. 5 they attacked and brought down two Ju 88s. According to the Germans, Ju 88 A-5 W. Nr. 6461 of 4./KG 3 'Blitz' went missing along with the crew. Another Ju 88 A-5 W. Nr. 3469 of St.I./KG 3, during its return to the base crashed near the city of Cherikov (Mogilev region).

On the night of 10/11 August eighty-three He 111s of KGr. 100 'Wiking', I./KG 28 and KG 53 'Legion Condor' carried out another air raid on Moscow. The main targets were aircraft factories in the suburbs of the capital, on which the German planes dropped 49 high-explosive and 14,000 incendiary bombs. The buildings of aircraft-gun plant No. 240 and the assembly shop of aircraft plant No. 22 'Gorbunov' were badly damaged. In addition they caused damage to thirty-two other businesses. The fires destroyed five warehouses and shops. Casualties were 54 killed and 298 wounded. 500 incendiaries and two SC1000 bombs fell on the large airfield at Kubinka, forming a crater with a diameter of 30m (100ft).

It was a great success for the Luftwaffe, which cost them one bomber. He 111 H-3 W. Nr. 2029 '6N+MN' of 1./KGr. 100 collided with a barrage balloon and fell into the Moscow river. Together with the crew died the *Staffel* commander Leutnant Oswald Lochbrunner (he was replaced by Oberleutnant Hans-Georg Bätcher). Another plane of 3./KGr. 100, He 111 H-3 W. Nr. 3207, was damaged by anti-aircraft fire, flew to German territory and crash-landed near Yelnya. In this raid KGr. 100 functioned as pathfinders, designating targets with flares and incendiary bombs. Despite the great destruction in Moscow, the command of the Russian 1st Air Defence Corps claimed that this air attack 'was repulsed by joint actions of fighters and gunners'.

On the night of 12 August, thirty German bombers made a new attack on Moscow and dropped fifty-five high-explosive bombs on it, including many SC1000s. One of them exploded in the square at the Nikitsky Gate in the area of 'Krasnaya Presnya'. A crater with a depth of 12m (39ft) and a diameter of 32m (105ft) was formed in the pavement, and anti-aircraft gunners of the batteries located in that area were killed. One of the targets was again the Kremlin – Stalin's residence. One bomb exploded at the entrance of the Grand Kremlin Palace (the Germans were sure that Stalin lived there).

Four-barrel Maxim anti-aircraft machine gun

Beams of searchlights in the sky of Moscow

Another large-calibre bomb hit the Arsenal building, which was completely destroyed. Many buildings inside the Kremlin were damaged: the building housing the commandant's office, garages, barracks of the soldiers of the garrison, warehouses and government buildings. Two government ZIS-101 and four GAZ M1 limousines were destroyed, and three other cars were damaged. Another high-explosive bomb exploded near the Borovitsky gate, through which Stalin entered the Kremlin. The telephone lines connecting the Kremlin with the government offices and the NKVD were damaged. In the Kremlin fifteen people were killed and fifty-three were wounded. In Moscow two bridges over the river were damaged, and eighteen houses and one factory were destroyed.

That night, anti-aircraft batteries fired 12,778 rounds of all calibres and claimed one downed aircraft. Night fighters had completed eighty-five sorties and claimed one victory. But in fact this successful German attack was without loss.

With this raid, Operation 'Clara Zetkin' ended. It had been a success for the Luftwaffe. In the first three big air attacks on Moscow alone, 5 factories and plants, 147 houses and many other important targets were destroyed or damaged. According to Soviet data, 336 people were killed and 1,360 wounded. Between 21 July and 12 August 1941, the Luftwaffe carried out seventeen raids on Moscow and lost thirteen bombers (some of which made emergency landings on German territory). Losses amounted to about 2 per cent of the attacking aircraft.

The air raids on Moscow are often compared to those on London, Coventry and other British cities in the autumn of 1940. Russian historians argue that Russian air defences 'did not allow the Germans to repeat the destruction of London and Coventry'. However, this is not true. In just one day, on 7 September 1940, German bombers flew 625 sorties over London. But for the six weeks of Operation 'Clara Zetkin' they carried out less than 600.

Chapter 2

'The New Attempts of the Fascist Vultures'

In mid-August, Operation 'Clara Zetkin' came to an end. According to the plan of 'Barbarossa', immediately after the capture of Smolensk German tank groups were to continue to move on Moscow. However, Army Groups Centre and South were advancing too slowly. Hitler feared a repeat of the fate of the French army of Napoleon Bonaparte in 1812. The French quickly captured Moscow, but found themselves in the deep and hostile Russian rear, without supplies and sufficient weapons. And then after the attacks on the flanks and by guerrillas they retreated back to the border. Therefore, the Führer ordered that the northern and southern forces first capture Leningrad, Kiev and the Crimean Peninsula and then the decisive attack on Moscow would be launched. The Luftwaffe also had to contribute to these missions.

Air raids on the Red capital continued, but only with small forces. On the night of 15/16 August the raid involved III./KG 26. Due to bad weather, the bombers could not find the target. He 111 H-6 W. Nr. 4106 of 9./KG 26 did not return. It was shot down by a Russian night fighter. The fate of the five crew was dramatic. Two were killed in the air, the pilot, Oberleutnant Fritz Ulrich, shot himself after landing in enemy territory. The gunner Unteroffizier Hans Balcke was captured. But the navigator Hauptmann Otto Stiller managed to hide in the forest and after two weeks reached German troops near Yelnya.

On 16 August, Russian fighters patrolled over the Volokolamsk–Rzhev, Kubinka–Gzhatsk, Maloyaroslavets–Yukhnov railway lines. In total, 222 sorties were carried out. At 09.30 Lieutenants Lukyanov, Goryunov and Tsymbal of the 34th IAP shot down Ju 88 A-5(F) W. Nr. 0309 'F6+FK' of 2.(F)/122 in the Istra district (north-west of Moscow). Three of the German crew were killed and one was captured.

At 23.40 in Moscow an air alarm was declared, which lasted until 03.35. Flak expended 7,916 rounds, and the 6th IAK PVO carried out sixty-nine sorties. The Russian pilots achieved one success. Lieutenant Benedict

Kovalev of the 11th IAP in the district of Naro-Fominsk attacked Ju 88 A-5 W. Nr. 6295 of 1./KG 3 'Blitz'. The bomber reached German territory but crashed during an emergency landing at Orsha. The Russians lost six fighters. Lieutenant Fokin, trying to ram a bomber, hit the cable of a barrage balloon but was able to bail out. Lieutenant Gulyaev of the 17th IAP and Lieutenant Maslov of the 25th IAP could not find the airfield in the darkness and made emergency belly landings. Lieutenant Avdeev of the 16th IAP crashed on landing. Lieutenant Sheshunov of the 24th IAP and Lieutenant Kobashev of the 121th IAP were both forced to bail out but Sheshunov's parachute did not open and he was killed. According to the MPVO bombs fell on Moscow. Factories and military facilities in the suburbs of Balashikha, Ukhtomsky and Ramenskoye were attacked.

On 17 August a public meeting was held in the Central Park of Moscow, dedicated to air defence. Town governor (the Chairman of the Executive Committee of Mossovet) V.P. Pronin said that 'the attacks of enemy aircraft did not break the steady rhythm of work and life of the capital' and the Luftwaffe 'received a worthy rebuff from the Moscow sky sentries'. Hero of the Soviet Union Viktor Talalikhin also made a speech, in which he swore an oath to boldly defend the city. This propaganda meeting was to boost the morale of the residents of Moscow, who were afraid of the air raids.

In the night of 17/18 August, the Luftwaffe carried out its eighteenth attack on Moscow with a single bomber. One high-explosive and 100 incendiary bombs were dropped, which destroyed No. 8 Usievicha Street and damaged water pipes in Velyaminovskaya Street. Night fighters carried out seventy-nine sorties. Lieutenants Saktalov and Nesterov mistakenly shot down a Russian Db-3 bomber. The navigator was killed in the air, but the rest of the crew bailed out safely.

The next night was also unsuccessful for the Russian air defences. 'Fascist vultures decided to try again to reach our capital', one of the air defence personnel wrote. Flak expended 2,974 rounds, and night fighters performed fifty-four sorties. But the pilots did not find the enemy. Politruk Murzin was blinded by the searchlights, lost orientation and crashed. Lieutenant Fomenko and Sergeant Kostennikov were also reported missing. A single bomber dropped one high-explosive bomb and 100 incendiaries on the Sokolniki district. As a result, eleven wooden houses caught fire, twenty-two people were killed and seventy-seven wounded. The bomb exploded on the positions of the 3rd Battery of the 176th Anti-Aircraft Regiment (ZenAP), damaging two guns, killing seven gunners and wounding eleven.

Missing Weather Reconnaissance Aircraft

Not only German bombers and reconnaissance aircraft flew in the Moscow region, but also weather reconnaissance aircraft from the *Wekusta* squadrons. These important strategic missions were carried out by small, specialized aircraft which were hard to spot. The *Wekusta* took measurements of atmospheric pressure, wind and temperature and then compiled current and long-term weather forecasts for the battlefields. In Operation 'Barbarossa' there were three such squadrons: *Wekusta* 1, *Wekusta* 26 and *Wekusta* 76. *Wekusta* 26 operated over the central sector of the front. Typically, such aircraft sought to keep away from the cities and avoid encounters with enemy fighters. Their losses were small in comparison with the losses of bombers and reconnaissance aircraft. But for *Wekusta* 26 the campaign around Moscow developed very unsuccessfully.

Wekusta 26's first weather reconnaissance flight over Russia began at 04.00 on 22 June 1941. A single plane flew on the route Warsaw–Bialystok–Minsk. On 30 June Do 17 Z '5M+J', the crew of which included Oberleutnant Hugo Dallhues, meteorologist August Hillecke and Oberfeldwebels Otto Brendehl and Paul Lotzkat, was damaged by ground fire and made an emergency landing on Russian territory in the Gomel region. But German troops were advancing rapidly, and on 2 July Hillecke and his crew returned to their base. On 3 July, Do 17 Z '5M+D' crashed due to the failure of both engines. On the same day, Bf 110 '5M+O' was attacked by Russian fighters and was forced to make an emergency landing on German territory. Both

LaGG-3 fighter 7-series

Bf 110 C 'Rositta' from Wekusta 26. *Staffel* emblem is clearly visible

The wreckage of a Ju 88 D (5M+?) from Wekusta 26, which was shot down on the Eastern front

crews were uninjured and returned to the squadron. On 8 July, *Wekusta* 26 completed its 46th flight on the Eastern Front and its 1,000th since the beginning of the war.

The squadron's losses on the Eastern Front were much heavier than in the West, due to their having to conduct their weather observations at lower altitudes to determine conditions on the 'surface', frequently bringing them into range of anti-aircraft guns. The aircraft had to operate from unprepared airstrips, often just grass-covered fields.

In mid-July Bf 110 S '5M+T' was damaged by anti-aircraft fire near Orsha and crashed. Do 17 Z '5M+N' crashed at Lida airfield when its undercarriage collapsed, and on 24 July, a new Ju 88 D was lost due to engine failure. On 8 August, Bf 110 C, W. Nr. 4422 '5M+T' on the way from the factory, made an emergency landing in East Prussia due to bad weather. But in all these cases, the crews (the most vital part) were uninjured.

The first serious loss in the new war of *Wekusta* 26 was suffered on 20 August. On that day He 111 H-3 W. Nr. 3183 '5M+A' (pilot Feldwebel Robert Dickler, senior meteorologist August Hillecke, Oberfeldwebel Hans Schopellin and Feldwebel Eduard Busemann), flew to the district of Ryazan, an ancient city located south-east of Moscow on the Oka river. Three hours after take-off, the crew reported that they had been intercepted by Russian fighters and one engine was damaged. After that, contact was lost and the plane failed to return to base.

In such cases, their colleagues could only wonder what had happened to those who had gone missing over the 'Russian expanses'. Killed in action? Killed by Russian peasants? Captured and sent to Siberia? Eaten by bears? Sometimes the downed pilots could be read about in Russian newspapers, which Soviet planes dropped on German territory. The press often published articles in which German fighters 'repented', cursed 'the dog Hitler' and urged their friends not to be at war with the Russians . . .

The fate of He 111 H-3 W. Nr. 3183 '5M+A' became known only after the war. Eduard Busemann was killed during the battle. August Hillecke, Hans Schopellin and Robert Dickler were captured. Schopellin later died in a Russian camp, and Hillecke and Dickler returned home. Their plane was shot down by the LaGG-3 of Lieutenant Pavel Demenchuk. The summary of the 6th IAK PVO reported: 'The Pilot 24 IAP Lieutenant Demenchuk near the village of Nekrasovo (25km north-west of Medyn) at 17.30 attacked and shot down an enemy Ju 88. At 17.45 met He 111 in the same district. After several attacks decided to ram the escaping He 111. When he hit Lieutenant Demenchuk died.' Demenchuk attacked the same aircraft several times, first identifying it as a Ju 88, later as an He 111. He 111 H-3 '5M+A' crash-landed 160km south-west of Moscow in the area between Kaluga and Tula.

On 28 August, *Wekusta* 26 lost another plane with a two-man crew. Bf 110 C-5 W. Nr. 2227 '5M+ON'(pilot Leutnant Albert Wollmann and meteorologist Albert Neuhaus) was shot down by Russian fighters, the I-153 of Lieutenant K.M. Treshow of the 127th IAP, and the Yak-1 of Lieutenant T.P. Obukhov of the 12th IAP. Both recorded a victory over a 'Me 110.'

On 1 September, Bf 110 C-5 '5M+T' suffered an accident at the Novgorod-Seversky airfield. The plane was destroyed by fire, but the crew survived. On 5 September, Bf 110 C '5M+Q' was damaged by anti-aircraft fire. The pilot Helmut Klemt was seriously injured, but was able to fly back to base and land, although he later died in hospital. In early September, *Wekusta* 26 relocated to the new airfield at Seschinskaya to the south-east of Smolensk, although it continued to fly from Smolensk-Nord. On 16 September, Do 17 Z '5M+K' was destroyed during a raid by Russian bombers. On 20 September, Ju W34 'NG+AG' crashed on landing. Oberleutnant Hans Oswald and meteorologist Werner Knichs were killed.

Wekusta 26 made several long-range flights from Seschinskaya to the Arzamas and Gorky areas. The *Staffel* continued to suffer losses on a regular basis. On 5 October Ju 88 '5M+Z' crashed due to engine failure, killing radio operator Oberfeldwebel Heinz Alfred Müller and flight engineer Oberfeldwebel Paul Lotzkat. On 18 October Bf 110 C-2 W. Nr. 2209 '5M+P' crashed near Smolensk whilst climbing to 5,000m (16,400ft) to measure weather conditions. The entire crew, pilot Feldwebel Werner Schloss, meteorologist Alois Schmidhuber and flight engineer Feldwebel Gunter Nimmer, were killed.

Since the beginning of Operation 'Barbarossa' *Wekusta* 26 had lost thirteen aircraft (five Bf 110s, four Do 17 Zs, two Ju 88s, one He 111 and one Ju W34) and fourteen crew. It was the largest loss to the Luftwaffe meteorological aviation since the outbreak of the Second World War. In November, the *Staffel* was transferred to the rear for rest and refitting. The losses of pilots in *Wekusta* 76, which served in the southern sector of the Eastern Front, were greater than in *Wekusta* 26. Between 22 June and 24 December 1941, it lost eight planes (five Ju 88s, two He 111s and one Bf 110) and seven crew: another 'bird' was destroyed on the ground in an air raid.

Heavy losses was not the only failure of Luftwaffe weather intelligence in Operation 'Barbarossa'. In the autumn of 1941 during Operation 'Typhoon', the high command of the Wehrmacht turned to the famous meteorologist Professor Franz Baur, director of the Weather Research Institute at Bad Homburg vor der Höhe, to predict what the winter of 1941/42 would be like in Russia. He compiled all the data, including information on the abnormally cold winters of 1939/40 and 1940/41 in Eastern Europe. Baur came to the conclusion that in Russia there were never more than two abnormally cold winters one after another. He predicted that the next winter would be 'normal' or warm. In his forecast, Baur used information about the abnormal amount of ice cover in the Baltic Sea in the previous winters, which was collected by *Wekusta* aircraft. Whether this was a result of two consecutive cold winters or a symptom of more complex models of the circulation of the Arctic anticyclone, which could lead to more severe winter, it was impossible to determine.

Although Professor Baur was right that there are no three identical winters in a row in Russia, he was very wrong to say that the third winter would be warmer rather than even more abnormally cold! Baur's erroneous forecasts were used in the preparation of the Wehrmacht plan of operations in November 1941 (against Tikhvin, Moscow and Rostov) and in the preparation of troops for winter conditions.

Luftwaffe Raids in September

In late August–early September 1941, there were no air raids on Moscow. For three weeks the city was left in peace, although the weather was fine and clear. Russian propaganda told people that the Germans were afraid to approach the city because of the very strong air defences. But the Luftwaffe were just busy with other missions.

Captured crew members of the bomber Ju 88 – Joseph Troche, Walter Rissik and Rudolf Tozer

Caricature in a Russian magazine about the downed German pilots

On the night of 8/9 September the twentieth air raid on Moscow took place. At 23.50 the sirens sounded and soon came the thunder of many anti-aircraft guns. Forty high-explosive and about 700 incendiary bombs were dropped on the city. As a result of the explosions and fires, the GPZ No. 1 ball-bearing plant and plant No. 161 were seriously damaged, and three houses and a garage were destroyed. The bombs hit a railway platform loaded with tanks. According to the rescue service, two people were killed

Обращение к немецким летчикам и солдатам четырех немецких летчиков

25 июня вблизи Киева приземлились на пикирующем бомбардировщике «Юнкерс 88» 4 немецких летчика: унтер-офицер Ганс Герман, 1916 года рождения, уроженец города Бреславля в Средней Силезии; летчик-наблюдатель Ганс Кратц, 1917 г. рождения, уроженец Франкфурта-на-Майне; старший ефрейтор Адольф Аппель, 1918 г. рождения, уроженец гор. Брно (Брюн)—Моравия и радист Вильгельм Шмидт, 1917 г. рождения, уроженец города Регенсбурга.

Все они составляли экипаж, входивший в состав второй группы 54 эскадрильи. Добровольно приземлившиеся летчики обратились ко всем немецким летчикам и солдатам с письмом, которое мы ниже публикуем.

К НЕМЕЦКИМ ЛЕТЧИКАМ И СОЛДАТАМ

Мы, немецкие летчики: водитель самолета Ганс Герман, наблюдатель Ганс Кратц, стрелок Адольф Аппель, радист Вильгельм Шмидт летаем вместе почти один год.

На бомбардировщике «Ю-88» мы вылетали для бомбардировки Лондона, Портсмута, Плимута и других городов Англии.

Еще ранее мы летали над французскими городами. Теперь нас послали на русский фронт для того, чтобы бомбить мирные русские города.

Мы часто задавали себе вопрос: почему воюет Гитлер против целого света? Почему он приносит всем народам Европы смерть и разорение? Почему должны лучшие люди Германии погибать от пуль, которые им посылаются навстречу народами, защищающими свое отечество.

На этот вопрос нам никто ответа не дал. Мы каждый раз видели, что спровоцированная Гитлером война приносит всем народам Европы, в том числе и германскому народу, только несчастья и смерть.

Нас часто беспокоила мысль, что из-за кровавой собаки Гитлера от наших бомб погибает много ни в чем неповинных женщин и детей.

Поэтому мы на сей раз сбросили бомбы так, что они не причинили вреда. Мы уже давно таили мысль бежать от Гитлера и начать мирную жизнь, но мы боялись.

Теперь, когда Гитлер объявил войну России, в которой он обязательно потеряет свою голову, мы решили предпринять побег.

25 июня наша группа, руководимая майором Крафтом, полетела в Киев.

Мы сбросили свои бомбы в Днепр и приземлились неподалеку от города.

Мы были поражены, когда нас немедленно окружили вооруженные крестьяне, которые тотчас же взяли нас в плен.

Это еще раз убедило нас, что советский народ един, подготовлен к борьбе и победит.

Теперь мы в России. Здесь нас хорошо приняли.

Братья летчики и солдаты, следуйте нашему примеру. Бросьте убийцу Гитлера и переходите сюда в Россию.

Ганс ГЕРМАН,
Ганс КРАТЦ,
Адольф АППЕЛЬ,
Вильгельм ШМИДТ.

An article in the newspaper *Pravda*, in which the crew of Ju 88 A from KG 54 urge comrades 'to throw out the killer Hitler and move to Russia'

and ten wounded. Anti-aircraft batteries were not fully alert, so only 7,335 rounds were fired. Red commanders honestly reported that they did not shoot anyone down. The 6th IAK PVO 33 made thirty-three sorties. Lieutenant Barchuk of the 176th IAP intercepted a Ju 88 near Dmitrov but after the first attack, the target disappeared into the clouds.

The next night III./KG 26 conducted another air raid on Moscow. Near the city it was cloudy and misty, and visibility was 3–4km (1.86–2.45 miles). The Germans were not able to locate their target, dropping bombs on the northern and eastern suburbs of Moscow. 'The enemy with single planes goes to the west and to the south of Moscow, comes to the east of Moscow, goes along the edge of the anti-aircraft artillery fire, but does not go to the city, tries to cause exhaustion, disruption of production work of Moscow,' reported the war diary of the 1st Air Defence Corps. Night fighters performed forty-six sorties, but found no one. 'In view of the strong haze, the search for enemy aircraft was difficult,' said the war diary of the 6th IAK PVO. Before reaching the target, the Luftwaffe lost He 111 H-6 W. Nr. 4110 of 8./KG 26, which was hit by anti-aircraft fire near Noginsk. Two of the crew managed to hide and get back to their lines, but the rest, including squadron commander Hauptmann Erhard Pochler, were killed.

On 11–14 September Luftwaffe aircraft conducted intensive reconnaissance in the Moscow region, mainly along the railway lines. Russian pilots made many sorties to intercept them, but only rarely did they managed to attack the target. On 14 September Lieutenants B.G. Pirozhkov and W.I. Dovgy of the 124th IAP, both rammed the same Ju 88 in their I-153s (at 12.50 and 12.55 respectively) near Tula. First Pirozhkov used his propeller to cut away the right-hand part of the tail, then Dovgy, seeing that the Ju 88 was still flying, hit the tail a second time. The first I-153 was able to return to base, but the second had to make an emergency landing. The long-range reconnaissance Ju 88 A-4 W. Nr. 1271 '8H+GH' of 1.(F)/33 came down near the village of Khanino. At this time it was considered that it was worth losing two or three Russian aircraft to down one German! Also, the armament of Russian fighters was weak and unreliable so pilots often resorted to ramming rather than shooting.

On the night of 19/20 September it was again cloudy with light rain in the Moscow area. The searchlights were not illuminated, and night fighters did not take off. But the Luftwaffe had some luck. At 23.20 the air alarm sounded, and at 23.55 two planes dropped two high-explosive and 200 incendiary bombs. The GPZ-1 ball-bearing plant was hit, where thirty-two fires broke out, and the assembly shop was destroyed. Twelve workers were injured. This was the third air raid on this strategically-important factory, and caused serious damage.

At 20.55 on 23 September, air surveillance posts reported a group of aircraft bearing 90° in the Vyazma area. In 21.02 the alarm was declared in Moscow. Twelve high-explosive and about 100 incendiary bombs were dropped. Kazansky railway station (track and platforms were destroyed) and the 'Kauchuk' rubber plant were hit. Two houses, a garage, a warehouse for the construction of the Palace of Soviets and a pier-restaurant on the Moskva river were also destroyed. According to the rescue service, four people were killed and eighteen wounded. The anti-aircraft artillery conducted heavy barrage fire, expending 14,208 rounds. But this twenty-second Luftwaffe air raid suffered no losses.

On this day, the first German fighter was shot down in the Moscow area, in the Ramensky district. It was Bf 109 E-7 W. Nr. 3757 of 9./JG 27, which had been transferred from the Leningrad front. Oberfeldwebel Franz Blazitko managed to hide and began to make his way to the front line, but two days later he was captured. Blazitko was credited with twenty-nine victories. Under interrogation, the pilot said that he served in JG 27, but the Russians did not believe him. According to them, JG 27 was in the Leningrad region, where a friend of Blazitko, Feldwebel Ernst Ripe, had been captured on 19 September. Why Blazitko was flying so far behind Russian lines remained a mystery. Maybe he lost his bearings.

On 24 September, a long-range reconnaissance aircraft, Bf 110 E-2 W. Nr. 3810 'F6+PK' of 2.(F)/122, was shot down near Tula. It was probably destroyed by two Yak-1s of the 12th IAP (pilots Loginov and Obukhov).

In late September the weather in Central Russia was getting colder and sometimes it even snowed, a reminder that the 'Russian winter', which the Germans feared, would soon arrive. Between 24 and 28 September, the Luftwaffe bombers carried out several aerial attacks on different targets in the Moscow area. For example, on the night of 26/27 September, 35 high-explosive and 500 incendiary bombs were dropped on the Kuntsevsky, Krasnogorsk, Podolsky, Pavlovo-Posadsky, Lukhovitsky, Leninsky, Ukhtomsky and Ramensky districts. Explosions and fires damaged several small towns and villages. On the night of 27/28 September forty-four high-explosive bombs were dropped on different targets around Moscow. An ammunition plant in the Zagorsk district was hit by eight large-calibre bombs. The target was severely damaged and partially burned, dozens of workers being killed and injured.

Russian pilots made numerous sorties, but only rarely did they make contact with the enemy. 'Stalin's Falcons' suffered heavy losses due to poor skills and technical problems. For example, at 17.00 on 27 September Lieutenant Taruev of the 423rd IAP encountered an He 111 in the Kaluga district which, after three attacks, disappeared into the clouds. The 6th IAK PVO lost four fighter pilots that day. Lieutenant Victor Kiselev of the 34th IAP had to make an emergency landing due to a technical failure near the village of Babinka. The plane was destroyed and the pilot was seriously injured. The Yak-1 of Lieutenant Gramzin of the 11th IAP collided with the Yak-1 of Lieutenant Benedict Kovalev during landing at Kubinka. Gramzin was killed, and Kovalev was seriously injured. Another pilot of the 177th IAP, during a night flight, had to bail out.

On 28 September the 6th IAK PVO completed 302 sorties, but only the I-16 of Lieutenant G.K. Startsev of 171th IAP intercepted an He 111 in

Russian propaganda poster 'RAM – weapon of heroes'

Destroyed district office of the Bolshevik party on Bolschaya Polyanka street

the Skuratovo area. The pilot rammed it and then bailed out. The damaged He 111 H-6 W. Nr. 4441 '6N+FH' of 1./KGr. 100 flew to German territory and crashed during an emergency landing. One crew member was killed and the pilot and navigator were injured.

On the night of 29/30 September during the flight to Moscow the Luftwaffe lost one plane. He 111 H-5 W. Nr. 3680 '1T+LL' of 3./KG 28[4] received a direct hit in the engine and made an emergency landing in Russian territory. Two crew members were killed, and the pilot and the radio operator were captured.

At this time, the 'calm' on the Moscow front, which had lasted 1½ months, came to an end. The Wehrmacht had completed preparations for the 'decisive' offensive, codenamed Operation 'Typhoon'.

---

4. 1./KG 28 was in the south sector of the Eastern Front for the entire period and operated for its intended purpose. He 111 dropped aerial mines in the harbour of Odessa and other places, and periodically carried out torpedo attacks in the Black Sea. Listed as part of the 28th *Geschwader* was training squadron Erg.Staffel./KG 28 of Hauptmann Heinrich Otto Bock stationed at Lüneburg airfield in Germany.

Chapter 3

The Luftwaffe in Operation 'Typhoon'

The plan for the capture of Moscow was typical of the Wehrmacht. Three tank groups had to break through the Russian defences to surround their main forces. Then the tank divisions were to make a leap forward and surround the Red capital. Despite the fact that the 'Russian winter' was approaching, Hitler still hoped to reach not only Moscow, but also the Volga river, capturing the cities of Yaroslavl, Rybinsk and Gorky. In this operation the Luftwaffe was given its regular role. First, it was to help the tank divisions break through the defences, then paralyze railway transport in the Russian rear. Later, its aircraft were to support the tanks' offensive into Russia. Attacks on cities and the factories that supplied the Red Army with weapons were the lowest priority.

By the autumn of 1941, Hitler's Luftwaffe had suffered serious losses and was significantly weaker than at the beginning of Operation 'Barbarossa'. But it was still strong enough for the attack on Moscow, for which II and VIII *Fliegerkorps* were concentrated. In direct support of the offensive were the Ju 87 dive bombers of StG 1 and StG 2, Hs 123 close support aircraft, Bf 109 Es of II.(Sch)/LG 2, Bf 110 C *Schnell-bombers* of SKG 210, and Bf 110 E *Zerstorers* of ZG 26. But the main role was again played by the bombers of KG 3, KG 4, III./KG 26, I./KG 28, KG 53 and KGr. 100. The Bf 109s of III./JG 27, JG 51 and II./JG 52 were to clear the sky of Russian aircraft. Operation 'Typhoon' was the last in which the veteran Do 17 Z bomber and the Hs 126 tactical reconnaissance aircraft were widely used.

In the autumn of 1941 the Russian air force was in crisis. Only fragments of the formerly powerful 'Stalin's Falcons' were left. Many fighter regiments had only between three and ten aircraft. In the Air Forces of the Western Front (WWS ZF), which supported the Moscow front, in early October there were only 106 fighters and 63 bombers serviceable. The most powerful Soviet aviation formation was the 6th IAK PVO. On 1 October it had 458 fighters, of which 300 were combat-capable.

THE LUFTWAFFE IN OPERATION 'TYPHOON'

Fighter Aircraft in the 6th IAK PVO on 1 October 1941

Type	Number
MiG-3	176
I-16	154
I-153	43
Yak-1	36
LaGG-3	29
Pe-3.	20
Total	458

The morning of the first day of October in the Moscow region was foggy. On one side of the battlelines Russian soldiers were preparing for the defence of their capital. On the other, German soldiers, already frozen in their overcoats, were preparing for the 'decisive attack' on Bolshevism. In the afternoon the weather was clear and cloudless. But the sky was peaceful apart from some German reconnaissance flights in the Rzhev and Vyazma areas.

Stalin had expected that on the first day of the offensive the Germans would make a massive air attack on Moscow. The cowardly dictator ordered his pilots to prevent the bombing 'at any cost'. But that didn't happen. On the night of 1/2 October only one *Staffel* of KGr. 100 'Wiking', based at Bobruisk, attacked the Red capital. The *Fliegerbuch* of the commander of 1./KGr. 100, Oberleutnant Hans Bätcher, records that the aircraft took to the air at 20.52 Berlin time. By this time, Bätcher had successfully completed many important missions against railway stations, factories, airfields and concentrations of Russian troops. Bätcher had proved to be a competent tactical pilot. Therefore, this attack on Moscow was different from the others he had carried out. The He 111s crossed the front line at very high altitude, so were not spotted by the ground observation posts. Reaching the target, the bombers approached with low engine revs. Because of this, Moscow did not sound an alarm, and anti-aircraft artillery opened fire only after flares began to be dropped. The bombs were dropped with great accuracy, hitting four factories. 'Anti-aircraft artillery conducted barrage fire, because the enemy planes were flying at an altitude beyond the reach of the searchlights', reported the war diary of the 1st IAK PVO. 'The consumption of 85mm shells – 910 . . . Searchlights did the search, but due to the high altitude of the targets were unsuccessful. Night fighters operated and made 36 sorties.

There were no meetings with the enemy.' The Bätcher squadron dropped 20 high explosive and 160 incendiary bombs. Anti-aircraft artillery did not have much time to shoot (the Germans noted 'weak anti-aircraft fire'), but destroyed six of their own barrage balloons. At 01.50–02.00 bombers of KGr. 100 returned to Bobruisk without loss, again demonstrating why it was considered an elite unit.

The real air battle began on 2 October. On that day, the weather in the Moscow region was good, although in some places there was cloud at an altitude of 200–600m (650–1,950ft). From dawn to dusk 'Stukas' of StG 1 and StG 2, Hs 123s and Bf 109 Es of II.(Sch)/LG 2 and Bf 110 Cs of SKG 210 attacked Soviet troop positions, command posts, communications centres and airfields. At the same time He 111s of II. and III./KG 4 'General Wever', KG 53 'Legion Condor', III./KG 26 'Leven' and I./KG 28, and Ju 88As of KG 3 'Blitz' bombed railway junctions, bridges, highways and Soviet reserves. The Luftwaffe suffered heavy losses. Near Medyn anti-aircraft fire brought down He 111 H-6 W. Nr. 5349 of 8./KG 53. The crew was reported missing. 9./KG 26 lost two planes – He 111 H-5 W. Nr. 3596 and He 111 H-6 W. Nr. 4429. Of ten crew, four were missing, one killed and four wounded. He 111 H-5 W. Nr. 3986 '1T+EL' of 3./KG 28 was shot down by a fighter, all

Diving Ju 87s bomb Soviet troop positions

Fighter I-16 in 1941 was considered 'ancient', but during Operation Typhoon made up about 40 per cent of the Russian fighter fleet

crew members being killed. 9./KG 3 lost two Do 17 Z-2s. Three of the eight crew members were captured, one was missing, but the remaining four were able to hide in the woods and reach their advancing troops. The absence of a continuous front line during the offensive facilitated crossing the lines.

On the night of 2/3 October, German bombers made a large air attack on the railway junction at Vyazma. But the raid on Moscow failed. It was cloudy, so the Russians did not turn on their searchlights (the light could not pass through the clouds). Thanks to this, German pilots found the target in bad weather. Now the searchlights were not shining, and only a lot of shell bursts could be seen. Russian anti-aircraft artillery fired 14,000 rounds, but only shot down thirty-three of their own barrage balloons. The German newspaper *Soldat im Westen* reported the next day: 'On the night of October 3, bombers made effective strikes on military facilities in Moscow, as well as a large military plant south-east of Kharkov.' German propaganda reports were often completely false.

On 3 October, the Luftwaffe operated as on the previous day. Reconnaissance aircraft flew in the Russian rear to the Rzhev–Vyazma –

Orel line. Near Rzhev, on the Volga river, Bf 109 fighters were seen for the first time. At 15.40 Berlin time KGr. 100 'Wiking' made a raid on the airfield in Orel, dropping high-explosive and fragmentation bombs. That evening in the city, where the trams were still running as if it was peacetime, German tanks suddenly appeared. Russian aviation was very active. The 6th IAK PVO carried out 391 sorties, mainly over targets behind the front line. Air Force Reserve and the Western Army Group carried out 487 sorties, most of which were ground attacks on German troops. Also the Russians carried out air raids on the airfields at Shatalovo and Borovskoye. 'Stalin's Falcons' claimed ten aerial victories that day, but the Luftwaffe lost only He 111 H-5 W. Nr. 3643 '1T+DK' of 2./KG 28.

On this day, Hitler made a speech on the radio on the topic of the beginning of the 'Third Winter Campaign'. He said that a 'giant offensive' had been underway on the Eastern Front for 48 hours.

On 4 October, the Luftwaffe attacked Russian troops, supply bases, railway junctions and trains near the cities of Vyazma, Sanznaya, Sukhinichi, Kaluga and Medyn. The disruption of railway transport was one of the main tasks of bomber aircraft during Operation 'Typhoon'. Attacks on such targets were carried out on a wide front from Bologoye station to Kursk. For example, in the morning KGr. 100 'Wiking' attacked the railway junction and airport at Kursk. Ju 87s of I. and III./StG 2 carried out 152 sorties, attacking Soviet troops near Beliy, Sychevka and Vyazma, while losing three aircraft.

Russian aircraft, including air defence fighters, also attacked ground targets. The pilots tried to stop the movement of German tanks. The biplane I-153s of the 120th IAP made fifty sorties in the area south of Beliy, making low-level attacks with rockets and machine guns against tanks and other vehicles. They were escorted by I-16s of the 495th IAP, which also engaged ground targets. There were also the armoured Il-2 ground-attack aircraft, which at that time was still considered a 'secret weapon'. On the same day on the southern flank of the Ninth Army (near Beliy) Germans for the first time recorded the appearance on the Eastern Front of British Hurricane fighters. In the autumn of 1941, the United Kingdom began to supply the Soviet Union with military equipment, including tanks and aircraft.

In the evening, the first German tanks reached the city of Yukhnov, which was only 190km (118 miles) from the Kremlin. This was accidentally discovered by the deputy commander of the 6th IAK PVO, Major M.N. Yakushin. He was flying from an advanced airfield at Shaykovka, when communications were suddenly cut off. Yakushin immediately

Commissar Koschman conducts educational conversation with the pilots of the 445th IAP. In the background, the MiG-3 fighter

Commander of the 178th IAP I. V. Smirnov (left) and Commissar Y. I. Basovich at Lipitsy airfield

reported this to headquarters. But Stalin did not believe this 'unpleasant information', and the chief of the NKVD Lavrenty Beria accused the pilot of 'spreading misinformation'.

On the night of 4/5 October, He 111s of I./KG 28 carried out another air raid on Moscow. The alarm in the city was sounded twice – at 01.00–02.12 and at 02.43 – 04.20. 'Anti-aircraft artillery barrage shelling repelled the raid, all the planes could not face the shelling and returned to the west,' reported the headquarters of the 1st Air Defence Corps. 'And only one plane managed to break through to the city to the northwest and to dump high-explosive and incendiary bombs. Anti-aircraft artillery fired artillery shells: 85mm – 534, 76mm – 807. Fighter aircraft were patrolling the searchlight fields, no interceptions, made eleven sorties. The searchlights were blocked by the clouds, targets were not illuminated.' The target of the raid was Aviation Plant No. 1, in the vicinity of which five high-explosive bombs were dropped. However, the bombs fell on the airfield near the target and only windows were broken in the factory. Military Warehouse No. 322 was also damaged. Ten people were injured. That night bombs were also dropped on the village of Myatlevo and other locations in the Moscow area. 2./KG 28 lost two bombers in the raid: He 111 H-6 W. Nr. 4230 '1T+CK' and He 111 H-6 W. Nr. 4445 '1T+LK'. Two crew men bailed out and were captured. The others were dead or missing. What brought these aircraft down is not known.

Burning He 111 bomber

School in Moscow, destroyed during a bomb attack

On 5 October the weather was good (3 to 10 points of cloud, visibility 16–24km [10–15 miles], temperature 10–12°), which was good for aviation. The Luftwaffe attacked Rzhev, Vyazma, Sanosnaya, Sukhinichi, Kaluga and Medyn. The Ju 87, He 111 and Ju 88 A groups mainly bombed railway facilities.

Russian aviation carried out 627 sorties, but only a few pilots were successful. Near Mosalsk fighters damaged Hs 126 B-1 W. Nr. 3311 of 1.(H)/14, which crashed while attempting an emergency landing on German-held territory. During the missions, two Ju 88 D-1s of 1(F)./33 were shot down and made emergency landings. The pilot of He 111 H-6 W Nr. 4482 2./KG 28, Oberfeldwebel Schubert, was wounded in an attack by a Russian fighter. He managed to reach the airfield at Seschinskaya, but crashed on attempting to land.

The most shocking discovery for Russian pilots was made during aerial reconnaissance of the Yukhnov district. At 14.00 the movement of a large column of tanks on the Yukhnov–Vyazma road was reported. The column had crossed the river Ugra and was already in the vicinity of the city. During repeated flights, between 18.30 and 18.50, the pilots saw that all the roads from Spas-Demensk to Yukhnov were packed with enemy tanks, armoured vehicles and trucks. There were Germans in the city, and a large group of Bf 109s from JG 51 were patrolling above it. The Russian front had been broken through along 150–160km, and from Yukhnov to the Kremlin was only 190km (118 miles). There were no Russian troops in their way.

On the night of 5/6 October, German bombers attacked a major transport hub west of Moscow. This raid ended with the loss of two aircraft: He 111 H-6 W. Nr. 4108 of III./KG 26 and He 111 H-3 W. Nr. 3172 '6N+FL' of 3./KGr. 100 'Wiking'.

On 6 October, the weather deteriorated, again signalling the approach of the 'Russian winter'. The Moscow area was enveloped by a cyclone, the air temperature dropped to 0–-2°. Visibility was reduced to 1km, and it was sleeting. There was little time left to achieve the 'victory before the beginning of winter' that Hitler had promised. The main targets of Russian aviation were German columns in the area of Yukhnov. The pilots were ordered to delay the advance of German tanks 'at any cost', as well as to monitor their deployment. Intelligence found that the Germans had moved 30km in the direction of Gzhatsk. To the west to of the city the advance guard of the 3rd Panzer Group was approaching. The Russian 19th, 20th, 24th and 32nd Armies had been encircled.

The I-153 biplanes of the 120th IAP and the Pe-3 heavy fighters of the 95th IAP attacked the enemy tanks. The Germans had brought up anti-aircraft artillery to the Yukhnov district, and the sky was constantly patrolled by Bf 109s, so the Russian air force suffered heavy losses. Eleven aircraft failed to return to base (six I-153s, three LaGG-3s, one Yak-1 and one I-16). Near Gzhatsk, in a battle with 'He 113s' (so Russian pilots called the new Bf 109 F) the LaGG-3s of Lieutenants Konstantin Kapustin and Georgi Trushkov of the 564th IAP were shot. Kapustin was wounded, but returned to his regiment, while Trushkov was killed. The Politruk A.S. Pasechnik of the 120th IAP and Lieutenant Veselkov also returned to their units without aircraft. On this day, the Germans captured Bryansk, forming another cauldron for the Russian troops.

On 7 October, a cold north-west wind blew in the Moscow region and it snowed. In the afternoon the Luftwaffe attacked railway stations and lines in the rear of the Soviet troops and carried out an air raid on the city of Rzhev. Ju 87s of StG 2 in groups of 25–30 intensively attacked the surrounded Soviet troops to prevent a breakout from the cauldron. The crews of the Stukas reported destroying 20 tanks, 34 artillery pieces and 650 vehicles. Twin-engine bombers and *Zerstorers* were also active.

The 6th IAK PVO carried out 273 sorties, 110 of them attacks on German divisions in the area of Yukhnov. Pe-3s of the 95th IAP attacked a convoy of vehicles near Ugryumovo station between 12.00 and 12.15 and another convoy west of Yukhnov between 17.45 and 18.00. A group of Yak-1s from 562nd IAP attacked a German airfield south of Yukhnov. During the air attack on Rzhev, the 34th IAP claimed three Ju 88s shot down, and the 495th IAP claimed another shot down Ju 88. In reality, the Luftwaffe lost two bombers in the northern sector: Ju 88 A-4 W. Nr. 1316 of 5./KG 3 and Ju 88 A-6 W. Nr. 2468 of St.I/KG 76. At the same time in the Yukhnov area the I-153 of Lieutenant Nechaev of the 120th IAP shot down Bf 109 E-7 W. Nr. 5009 of Spanish 15.(Spain)/JG 27 with a volley of rockets. In the Dukhovshchina area was Bf 109 E-7 of 8./JG 27 was shot down and Bf 110 E-2 W. Nr. 4513 '3U+EM' of 4./ZG 26 'Horst Wessel' also failed to return to base. One damaged Bf 110 E-2 of 6./ZG 26 made an emergency landing at Smolensk airport. According to Soviet information, at 17.25 a group consisting of five Yak-1s of the 11th IAP (Captain Konstantin Titenkov, Lieutenants Boris Vasiliev, Lapochkin, Stepan Verbludov and Sergei Kazeval) attacked and shot down an 'Me 110'. The pilots were credited with one-fifth of a victory each. In the southern sector of the front, near Somovo and Gorbachevo ground fire brought down two He 111s (W. Nr. 4403 and W. Nr. 6879) of KGr. 100 'Wiking' which were supporting the attack of General Heinz Guderian's Second Panzer Army at Tula.

Despite the difficult weather conditions, the aircraft of both sides continued to operate actively. On 8 October, the Soviet 6th IAK PVO carried out 329 sorties, but only a few pilots were successful. Near Rzhev Lieutenant Victor Korobov of the 34th IAP shot down Ju 88 A-5 W. Nr. 4276 'F1+JH' of 1./KG 76: the crew was captured. Over the Ugra river a Bf 109 E-7 piloted by K. Maruan of III./JG 27 was shot down. The pilot was also captured. Near Novo-Petrovsky Lieutenant Nemyatiy of the 519th IAP in his MiG-3 rammed Ju 88 A-5 W. Nr. 4350 of St./KG 3, which the Germans listed as missing in the Kashira area. The Russian pilot survived and was awarded the Order of the Red Banner.

A Breakthrough at Kalinin

On 8–10 October Russian fighters and ground-attack aircraft continued to attack German troops in the area of Yukhnov. But these attacks did not affect the course of events. By the evening of 10 October, German troops had reached the line Olenino–Sychevka–Gzhatsk–Medyn–Kozelsk. Advanced units of the Second Panzer Army reached the outskirts of Mtsensk. At this defining moment, Hitler himself prevented the breakthrough of tanks to Moscow. On the evening of 8 October, he intervened in the course of the battle, declaring the main focus of effort ('*schwerpunkt*') to be the movement to the north and north-east of Kalinin and Torzhok. The *Führer* had become interested in the idea of capturing an extended area between Novgorod–Tikhvin and Kalinin–Rybinsk, to reach Vologda and Yaroslavl by the beginning of winter. On 9 October, the Reichsminister of Propaganda Joseph Goebbels announced on the radio: 'The outcome of the war is decided and Russia is finished.' Just as in September with Leningrad, Hitler decided: 'The goal is achieved, but not yet captured' . . .

On 12 October, the weather in the Moscow area improved, with clear skies over the area of fierce fighting. The Luftwaffe supported their troops in the area of Kalinin, Mozhaisk and Maloyaroslavets. Ground-attack planes and dive bombers made attacks on defensive positions, roads and troop concentrations. Reconnaissance aircraft flew over the railway lines around Moscow, in the areas of Serpukhov, Kashira, Kolomna and Ryazan. Air attacks were made on the airfields at Klin, Kubinka and Bronnitsy, and everywhere German planes scattered propaganda leaflets calling for an end to the fighting. The Kubinka airfield was especially hard hit when at 08.15 nine Ju 88s dropped 200 fragmentation bombs, destroying many Russian aircraft including three Yak-1s of the 563rd IAP. The Luftwaffe also suffered serious losses. While attacking Soviet troops around the city, two Bf 110s of 6./SKG 210, W. Nr. 3719 'S9+MP' and W. Nr. 3788 'S9+EP', were shot down by anti-aircraft fire. All the crews were killed or reported missing.

In the afternoon of 13 October, German tanks, having advanced 100 km (62 miles) along the right bank of the Volga, reached the south-western suburbs of Kalinin. This was the ancient city of Tver, which the Bolsheviks had renamed Kalinin in honour of the 'all-Union elder' Mikhail Kalinin – one of Stalin's close associates. This large city was located on the banks of the Volga and was an important transport hub. Through it passed the railway from Moscow to Leningrad, which delivered troops to the Leningrad front.

This breakthrough was unexpected by the Russians. Five I-16s of the 495th IAP at the Migalovo airfield (near Kalinin) took off at the last moment, under fire from German tanks. Soviet troops in Kalinin tried to resist, but with the support of Hs 123s and Bf 109 Es of II.(Sch)/LG 2, which attacked the Russians with strafing, the Germans managed to enter the city. Stalin, learning of the capture of Kalinin, immediately ordered it to be recaptured 'at any cost'. After that, fierce battles on the ground and in the air broke out around the city. The Luftwaffe was very active in this sector. They defended the captured bridgehead on the southern bank of the Volga and sought to 'isolate' the area.

On the morning of 14 October, Bf 110 E-3s of 3./ZG 26 'Horst Wessel' attacked trains on the Torzhok–Rzhev railway line. Two aircraft failed to return:

- Bf 110 E-3 W. Nr. 4393 '3U+HL' (pilot Leutnant Komle, navigator Gefrieter Hilgers);
- Bf 110 E-3 W. Nr. 4336 '3U+LL' (pilot Leutnant Huck, navigator Gefrieter Fogelsang).

More fortunate was Leutnant H. Franck of St.II.(Sch)/LG 2. His Bf 109 E-7 W. Nr. 6416 was shot down by ground fire near Kalinin, but he was able to return to his squadron.

According to German plans, the airfield at Migalovo was to become an important Luftwaffe airbase for further advances to Vyshny Volochek, Kalyazin and Yaroslavl. In the evening of 14 October, a day after the last Russian fighters evacuated Migalovo, the first element of Ju 87s from I./StG 2 landed there. Then transport aircraft brought in some of the ground staff. However, in addition to aircraft maintenance the technicians also had to organize the all-around defence of the airfield. 'Kalinin was seized in a rapid attack, and the bridge over the Volga had been captured intact', the war diary of StG 2 'Immelmann' recorded. 'However, the surrounding forests were swarming with Russian soldiers. The airfield, where the headquarters and I./StG 2 were located, was constantly under fire. Anti-aircraft guns were positioned on the edge of the airfield and continuously fired at the attacking Russians, whilst the Stukas themselves attacked them constantly from the air.'

Some of the Bf 109 E-7, Hs 123 A-1 and Hs 129 B-1 ground-attack aircraft of II.(Sch)/LG 2 commanded by Major Otto Weiss relocated to Migalovo. Arriving in this inferno, right on the front line, their pilots flew several sorties a day. Often they had to fly in heavy fog at a height of 30–50m (100–150ft) above the ground, attacking the Russian troops around Kalinin. On 16 October Bf 109s of II./JG 52 and the Spanish volunteers of 15.(Spain)/JG 27 also arrived.

Soon the Russians became aware of the high concentration of Luftwaffe aircraft at Kalinin and the airfield was subjected to regular air raids. On 18 October, a group of MiG-3s and I-16s of the 27th IAP attacked Migalovo airfield. Four Bf 109 E-7s of 4 and 5 (Sch)./LG 2 were destroyed or damaged. Lieutenant Arkady Kovachevich claimed one victory. Russians also suffered losses: Sergeant Potapov was reported missing.

At this time the armoured group that was in Kalinin (the 1st Panzer Division and the 36th Motorized Infantry Division) was isolated from the rest of the German army. Indeed, the crossing over the Volga between Staritsa and Kalinin was still in Soviet hands. The Germans were kept supplied by Ju 52 transports and He 111 bombers, which landed at Migalovo.

On 19 October Stalin gave strict orders: Kalinin was to be recaptured within two days. 'This task is to be entrusted to those capable of carrying it out,' the order read.

On 21 October, fighters of the 27th IAP (from Klin airfield) carried out repeated raids on Migalovo airfield. The pilots claimed fifteen Me 109s destroyed on the ground and two shot down in the air. In fact the only German losses in the Kalinin area were two Bf 109 Es of 15(Spain)/JG 27.

During this period there was fierce fighting around the town. The Russians sent to Kalinin six infantry divisions and one tank brigade. In several

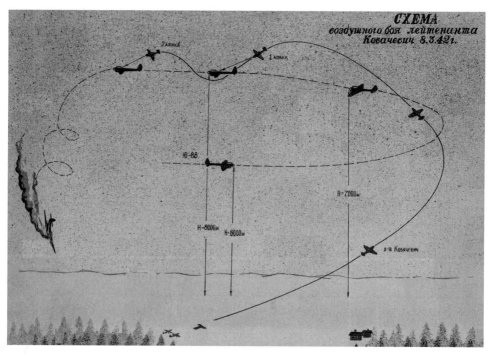

The original scheme of attack MiG-3 Lieutenant Arkady Kovachevich against Ju 88 D-5 W.Nr. 1719 of 4.(F)/14

instances, they managed to break into the outskirts of the city, but the Germans, with the active support of the Luftwaffe, launched counterattacks and threw them back to their starting line. During the day the positions of the Russian 5th Infantry Division were bombed and strafed twenty times by the Bf 109 Es, Hs 123 A-1s and Hs 129 As of II.(Sch)/LG 2. At the same time, He-111 bombers dropped cargo containers with ammunition and food to the troops holding the city.

On 24 October, Pe-3s of the 95th IAP and 208th IAP, accompanied by MiG-3s of the 27th IAP and 28th IAP, launched a new attack on Migalovo airfield. During the first approach they dropped bombs, followed by strafing attacks on the second pass. The fighters also strafed the airfield and were engaged with German fighters over Kalinin. Russian pilots said that thirty aircraft were destroyed on the ground and two shot down. But the German data disproves these statements. For the attackers, this raid ended in disaster: twelve aircraft (seven MiG-3s and five Pe-3s) failed to return to base and one heavy fighter crashed while trying to land. The commander of the 208 IAP, Major Stepan Kibirin, and his navigator Captain Feodor Kononov, were killed. German aircraft on this day were active around Kalinin, bombing and strafing the Russian troops around the city. Bf 110 E-2 W. Nr. '3U+UL' of 3./ZG 26 'Horst Wessel' was hit by anti-aircraft fire. Oberleutnant F. Ayunger and Gefreiter Adler were recorded as missing.

On 25 October three Russian armies attacked Kalinin, the 31st Army from the north-west, the 30th Army from the north-east and south-east, and the 29th Army from the south-west. In the brutal assault involving ten divisions, the fighting went on day and night. By the end of the day, the Soviet 133rd Infantry Division had managed to capture several blocks in the north-western part of Kalinin. But the Russians suffered from heavy attacks by German bombers and ground-attack aircraft. Especially hard hit was the 119th Infantry Division, which occupied positions south of the city. The German 1st Panzer Division and the 36th Motorized Infantry Division were still cut off, and supplies for them continued to be delivered by air.

On 26 October the battle for Kalinin culminated. Two infantry divisions of the German Ninth Army river approached the outskirts of the city along the bank of the Volga. They attacked the positions of the Russian 119th Infantry Division with the support of Ju 87s and Bf 110s. Because of the low clouds, the *Zerstorers* operated at low level, sometimes at only 20m (65ft).

On 27 October, despite heavy casualties, the Russian 133rd Division managed to break through to the Ogorodny alley and the tram lines in the north-west of the city. The divisions of the 30th Army that attacked Kalinin from the north-east were pinned down by German air attacks. The Russians desperately sought to recapture the city before the arrival of German reinforcements. But they lacked air support.

By 29 October, the Germans were able to establish land communication with the garrison and deliver reinforcements to the city. The Russian offensive was exhausted. This phenomenally brutal battle was a rehearsal for the future battles for the 'fortresses' of Demyansk and Rzhev . . .

Russian Field Artillery against the Luftwaffe

Stationing German aircraft in Kalinin was risky. The Migalovo airfield was on the south-eastern outskirts of the city and within range of Russian field artillery. On the evening of 22 October, Soviet intelligence learnt that sixty-eight German transport aircraft had landed at Migalovo. The 531th Light Artillery Regiment (531th LAP) was ordered to carry out a bombardment of the airfield at 03.00. At this time the Russians were short of heavy artillery due to the immense losses suffered during Operation 'Barbarossa'. Artillery regiments had to be equipped with old Tsarist-era guns taken from warehouses and training regiments and sent to the front.

The shelling of the German air base was carried out exactly as planned by the 76mm guns of the 1st, 2nd and 4th Batteries of the 531th LAP. The 2nd battery, under the command of Lieutenant Nemchenko, fired 150 rounds from three guns. The shelling lasted for 12 minutes, but the Russians were unable to observe the results. In fact, the shells hit only one German aircraft – Ju 52/3m W. Nr. 2867 of 16./KG zbV1.

On the night of 25/26 October, the 1st and 4th Batteries of the 531th LAP carried out repeated shelling ('fire raids') on Migalovo with 76mm guns. 'Loud engine noises were heard during the attack,' read the Russian report. 'Later, the human intelligence service found out that the attack was successful.' In fact, only two aircraft were destroyed: Ju 87 B-2 W. Nr. 5727 of 2./StG 2 and Fi 156 W. Nr. 4348 of Verbst.58.

The most successful attack on the German air base came on 30 October. The 107mm guns of the 108th Artillery Regiment (108th AP) destroyed nine Bf 109 F-2 fighters (eight from II./JG 52 and one from II./JG 54) and two Ju 52/3m glider tugs from I./LLG1. Casualties were two killed and two wounded. The next day, the Russians captured a 'Polish prisoner' from the 36th Motorized Infantry Division. He said that ten aircraft were destroyed at the airfield, and ten more were damaged, which was not far from the truth.

'Vikings' over Moscow

On 14 October, the headquarters of Army Group Centre issued an optimistic order, which began with the words: 'The Enemy in front of the army group has been defeated. The remains retreat . . .' All troops were ordered to 'pursue' the Russians and move to many distant objectives. Ninth Army and 3rd Panzer Group were to attack north to the area of Vyshniy Volochek. Fourth Army and the 4th Panzer Group met to encircle Moscow from the north, west and south, and the 2nd Panzer army from the east, moving through Orekhovo-Zuyevo and Noginsk. Then motorized troops were going to move on to Yaroslavl, Rybinsk and Gorky. In the southern sector the 2nd Army was to move to Voronezh. The Luftwaffe's priority was to support the advancing divisions.

The same day, a new series of air raids on Moscow began. It was opened by KGr. 100 'Wiking', which on the evening of 8 October had moved from Bobruisk to an advanced airfield at Seschinskaya (Bryansk district). The target of the attack was railway facilities south of Moscow. The *Fliegerbuch* of the commander of the 1st *Staffel*, Oberleutnant Bätcher, records the destruction of ninety wagons during this raid. In the evening KGr. 100 attacked the same targets using SC500 high-explosive and SD50 fragmentation bombs. The average flight time of the He 111s was 3.5–4 hours.

The next air attack on Moscow occurred on the night of 14/15 October. The war diary of the 1st Air Defence Corps read:

> Anti-aircraft artillery fired a massed barrage. Fighters did not take off because of low unbroken clouds, searchlights for the same reason were not lit. As a result of the battle 4–5 planes broke through to the city and dropped high-explosive and incendiary bombs. There was damage and casualties among the civilian population . . .The city declared an air alert from 4.03 to 4.55. Anti-aircraft artillery during barrage fire spent shells: 85mm – 11 541, 76mm – 6,656, 75mm – 59, 105mm – 76.

According to the Russian rescue service, seven high-explosive and more than 300 incendiary bombs were dropped on the city. As a result, in the Rostokinsky district there was a big fire at plant No. 58. Two warehouses of the Kalininkaya railway and twelve houses were destroyed. Twenty people

lfd. Nr. des Fein d. fluges	Wartung als Frontflug	Bau-muster	Tag	von ... bis	Zeit über Feind- bzw. feind-gefährdetem Gebiet	Flugweg	Ein-dring-tiefe km	Feindberührung (Jagd- und Flak)	Ergebnis des Fluges (z. B. Abschüsse, Artillerieeinschießen, Auf-klärung, Bombenwurf unter Angabe von Angriffshöhe, Wurfart, Zahl der Anflüge, ob Luftbildbestätigung des Erfolges usw.)	Bestätigung durch Dienststelle und Augenzeugen
75	2	He 111	8.10.	0532 – 1040				leichte Flak	B.w. Aufkl. Angr. a. Mch., Zug.; Glis d. 1 SD 50 muhn-bmhm; 1 SC 50, 4 SD 50, 4 SD 50	
76	1		14.10.	1015 – 1110				keine Flak	Bahnanlagen snll. Mnhm Bomben i. Bhf.; 90 Wagen zerstört; Tiefangriff auf fahrenden Zug	
77	1		14.10.	1510 – 1838				keine Abwehr	Angr. Gleisanlagen · Züge südl. Mnhm; 1 SC 500 · 16 SD 50 a. Truppen u. Bahnanlagen	
78	1		17.10.	0749 – 1040				schwere Flak	Störangriff auf Mnhm 1 SC 500, 2 SC 250 · 8 SD 50 im Ziel	

Records in the *Fliegerbuch* of Oberleutnant Hans Georg Bätcher with remarks on the attacks on Moscow on 14 and 17 October

Pilots of the 178th IAP read the newspaper against the background of a LaGG-3 fighter

were killed and sixty-five injured. 'On the night of October 15, bombers attacked important military facilities in Moscow,' reported the OKW. 'There were several fires.' This raid was performed by KGr. 100 'Wiking', and the He 111s used the high-powered SC1800 bombs. 'The results of the attack could not be observed,' says the KG 100 war diary. 'Strong anti-aircraft artillery cover, searchlights and night fighters patrolling over the target greatly hampered the actions of the crews.' In fact, the searchlights actually helped them locate the target in heavy cloud. If the targets in Moscow were not distinguishable, the Germans aimed at the centre of the vast field of light.

On the morning of 17 October, the commander of 1./KGr. 100 'Wiking', Oberleutnant Hans Bätcher, made a solo air attack on Moscow. His *Fliegerbuch* recorded that his He 111 took off at 07.49, and dropped one SC500 bomb, two SC250s and eight SD50s on the southern part of the city. At 10.40, after a flight of 2 hours and 51 minutes Bätcher returned to Seschinskaya. The bomber had not been detected as it entered the airspace over the city, so the air alarm did not sound. At 09.45 Moscow time, explosions suddenly occurred in the south-western area of the capital (according to the Russian rescue service, nine high-explosive bombs were dropped). The flour warehouse of Bakery No. 6 was destroyed, and 'Vorobyovy Gory' railway station was damaged. Two people were killed and six injured. Bätcher reported that 'light anti-aircraft fire was met over the target'.

On the same day, Bätcher made a second flight, dropping a similar 'kit' of bombs on railway facilities in the south of Moscow. The raid by a single He 111 on the Russian capital was reported as follows in the OKW communique of 18 October: 'Powerful bomb attacks were inflicted during yesterday and last night on important military facilities in Moscow. Due to the explosions of a large number of high-explosive and incendiary bombs in the city centre and in the bend of the Moscow river there were major fires.' German propaganda sought to exploit any event for its own purposes.

After the capture of Kalinin, Maloyaroslavets and Mozhaisk, the Russians no longer had air surveillance posts on the borders but only 100–120km from Moscow. Therefore, the warning system did not work, as the German bombers needed only 25–30 minutes flying over Russian territory to reach the city.

Russian aviation was still active, but only in rare cases were the pilots lucky. On 17 October, the 6th IAK PVO carried out 568 sorties and claimed twelve victories (including three 'He 113s' and three Hs 126s). In reality, the Luftwaffe lost only Bf 109 F-2 W. Nr. 5420 flown by Unteroffizier Heinz Jon

Gerasim Grigoriev during the air battle for Moscow shot down 8 German aircraft (5 of them confirmed)

Barrage balloon is lying on the playground in Moscow

of I./JG 51. Over Reshetnikovo station a pair of MiG-3s (Lieutenants Alexey Katrich and Fedor Chuikin of the 27th IAP) shot down this 'He 113'.

On 18 October, Moscow air defence pilots carried out almost 700 sorties, but shot down only one German aircraft. Near Aprelevka Lieutenant Alexandrov of the 34th IAP brought down an 'Me 110'. It was probably the schnell-bomber Bf 110 E-6 W. Nr. 2254 'S9+AM' of 4./SKG 210. In addition, Bf 110 E-2 W. Nr. 2729 '6K+YA' of 5.(H)/23 disappeared without trace.

Anti-Soviet Riots in Moscow

In mid-October, Stalin's propaganda continued to zombify the population in the spirit of 'all is well' and 'victory will be ours'. The radio and the newspapers said Hitler had run out of men and that the troops advancing on Moscow were cripples, mental patients, degenerates and alcoholics. But the people no longer believed the propaganda. On 16 October, anti-Soviet protests and mass riots broke out in Moscow. After learning that the front had collapsed again and that German tanks were approaching the city, thousands of people decided that the dictatorship of the Bolsheviks and Stalin was over. Some rushed to loot shops, others to flee the city.

The director of one of the aircraft factories, Perovskiy, took the official seal of the institution, got into his car and fled. Following his example, the chiefs of the shops and departments also ran, leaving the workers in the lurch. In many factories workers beat up the managers and looted stores. The employees of the famous Moscow 'Mikoyan' meat processing plant stole five tons of sausages and went home. At the 'Burevestnik' shoe factory in the Sokolniki district a crowd of workers gathered and demanded their pay. But money was not enough: people broke down the gates and stole all the ready-made shoes along with semi-finished products. The director of the First Moscow Medical Institute, V.V. Parin, his assistants and the secretary of the Pashintsev party organization fled the city in a stolen car, leaving behind the hospital with the wounded, a clinic with patients, faculty and their students. At the gates of the 'Stalin' (ZiS) automobile plant 1,500 workers gathered, demanding their wages. The watchman and policemen were beaten with shovels.

That night mass riots broke out in the streets of Moscow. People broke shop windows, broke down doors and emptied out the shops. There were many gangs of looters. In Moscow, the trams, trolleybuses and metro stopped. The journalist N.K. Verbitsky wrote in his diary: 'Yes, October 16 will go down as the most shameful date, the date of cowardice, confusion and betrayal in the history of Moscow. The people who were first to shout about heroism, resilience, duty, honour were the first to flee the city.'

The panic was fuelled by the 'news' that the Germans had already entered the city and were heading for the Kremlin. Thinking that this was the end of Stalin, people surged into the streets with renewed vigour. A worker at one of the Moscow factories recalled:

> Germans in Moscow? What to do? I decided to go to my father and ask him. My father worked at the headquarters of air defence of the Northern railway, which was located in Kalanchevke, he lived in barracks. I went to him on tram number 32, in order to find out what to do. Broken windows, robberies and fun. I saw how people carried on shoulders not only bags, but also whole hams, saw the women holding the linked fingers of hands over the head, sausage circles were put over them. Working people robbed and had fun, as if they were not in danger.

While some people were looting and waiting for the Germans, thousands of people fled to the east towards Gorky in cars and carts and on bicycles.

Self-defence group holds a meeting in one of the Moscow yards

Many walked, laden with bags. On the highway from Moscow to Gorky, there were mass pogroms. The angry crowds overturned the cars of fleeing Communist Party functionaries and other Soviet bosses, stole the contents and then dumped them in the ditch. 'Priority' was given to those who looked Jewish. Order in Moscow was only re-established by the end of October thanks to brutal repression and executions.

NKVD mounted patrol monitors law and order in Moscow

At this time, the victorious attitude of the German command was quickly replaced by the understanding that 'the Russians do not give up'. 'There are no signs of the enemy's withdrawal . . . the enemy still puts up strong resistance . . . it should be expected that the enemy, who will also be able to use in defence the numerous rivers flowing across the path of the offensive, will continue persistent resistance', read the OKH operational summary on 18 October. Furthermore, the report of the Fourth Army first noted 'the active operations of enemy aircraft that attacked the marching columns and command posts'. After gathering all available forces (the rear-echelon units, military schools, regiments of people's militia [the Russian 'Home Guard']), the Soviet high command were able to create a new line of defence on the approaches to Moscow. At this time, the German tanks were stuck in the mud and left without fuel. Only the Nazi newspaper the *Volkischer Beobachter* continued the optimistic trend set by the *Führer*: 'The whole world has already realized that in this operation the last fully combat-ready Bolshevik troops – Tymoshenko's army group – were destroyed, and thus the fate of the Eastern campaign was decided.'

On the morning of 21 October the weather in the Moscow area was 'normal': 10 points of cloud and periodic rain. In such conditions, even taking off was difficult and dangerous. But the Germans had captured the airfield at Seschinskaya, a Russian long-range bomber base. It had a concrete runway, unaffected by the 'Russian thaw'. At lunchtime the bombers of KGr. 100 'Wiking' took off from Seschinskaya and carried out an air attack on Moscow. Taking advantage of the clouds, they arrived undetected over the city and dropped sixty-six high-explosive and fragmentation bombs. There was no air-raid warning and the people could not take shelter in time. The anti-aircraft artillery did not open fire.

The air raid affected the north-eastern regions of Moscow. The main office of aviation plant No. 1 'Osoaviakhim', plants Nos 51 and 58, the water supply of the Rublevskaya station, the bus station and several residential barracks were destroyed. According to the Russian rescue service, twenty-nine people were killed and seventy injured. In this attack, the Germans used not only the usual high-explosive and fragmentation bombs, but special SBe50 concrete fragmentation bombs. They were charged with ammonium nitrate with a mixture of wood pulp and aluminium powder. The 4–5cm (1.5–2 inches) concrete body of the bomb had steel fragments embedded in it, resembling modern terrorist devices.

Russian fighters played no part in repelling this air attack on Moscow. The war diary 'forgot' to include it to hide this latest failure. Russians carried out numerous flights 'to provide cover' and 'patrol' during which there was an unaimed barrage over certain areas.

A Russian family descends into a primitive earthen shelter

View of Moscow from a German plane

On 22 October the Luftwaffe continued its attacks on Moscow and carried out several raids. Eight districts of the city were damaged, forty-five high-explosive, fragmentation and concrete bombs being dropped. The most severe damage occurred at the Moscow-Tovarnaya railway station, where the tracks and platforms were damaged. On Butyrskaya Street in the Oktyabrsky district three houses were destroyed, and eight houses in the in Dzerzhinsky district. Dozens of other buildings were damaged. According to the Russian rescue service fourteen people were killed and forty-six injured. The warning was sounded too late for people to reach the shelters in time.

But this day was not without loss for the Luftwaffe. The 6th IAK PVO carried out 441 sorties. Russian fighters covered Moscow and the troops in the district of Naro-Fominsk and engaged with German aircraft over the front line. Pilots reported seventeen aircraft shot down. The 34th IAP of Major L.G. Rybkin engaged in twenty-four dogfights over the Minsk highway and reported twelve victories. These were by Lieutenant N. Alexandrov (personal victory over a Do 215 in the Naro-Fominsk district, and a shared victory over a Ju 88 in Vnukovo), Z.A. Durnaykin, Tikhonov (an He 111 near Tikhonovo), Y. Gerasimov, Lieutenants A.F. Code, Victor Korobov (an He-111 near Aprelevka), A.N. Potapov and Y.S. Seldakov. The Luftwaffe had indeed suffered major losses. In total it had lost twenty-seven on the Eastern Front on this day, fifteen of them in the Moscow region. South-west of Moscow Do 17 Z-2 W. Nr. 2627 of 8./KG 3 and Ju 88 A-4 W. Nr. 1252 of 2./KG 3 were shot down. In the Aprelevka and Tikhonovo areas two He 111 H-6s from III./KG 53 'Legion Condor' and III./KG 26 were brought down, and in the Podolsk district Hs 126 B-1 W. Nr. 3136 'V7+2B' of 2.(H)/23 was reported missing with its crew. Bf 109 F-2 W. Nr. 8976 was shot down in the Mozhaysk area and Bf 109 F-2 W. Nr. 12960 in the Maloyaroslavets district (both from I./JG 51).

On this day, units of the German Fourth army broke into the western outskirts of Naro-Fominsk, and ended up only 60km (37 miles) away from Moscow.

At this building the shock wave tore off the facade

Bf 110 E-1 W.Nr. 4080 '3U+CP' of 6./ZG 26. This plane was shot down near Moscow on October 27

Bätcher's Raid on the Huge Soviet Granary

In the second half of October, the Luftwaffe targeted grain silos located around Moscow, to deprive the Soviet troops and the civilian population of food on the eve of winter. Air raids were carried out against the granaries at the Tikhonova-Pustin (Kaluga) station, Alexandrov, Yaroslavl, Ivanovo, Tula and other places. The attacks were usually carried out by single bombers with experienced crews who suddenly appeared over the target from out of the clouds or at dusk.

A raid on one of these targets, a huge granary in the village of Volodar (360km [224 miles] east of Moscow) was carried out by the commander of 1./KGr. 100, Hans Bätcher. By this time, he had carried out eighty sorties 'against the enemy' (*Feind-flug*) and was considered an expert in the destruction of point targets (e.g. factories, railway stations, airfields and troops concentrations).

At 13.38 on 22 October, Bätcher's He 111 H took off from Seschinskaya. The flight time to the distant target was 2½ hours. The main reference point was the straight line of the railway from Moscow to Gorky, near which towered the huge granary building. Next to it was the airfield at Seima, where Soviet aviation regiments received new LaGG-3 fighters from aviation plant No 21. No less than 100 fighters were there! But the Russians did not expect that a German bomber could appear in such a remote area. The pilots only saw Bätcher's He 111 when it was over the target. The plane dropped to 1,000m (3,300ft) and dropped one SC 1000 high-explosive bomb and four SD250 fragmentation bomb son the huge granary.

Local resident Valentina Smirnova recalled:

> We went to school in the afternoon, there was a lesson. It was already evening and it began to get dark. Suddenly there was a terrible roar at which the glass trembled and the plaster fell. The teacher immediately shouted: 'run outside'. In many houses in the village the lights went out and the windows were shattered. I started to panic. The teachers and children ran shouting out of the school. Residents were hastily evacuating the houses with suitcases and bags . . . People thought the Germans had arrived.

She continued:

> For a moment, the children stopped at the unexpected and unknown terror before them: the eastern side of the nearest granary, a week ago covered with gray-yellow camouflage, was on fire. A giant mushroom of black smoke swelled into the air, covering half the sky over the village. Large bright red flames licked at the base of the mushroom, the heat of which could be felt from a distance – the glow of the fire played eerily in the glass windows, the rays of light on roofs and dark wood walls.

The target that Bätcher attacked was mill plant No. 4 and base No. 154, belonging to the territorial administration of state material reserves. The granary, in which 100,000 tons of grain were stored, was completely destroyed. This raid was listed in Bätcher's *Fliegerbuch* as one of his most meritorious actions. His He 111 returned to Seschinskaya at 18.25, when it got dark.

The Soviet authorities were very frightened. Soon the raid on the granary was discussed at a meeting of the Gorky regional committee of the Communist Party. The First Secretary (Stalin's local representative) Mikhail Rodionov accused the pilots of treason, 'collapse of discipline' and drunkenness. Because not one fighter took off to intercept the He 111, Rodionov shouted:

> What was the aviation regiment doing? . . . This was a wonderful chance to attack the enemy. It seems a lucky chance that they did not destroy this airfield and the aircraft. Why this drunkenness and other phenomena? This means that the commanders do not lead their subordinates. For such sloppiness, for such a state of discipline commanders should be sent to prison!

The Germans achieved their objective. Many stocks of grain were destroyed. But bread was already scarce before this. At the end of October in Moscow the workers' bread ration was reduced from 800g to 600g (1.75lbs to 1.35lbs) per day. In other cities, the population also starved. Instead of good bread people began to be given low-grade substitutes.

Raids on the Kremlin and the Central Office of the Communist Party

On 23 October it was cloudy and raining in the Moscow region, but the aircraft of both sides were active. The Russians desperately tried to stop the advance of Guderian's tanks at Tula. The main target of Luftwaffe on this day were Soviet troop positions near Mtsensk. KGr. 100 'Wiking' attacked this target three times. Oberleutnant Bätcher's *Fliegerbuch* states that his He 111 took off from Seschinskaya at 07.07 Berlin time. North-east of Mtsensk, he dropped one SC500, two SD250s and eight SD50s on Russian tanks and infantry positions. Because of the heavy clouds the attack was carried out at an altitude of 600m (1,968ft). At 08.55 Bätcher landed at Seschinskaya and at 10.14 took off again with his plane loaded with high-explosive and concrete fragmentation bombs. The duration of the flight was a little less than two hours. After a three-hour rest, at 15.13 the He 111 of the commander of the 1st squadron took off once more and an hour later dropped on the soviet troops one SC500 and ten SBe50s on Soviet troops. In total, this single bomber dropped 3.7 tons of bombs on one day. In Mtsensk district, ground fire damaged He 111 H-6 W. Nr. 4166 of 2./KGr. 100. One crewman was wounded. Their efforts were not in vain. In the evening, Guderian's Second Panzer Army broke through the Russian defences and advanced to Tula.

THE LUFTWAFFE IN OPERATION 'TYPHOON'

At 18.23 five He 111s of III./KG 26 made another air raid on Moscow, dropping forty-three high-explosive and fragmentation bombs and 1,500 incendiaries. The main target was the food warehouses of the Moscow state administration of reserves on Volochayevskaya Street. There was a big fire. Also damaged were the 'Orgaviaprom' factory and the Danilovsky market. A large house, No. 84 Osipenko Street, was destroyed. Twenty-three people were killed and eighty-three wounded. During the raid He 111 H-6 W. Nr. 4107 came down for an unknown reason. Two of the crew (including the pilot Leutnant H. Lohr) were missing, but the others were able return to German territory.

The 6th IAK PVO carried out 400 sorties and claimed five aircraft shot down. Their own losses amounted to eight fighters, including five Yak-1s. The pilots who failed to return were Politruk V.I. Gerasimov of the 34th IAP, Lieutenant N.V. Guriev and Sergeants Ivanov and Mackowski of the 562nd IAP, Sergeant Vnukov of the 233rd IAP, Lieutenant Dovzenko of the 177th IAP, and Junior lieutenant V.N. Mikelman and Sergeant Evstigneev of the 11th IAP.

German fighters also suffered losses. Over the Ugodsky factory Bf 109 F-2 W. Nr. 9189 piloted by Unteroffizier Gunter Schak of 7./JG 51 was shot down. The pilot bailed out. In the future, he was to be one of the best Luftwaffe aces. By the end of the war, he had 175 victories. Fate was crueller to Oberfeldwebel Heinz Schawaller of 1./JG 51, who was killed in the wreckage of his Bf 109 F-2 W. Nr. 6663. Probably he was shot down near the village of Malkovichi by Lieutenant A.I. Scherbatykh of the 34th IAP. Schawaller managed to win twelve victories.

The Russians tried to disguise the Kremlin with camouflage of different colors

The Russians tried to disguise the Kremlin with camouflage of different colors (2)

But the worst day was had by the German bombers. In one district (Odintsovo-Nemchinovo) ten bombers (eight He 111s and two Ju 88) were lost. Thirty-seven crew were killed and missing, including the commanders of two squadrons (7./KG 53 and 8./KG 53). The exact cause of the loss of so many aircraft in one place is unknown. Some were shot down by Russian fighters of the 34th and 41st IAPs, while others probably crashed due to a sudden change in the weather conditions.

The Loss of German Bombers in the Odintsovo-Nemchinovo District, 23 October 1941

Aircraft	W. Nr.	Code	Squadron	Casualties	% Damage
He 111 H-6	4243	A1+FP	6./KG 53	2 injured	100
He 111 H-6	4248	A1+IP	6./KG 53	5 dead	100
He 111 H-5	3991	A1+BR	7./KG 53	–	70
He 111 H-6	4284	A1+CR	7./KG 53	5 dead	100
He 111 H-6	4285	A1+KR	7./KG 53	5 dead	100
He 111 H-6	4369	A1+IR	7./KG 53	5 dead	100
He 111 H-6	4477	A1+HS	8./KG 53	5 dead	100
He 111 H-6	4107	1H+HT	III./KG 26	2 dead	100
Ju 88 A-4	3574	5K+CB	St.I/KG 3	4 dead	100
Ju 88 A-4	2563	5K+??	I./KG 3	4 dead	100

On the evening of 24 October III./KG 4 'General Wever' made another air raid on Moscow, dropping 25 high-explosive bombs and 600 incendiaries. The main target was again the Moscow-Tovarnaya railway station, where the tracks and buildings were destroyed as was a nearby block of houses in Samotechny Lane. According to the Russian rescue service, eight people were killed and seventeen wounded. 'During the night, the bombers attacked military facilities and military plants in Moscow,' the OKW reported the next day.

On this day, Russian air defence fighters, despite the bad weather, carried out 550 sorties and claimed 32 aircraft shot down! Army aviation on the Moscow front carried out 318 sorties, attacking ground targets in the Ruza, Mozhaisk, Vereya and Maloyaroslavets areas. In fact, the Germans suffered no losses, and their fighters were successful. In aerial combat west of Moscow Lieutenant A.I. Shcherbatykh of the 34th IAP,

Lieutenant M.M. Babuschkin of the 16th IAP and Boris Vasilyev of the 11th IAP were killed. In combat with a Bf 109 the MiG-3 of Lieutenant Georgi Primak of the 16th IAP was shot down but the pilot managed to bail out of the burning aircraft and was unhurt.

The only loss the Luftwaffe suffered was in the Serpukhov area. Schnell-bomber Bf 110 E-2 'S9+AM' of 4./SKG 210 was shot down while attacking ground targets. The crew of Leutnant H. Fischer and Unteroffizier F. Beyer were never found. With air support, the Germans occupied Tarusa on the outskirts of Serpukhov – an important railway junction south of Moscow. The Wehrmacht continued to slowly push the Russians to the east.

At this time, Hitler suddenly realized the 'huge strategic importance of Voronezh'. The commander of the Second Panzer Army, General Guderian, was ordered to urgently allocate for this purpose, six infantry divisions, one panzer division and one motorized division. These large forces were transferred to the Second Army. The attack on the south-east stretched the long front of Army Group Centre and created many problems for the rear services and the Luftwaffe. The *Führer* continued to be 'optimistic' and to believe that it was still possible to occupy many cities before the 'Russian winter'.

The Russians continued to exaggerate and inflate their 'successes'. Reports told about a series of air victories. On 25 October the 6th IAK PVO set a record by carrying out 716 sorties. Pilots claimed about twenty victories for four of their own planes lost. In reality, Luftwaffe lost only one He 111 P-4 W. Nr. 2968 from 9./KG 4 'General Wever'. To the east of Serpukhov it was damaged by the LaGG-3 of Lieutenant Gerasim Grigoriev of the 178th IAP. The bomber reached German-held territory but was completely wrecked in an emergency landing. One of the crew was killed and another wounded.

On 27 October, Russian pilots carried out almost 700 sorties, 56 of which were attacks on ground targets. Fighters of the 120th IAP together with six Il-2s of the 65th SHAP made five attacks on German troops around Tarusa and Ruza. The air defence fighters dropped 90 fragmentation bombs and fired 250 rockets. The rest of the fighters carried out patrols. 'Success' was again small. The pilots claimed seventeen victories but again only one German aircraft was actually shot down, Bf 110 E-1 W. Nr. 4080 '3U+CP' of the 6./ZG 26 'Horst Wessel'. This was the only real victory of those claimed by the pilots of the three regiments (the 34th, 42nd and 171th) in different areas (Naro-Fominsk, Teploye station and Volokolamsk). Their losses were four fighters. Hero of the Soviet Union Lieutenant Viktor Talalikhin of the 177th IAP was killed when his I-16 was shot down in combat with a Bf 109.

Masking on the Bolshoi theatre

The morning of 28 October in the Moscow region was cloudy and wet with fog, but by lunchtime the sky had cleared. This allowed the Germans to send up a lot of their bombers on air raids on the Red capital. Air alerts were declared in the city on four occasions, and the bombing attacks lasted from morning till late evening. Among the first over Moscow were the planes of 1./KGr. 100 'Wiking'. The He 111 of Oberleutnant Hans Bätcher took off from Seshchinskaya at 09.40 (Berlin time), and at 11.00 dropped one SC500, four concrete SBe50s and four SD50s on the city. Between 14.45 and 18.15 the *Staffel* carried out a second raid on Moscow, during which Bätcher, on his 87th combat sortie, dropped three high-explosive and eight fragmentation bombs.

During the day, the Germans dropped 110 high-explosive and fragmentation bombs and more than 1,200 incendiaries on Moscow. In the Tagansky district railway lines, residential buildings and a meat processing plant were destroyed, along with a brick factory in the Leninsky district and school No. 155, four houses and the Institute of Foreign Languages in the Leningrad district. But the main target of these air attacks was the centre of the city and the Kremlin – the lair of the Red dictator. The Germans sought to create panic amongst the government and paralyze the work of the authorities. Bätcher and his colleagues managed fifteen hits on the Kremlin. The bombs exploded in the square near the 'Orusheinaya palata', on Red Square ('Krasnaya ploschad') near the Spasskaya tower, next to the Tsar-gun, and hit the Arsenal building. The leader of the Moscow Bolsheviks (Secretary of the Moscow City Party Committee) A.S. Shcherbakov and the town governor (the Chairman of the Executive Committee of Mossovet) V.P. Pronin were shell-shocked. One of the high-explosive bombs exploded in the city centre in the middle of Gorky Street (now Tverskaya Street) opposite the central telegraph office. On the street several cars were overturned, and many people queueing outside the shops were killed or injured. The side of the famous Bolshoi theatre was destroyed. The main facade and the ceiling of the lobby collapsed. Several houses on the embankment of the Moscow river were also destroyed.

The rescue service reported 26 dead and 144 wounded, but the real casualty figures were much higher. In the Kremlin alone there were 41 dead, 4 missing and 101 wounded. These air attacks were heavy, but they cannot be compared to the bomb attacks on London in the autumn of 1940. Moscow residents never experienced the disasters suffered by the residents of the capital of Great Britain.

Russian fighters had no effect on the air raids. Their only success was the Spanish Bf 109 E-7 W. Nr. 2796 of 15.(Spain)/JG 27 shot down in the Volokolamsk area. He was probably a victim of the MiG-3 group of the 27th IAP. Russian losses amounted to four fighters which failed to return to base.

On 29 October the weather in the Moscow area was clear, and on this day there was one of the biggest air battles. The 6th IAK PVO carried out 663 sorties, claiming 44 aircraft shot down. But this time the Luftwaffe really did suffer serious losses near Moscow, including from Russian fighters. Analysis of the documents allowed us to determine the following:

- Lieutenant Ivan Polyakov of the 28th IAP brought down Hs 126 B-1 W. Nr. 4339 of 3.(H)/12 near Volokolamsk;
- Lieutenant Eremenuk shot down Hs 126 B-1 W. Nr. 3317 of 7.(H)/13;
- The MiG-3 group of the 16th IAP shot down Bf 110 E-3 W. Nr. 4102 '3U+KL' of 3./ZG 26 'Horst Wessel' over Volyntsevo airfield;
- Politruk Nikolay Baskov of 445 IAP shot down Ju 88 D-2 W. Nr. 0826 of 1.(F)/22 in the Ferzikovo area (Kaluga region);
- Three I-16s of 177th IAP shot down Bf 109 F-2 W. Nr. 9218 of 1./ JG 51;
- A MiG-3 of either the 42th or 27th IAP shot down He 111 H-6 W. Nr. 4386 'A1+LN' of 5./KG 53 'Legion Condor' in the Serpukhov district.

Numerous other victories claimed by 'Stalin's Falcons' cannot be confirmed from German sources, such as Lieutenant Ivan Zabolotnyy of the 16th IAP's claim of three aircraft (two 'Me 109s' and a Ju 88) and MiG-3 pilot Lieutenant Ivan Golubin of the 16th IAP's four individual victories! The young pilot was credited with three 'Me 109s' and a Ju 87. As usual, Russian losses were higher than those of the Germans. Three pilots were killed in aerial combat, eleven 'failed to return to base' and two crashed on landing.

In the evening, another air raid on Moscow took place, during which 27 high-explosive and fragmentation bombs and 1,300 incendiaries were dropped on the city. This time the crews of III./KG 26 made a direct hit on the headquarters of the Central Committee of the VKP (b) (the Central Office of the Bolshevik Party) on Staraya Square. In one of the rooms there was a meeting discussing the defence of the near approaches to Moscow and in the city itself. 'The meeting began in the evening in the office of A.S. Shcherbakov,' recalled B.N. Chernousov, in 1941 Secretary of the Moscow Committee of the VKP (b).

> The commander of the Moscow military district, General P.A. Artemyev described in detail how the defence of the capital was built, what forces we have . . .I looked at the faces of the comrades present at the meeting. They were all calm and resolute. Artemyev had not finished his report when there was a loud explosion and the lights in the office went out. Pieces of plaster fell down. Everyone realized that a bomb had hit the Moscow Party building. We got out of the office through an emergency exit because the main door was jammed. Downstairs we were told that several employees of the Moscow Committee had been killed and wounded. Among the damaged cars we found an intact one and went to the Mossovet.

In addition to the Party office the 'Stankonormal' plant, the 'Neprerywka' factory and several houses were destroyed. The Luftwaffe lost He-111 H-6 W. Nr. 4491 of III./KG 26, piloted by the commander of the 9th *Staffel*, Hauptmann Otto Stiller. But the circumstances of this death cannot be established. 'Large forces of bomber aircraft in the daytime and at night struck Moscow with high-explosive and incendiary bombs,' reported the OKW on 30 October. 'There was evidence of large fires and heavy explosions.'

'The raids of the Germans are heavier and longer every day,' the Moscow doctor E. Sakharova wrote in her diary that day.

> Yesterday the Bolshoi theatre was destroyed. A bomb fell on the street near the Telegraph Office, by the queue at a health-food store, there were many injured and killed . . . Moscow has an unusual appearance and mood: barricades on side streets too. Moscow is preparing for a great battle. In the evening, at dusk, whole families are with the children in the shelters, with suitcases for the night. Everyone's whole life is knocked out of its channel.

On 31 October there was another raid on Moscow in which 117 high-explosive and fragmentation bombs were dropped. Three factories and seven houses were damaged. Eleven people were killed and fifty wounded.

Guderian's tanks approached Tula. Their attack was supported by the *Schnell-bombers* of SKG 210, which bombed and strafed Russian troop positions around the city. During such a mission Bf 110 E-1 W. Nr. 3880 'S9+DA' was shot down. The crew, Gefreiters J. Meir and K. Schultze, were wounded but survived.

Statistics for October

During October the 6th IAK PVO flew 11,908 sorties, including 637 to attack ground targets. Russian pilots reported 275 victories and 45 aircraft destroyed on the ground. In fact, the vast majority of flights by Russian fighters had no results. The real losses of the Luftwaffe in the Moscow region, in which Russians fighters shared, were roughly 100 aircraft, which includes aircraft shot down by Russian army aircraft and anti-aircraft artillery and those reported missing. These include twenty-nine He 111s, seventeen Bf 109s, twelve Bf 110s, eight Ju 88s, four Hs 126s and three Do 17s.

The Germans Slow Down

In October, Operation 'Typhoon' did not achieve its goal. The Germans came close to Moscow. At the end of the month the Wehrmacht had halted only 60km (37 miles) from the city. Hitler wanted to cut off the Urals from the northern and southern regions of the Soviet Union before the onset of the 'Russian winter'. He intended to surround Moscow and cut the railways going from Moscow to Vologda in the north and to Rostov in the south. The 3rd and 4th Panzer Groups were preparing to cross the Moscow-Volga canal at Yaroslavl, and Second Panzer Army to Ryazan and Kashira. But the tanks did not have fuel and the artillery did not have enough shells. A pause was needed to prepare for the 'last' offensive in 1941.

Due to the terrible condition of the roads the supply of the combat units of the Second Panzer Army and the 3rd and 4th Panzer Groups was carried out by air by Ju 52s. In the autumn, Go 242 cargo gliders of LLG 1 and LLG 2 and the huge Me 321 'Gigants' of *Sonderstaffel* (GS)/KG zbV2 were used to deliver supplies to Army Group Centre. The 'Gigants' had to be towed by three Bf 110s, with a Bf 108 'Taifun' leading them. The priority for the gliders was carrying fuel for the Panzer divisions.

The Composition of the 6th IAK PVO on 1 November 1941

Regiment	Airfield	Aircraft Type	Number	Serviceable
11th IAP	Kubinka	Yak-1	7	4
16th IAP	Lyubertsy	MiG-3	32	27
		I-16	4	3
27th IAP	Klin	MiG-3	24	21
		I-16	7	6
28th IAP	Monino	MiG-3	20	19
34th IAP	Vnukovo Sukovo	MiG-3	17	15
95th IAP	Monino Chkalovskaya	Pe-3	16	14
120th IAP	Central Airfield of Moscow	I-153	18	15
		MiG-3	13	11
126th IAP	Chkalovskaya	P-40	12	10
171st IAP	Kashira	MiG-3	9	8
		I-16	3	2
176th IAP	Yurkino	I-16	19	8
		MiG-3	14	13
177th IAP	Dubrovitsy	I-16	13	8
		MiG-3	8	6

Regiment	Airfield	Aircraft Type	Number	Serviceable
178th IAP	Krutihki	I-16	15	4
		LaGG-3	9	4
208th IAP	Chkalovskaya	Pe-3	9	7
233rd IAP	Tushino	I-16	26	13
		MiG-3	7	7
309th IAP	Gridino	I-16	16	14
		I-153	13	12
423rd IAP	Volyntsevo	MiG-3	11	9
		I-16	11	5
428th IAP	Sukovo	MiG-3	19	11
436th IAP	Klin	Yak-1	8	6
445th IAP	Kashira	MiG-3	20	14
		I-16	12	9
495th IAP	Pohinki	I-16	11	6
		MiG-3	10	10
562nd IAP	Cubinka	Yak-1	9	5
564 IAP	Ostafievo	LaGG-3	14	8
		I-16	3	2
565th IAP	Ramenskoe	MiG-3	19	16
Headquarters 6th IAK	Central Airfield of Moscow	MiG-3	2	2
		Total	480	354

In early November, the Russian 6th IAK PVO remained the most powerful unit of Stalin's aviation. It had 480 fighters, 354 of them combat ready. At that time these were the best aviation regiments. The location of the aviation corps had changed due to the retreat. The main part of the aviation regiments were concentrated around Moscow and to the east. Even the important Vnukovo air base was only 40km (25 miles) from the front.

Fighter Aircraft in the 6th IAK PVO on 1 November 1941

Type	Number	Serviceable
MiG-3	225	189
I-16	140	80

Type	Number	Serviceable
I-153	31	27
Pe-3	25	21
Yak-1	24	15
LaGG-3	23	12
P-40 Tomahawk	12	10
Total	480	354

In early November, the weather on the Eastern front deteriorated again. In the Moscow region there was continuous cloud cover, heavy fog and sleet. '*Luftflotte* 2 didn't act because of bad weather,' read the daily report of Army Group Centre.

On the night of 3/4 November the Luftwaffe carried out another air raid on Moscow, dropping twenty-three high explosive and fragmentation bombs. There were many fires, with a few blocks destroyed in the Octyabrsky, Sokolnitchesky and Krasnopresnensky districts. The Russian rescue service reported four dead and fourteen wounded.

On 4 November, the weather improved. Russian and German air activity intensified, and there were many air battles. Some of the air defence fighters, armed with bombs and rockets, attacked Inyutino airfield, recently a base for 'Stalin's Falcons' but now in the hands of the Luftwaffe. The I-153 biplanes of the 120th IAP attacked German troops to the west of Serpukhov. Two pilots, Lieutenants Nikolaev and Nabatov, never returned to base.

The fighters of the 177th IAP performed thirty-nine sorties and claimed two victories (an 'Me 109' and an Hs 126). In this battle, Bf 109 E-3 W. Nr. 3293 flown by Spanish pilot Commandante Angel Salas Larraabal of 15.(Spain)/JG 27 was shot down. He made an emergency landing on neutral ground, and the next day he was rescued by German infantry. The Russians paid a heavy price for this victory. Sergeant Zubkov was shot down and killed, and Lieutenants Savinov, Sevastyanov and Turkov were missing. In the Naro-Fominsk district the MiG-3 of Lieutenant Korshunov of the 16th IAP was reported missing. They were probably victims of the fighters of III. and IV./JG 51, which were operating over the south-western suburbs of Moscow on 4 November. III./JG 51 claimed eleven victories with the loss of two Bf 109 (one pilot was shot down by anti-aircraft fire and was killed, the second made an emergency landing in friendly territory). IV./JG 51 claimed nine victories for one loss.

The Yak-1s of the 11th IAP scored two victories over the Do 215. Russians often confused this plane with the Bf 110 and Do 17 because of its similarly-shaped tail. In this episode the *Zerstorers* of II./ZG 26 'Horst Wessel' were attacked. Two Bf 110 D-3s returned to the airfield at Dugino (17km [10.5 miles] south of Sychevka near the Rzhev-Vyazma railway) with combat damage and crash-landed. In the Serpukhov area Lieutenant P.E. Zhidkov of the 445th IAP in his I-16 attacked a Ju 88. But the fighter was shot down by return fire, crashed and exploded. The pilot was killed.

'Large forces of *Luftflotte* 2 operated in all sectors of the front,' read the daily report of Army Group Centre. 'Raids were made on clusters of troops, columns, field and artillery positions, barracks, camps and occupied Russian settlements. Traffic on the railways to the south and east of Moscow was disrupted. Raids on several airfields were made. In the afternoon, large formations have dealt a powerful blow to the factories in the city of Gorky.'

On 4 November *Luftflotte* 2 carried out 339 sorties, and Russian aviation 824. 'Stalin's Falcons' sought to 'dominate the air'. Russian command thought: who flies more, owns the sky. But most of the flights of Russian fighters had no result. The Germans flew less, but got results. On 5 November Russian aircraft in the Moscow region carried out 1,172 sorties, but for that huge number of flights only twelve victories were claimed (none confirmed!). The Germans in their reports noted only an air raid on Orel and heavy bomb attacks on the LIII and XLIII Army Corps in the Tula region. Other activity by Soviet aircraft seems to have passed unnoticed. The large number of Russian fighters in the air did not interfere with the air raid on Moscow. At lunchtime, a single bomber dropped nine high-explosive bombs on the city from a great height. Several houses were damaged, five people were killed and one wounded. There was no air-raid warning in the city.

On 6 November, Russian air forces carried out a record number of flights – 1,374! About half of these – 613 sorties – were by the fighters of the 6th IAK PVO. Air defence pilots fought thirty-three air battles and claimed twenty-five victories. In fact, the Luftwaffe's losses were four aircraft. For example, in the Klin district Bf 109 F-2 W. Nr. 9184, flown by the commander of I./JG 52 Oberleutnant Karl-Heinz Lismann, was shot down. He was seriously wounded, but escaped being captured.

Chapter 4

Air Attack on the 'Molotov' Automobile Plant

Thanks to the pause in the attack on Moscow, *Luftflotte* 2 had the opportunity to carry out a series of strategic attacks on major Russian industrial centres. The main target was the city of Gorky (Nizhny Novgorod), located 400km (250 miles) east of Moscow, near the confluence of the Oka and Volga rivers. It was a large city with a population of 600,000 and there were many important factories. Military equipment was delivered from there to the Moscow front and significantly strengthened the Russian defences. Aircraft plant No. 21 'Ordzhonikidze' produced the LaGG-3 fighter, artillery factory No. 92 'Stalin' 76mm guns, the 'Krasnoje Sormovo' plant T-34 tanks, and the 'Engine of the Revolution' plant 120mm mortars. The main factory in Gorky was the famous Gorky 'Molotov' automobile plant (GAZ). It had been built by the Ford company in 1932 on the banks of the Oka river and produced GAZ-AA and GAZ-AAA trucks (similar to Fords), T-60 tanks, motors, parts for artillery and aircraft, and other important products. Gorky consisted of two parts. On the mountainous right bank of the Oka river was the ancient quarter of the city, where towered the Kremlin fortress, built in 1513 for defence against the Tatars. In the old part there were narrow streets and old houses, but there were also some new quarters.

Nizhny Novgorod has long been famous for trade and merchant traditions. Due to its location at the confluence of two large rivers, it was an important trade and transport centre in Russia. The Nizhny Novgorod fair, which was held on the left bank of the Oka river, was known throughout Europe and Asia. Under the Bolsheviks, the city was renamed Gorky, in honour of the writer who had been born there, and turned into a large military centre. Many plants were classified and known only by code numbers 'Factory No. 2, Factory No. 112, Factory No. 205'. Under the threat of punishment, workers were forbidden to talk about their products. But despite the Bolsheviks' precautions, German military intelligence (the *Abwehr*) had a complete dossier on all their 'secret' industries.

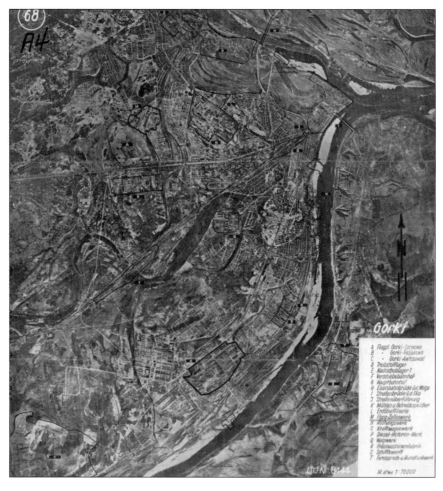

German aerial photograph of Gorky city. At the bottom of the letter "O" is marked the 'Molotov' automobile plant

Gorky was one of the ultimate goals of Operation 'Barbarossa' and the end point of the advance of Guderian's Second Panzer Army. But in early November 1941, German forces were still a long way away. Therefore, the Germans decided to disrupt the work of the factories in Gorky with air raids.

At the end of October, after the German Blitzkrieg on Moscow, a large line of fortifications and obstacles began to be constructed in the Gorky region. Thousands of women, children and the elderly were digging trenches and building bunkers over a large area. Gorky was poorly protected from air

Three-dimensional drawing of Aircraft plant No. 21 'Ordzhonikidze'

attack. The Gorky air defence brigade consisted of three regiments of anti-aircraft artillery (the 90th, 196th and 742th ZenAP) and two independent anti-aircraft artillery battalions. These units had few weapons and aircraft. Half of the guns were 76mm guns from the First World War and Finnish Bofors captured during the 'Winter War' of 1939–40. The only fighter aircraft were in 'Aviation Detachment Aircraft Factory No 21' manned by the pilots attached to the factory. By early November, the detachment (commanded by Major Nikolai Alifanov) consisted of nine LaGG-3 fighters.

The air raid on Gorky was allocated to KGr. 100 (Major Helmut Kuster), III./KG 26 (Major S. Bochme) and I./KG 28 (Oberst Ernst Rot). These three units were based at Seschinskaya, with Rot in overall command. The distance to the target was 750km (466 miles).

Bomb attack on Gorky 4 November, 1941 drawing by the painter Permowski, who was an eyewitness

The first attack occurred at 01.40 (local time) on 4 November. A single He 111 dropped three high-explosive bombs on the 'Molotov' automobile plant. The first fell on Engine Shop No. 2 (crankshafts), the second exploded outside, and the third hit the corner of the wheel shop. The bombing was unexpected, and there was no air-raid warning. The workers ran out of the shops in a panic, heading for the shelters or just to get away. Then fire engines arrived with bells ringing, weaving through the panic-stricken crowds. The managers rushed to the phones to report the attack to the local Communist Party office.

At 02.14 workers heard the noise of engines from the south-west. A moment later the silhouette of an He 111 appeared overhead, had not previously been noticeable. Over the Novosokolnik factory the plane suddenly jerked upwards – bombs away! Hearing a terrible whistle, people threw themselves to the ground. The first bomb exploded between the shops, the second outside the plant on the tram platform. The roar of the explosions could be heard from a great distance. Residents of the city ran out into the street, where they saw the bright glow of the fire at the car factory. The people realized: the war had come to their city . . .

In the morning, after the fires had been extinguished, the workers examined the damaged buildings. In Engine Shop No. 2, 1,700m² of the roof had been destroyed along with much of the equipment in the shop. Significant damage had also been caused by the water used to put out the fire, the basement being flooded and more machinery destroyed. Twenty-seven people were killed, and forty wounded. In the wheel shop part of the roof collapsed and the steam, water and heating supplies were cut off. Two workers were killed and ten were injured.

At lunchtime on 4 November, Oberst Rot decided to carry out the next raid at sunset. The designated targets were the 'Molotov' automobile plant, 'Engine of the Revolution' and the 'Lenin' radio factory (formerly 'Siemens und Galske'). Rot ordered his crews to destroy the power plants using BM1000 aerial mines and heavy high-explosive bombs to cripple the important factories.

At 16.10 (local time) the first bomber reached the vicinity of Gorky. The He 111 followed the high bank of the river to find the 'Lenin' radio plant. Making two or three circles over the target, the bomber dived. The BM1000 hit the main four-storey building of the plant, destroying it in a powerful explosion. Only after that, was the air-raid alarm sounded and the anti-aircraft guns opened fire. A resident of Gorky Anatoly Kurmaev recalled:

> First I saw in the sky the black clouds of anti-aircraft shell bursts. Then I saw a tall column of black smoke, fire and dust rising in the mountainous part of the city above the 'Lenin' plant. And after the first explosion I could see a few more, throwing into the sky new columns of flame and smoke. Just then we heard the air-raid alarm.

The No. 326 'Frunze' radio equipment plant was located opposite the 'Lenin' plant. All the windows were broken by the explosion and plaster rained down. The frightened workers stopped working and ran to the exits, clambering over a high fence to escape. At the 'Myza' railway station in the same area the station employees fled. Chaos ensued. A trainload of wounded soldiers was stuck at a signal, so the passenger jumped out of the carriages and scattered in all directions. Those who could not run, crawled . . .

At this time, the pilot of the He 111 flew over the city centre, visiting the sights of the ancient city. Over the Nizhny Novgorod Kremlin, he made an 'honorary circle', demonstrating his impunity. Anna Korobova, an employee of the Bolshevik Party office in Gorky, recalled: 'During the break between meetings, we went outside and to our horror saw a black plane with a swastika describing a circle over the Kremlin. The German pilot leaned out of the cockpit and waved at us! After that, we returned to the building, and we were told the plane had attacked the plant 'Lenin', its director Kuzmin had been killed. . .'.

At that moment, two more bombers were approaching Gorky. They flew over the villages at low level, frightening the peasants, and reached the Avtozavodsky district at 16.20. The planes roared over the people's heads, moving towards the GAZ factory. The first He 111 was flying over Zhdanov Street, the second – 400m away – over Kirov Avenue. At this moment Raphail Rivin stepped out of the clinic.

> Suddenly I saw a plane flying at a very low level over the fence of the clinic. When it swept past me with a terrible roar, I distinctly saw the figure of a pilot in a headset, and then the Nazi symbols. After that, I started waving my arms, attracting the attention of passers-by, shouting: 'Plane, plane!' The bomber flew over the side of the plant, and on the street people began to panic. One woman in a long dress tried to climb over the high fence of the clinic and got stuck on the top.

Anna Sorokina was in the street at that time and saw the He 111s flying over the house: 'They flew, as if in a display, their bellies almost touching the roof and chimneys.'

Automobile factory worker Nadezda Nadezhkina, who was at her lookout post on the roof of the GAZ plant, saw in the evening sky two aircraft approaching low from the west. The girl looked at the recognition pictures in front of her, trying to identify them. At the same time the second fighter post reported the danger to headquarters by phone. A few seconds later Nadezhkina saw four bombs fall from the first plane, plummeting with a howl on to the mechanical repair shop. And a moment later, pillars of smoke and flame rose into the air. 'The low-flying aircraft, the separation of the bombs, their howling and falling is still clearly in my memory,' recalled Nadezhkina. 'Panicking, the workers ran to the exits.'

Painter Permowski was in the concert hall near the plant:

> Everything was peaceful and quiet. . . . The radio announcer said . . . a plane flew over the roof. It was flying at low level. We heard the roar of the engines. Then everything calmed down. This happened regularly over our roof. We were close to the airport. Then suddenly a heavy, dull explosion. The earth shook. The electric lights went out. The voice of the radio announcer faded away. Something had happened. We ran out into the street. Over the factory spreads a giant mushroom of black smoke. Anti-aircraft guns began to fir. And we realized: it's a German plane bombing our factory . . .

Three SC250 bombs hit the centre of the mechanical repair shop, a fourth exploding in the street near the electrical substation of the assembly and stamping shop. The east wall and 800m² of ceiling collapsed. One of the bombs exploded in the canteen, where all the workers were torn to pieces. The second He 111 dropped bombs on the power station of the plant. One exploded in the unfinished west wing of the building and destroyed it, the second broke through the roof but stuck in the rafters over the boilers and did not explode.

The pair of He 111s made a circuit over the factory, shooting at the main factory entrance and the fleeing cars and horse-drawn carts. 'Here he flew at a low level over the Social City, Univermag (department store), over the clinic,' the artist Permowsky wrote in his diary. 'For a moment his dark green silhouette could be seen, in the ominous roar of explosions and gunfire. The smoke is spreading, went to the side of the Oka river. Flashes of anti-aircraft guns lit up the dead lustre of the coming darkness of evening.'

At 16.40 a fourth He 111 arrived, heading south towards the target. Residents saw the 'air monster' roar over the 'Myza' railway station with a thick bomb hanging under the fuselage. The plane flew over the Oka and in a shallow dive dropped a BM1000 mine on the 'Engine of the Revolution' factory. The massive explosion occurred in the power station, which

Anti-aircraft searchlight in Gorky

The Soviets actively used women in air defence units. This photograph shows radio operators. Right (bottom row) Maria Ganina, left (top row) Anna Mitina

contained steam boilers, diesels, compressors and transformer substations. Workers who were in the neighbouring shops were thrown to the ground and showered with fragments of glass from the shattered windows. In the assembly department of Shop No. 6 there was a fierce fire which spread to the roof of a nearby warehouse. The shock wave and shrapnel had damaged the power lines.

After that, panic spread throughout the city. Passengers jumped from moving trams, drivers abandoned their vehicles and ran away, and crowds fled to shelters. At the automobile plant, the soldiers of the militia battalion were ordered to take rifles, climb onto the roofs of the buildings and shoot at the aircraft. Among them was Raphail Rivin: 'After the first bomb attack, I grabbed a rifle (it was a Polish carbine) and ran to my post. Other fighters brought boxes of ammunition and stuffed their pockets with it, climbed on the roof of the workshops to fend off the raid with the weapons that we had.'

The consequences of the twilight raid were terrible. At the 'Lenin' factory 101 people were killed, including the whole of the management, and 190 workers were wounded. Many people were buried under the rubble in the basement of the destroyed main building. At the 'Molotov' automobile plant there was a lot of damage. In the mechanical repair shop the floors were broken, 400m^2 of internal partitions collapsed, and forty-five units of equipment, tools, materials, semi-finished products, finished products (mortars) and technical documentation were destroyed. Among piles of debris lay the mutilated corpses of the workers, body parts and bloodied pieces of clothing. The air raid put Factory No. 718 'Engine of the Revolution'out of action. The total destruction of the power station cut off the supply of electricity and heating so to avoid freezing of the heating system all the water was drained from the pipes. Seventeen people were killed and forty-six were injured. Among the dead were the head of shop No. 8 Zuev and the assistant chief of the 2nd mechanical shop Sidorov.

No Retreat From The Factory!

During the war the Soviet Union adopted strict laws to enforce industrial discipline. Layoffs and vacations were banned. Absenteeism and leaving the workplace without permission were considered treason. In August 1941, the Bolshevik leaders noticed that during air raids the workers were running away from their jobs and taking cover. As a result, production of military equipment was interrupted. On 18 August, Deputy People's Commissar of Ammunition Gamov wrote: 'Some plants, when the air alarm was reported, stopped work even though it was not necessary, causing a large loss of production.' Deputy People's Commissar of the Aviation Industry Kuznetsov: 'The enemy's air raids showed that rear targets are attacked mainly at night. Bomb hits on them are at random. In these circumstances, it is impossible to determine the time of the threat of a direct air attack.'

In the autumn of 1941, the NKVD forbade workers to evacuate during air raids. On 5 October 1941 they issued Order No. 29/5493:

> To build individual shelters and compartments inside the workshops.
>
> At the signal 'Air alarm' the work does not stop, except for people who are in the fire protection and rescue service [MPVO].
>
> Workers to remain at their places until the moment of direct attack [bombing]. The work of the enterprise shall be terminated, except for units whose processes may not be suspended.

Work had to be resumed without waiting for the signal 'Cancellation of the air alarm'.

The head of the Main Department of the MPVO, NKVD Lieutenant General Osokin issued a 'temporary instruction' on the operation of plants on the signals 'air alarm' and 'immediate threat of attack':

> In order to protect building and valuable equipment against blast and fragmentation, cut-off walls and boxes of earth and sand are to be installed. When the 'air alarm' is sounded, finished products are to be dispersed and arrangements made for their immediate evacuation from the site.

If the German bombers were approaching, the workers had no right to leave their workplace. They could only evacuate once the bombs started falling on the factory! Often the workshops were locked from the outside, preventing the workers from escaping.

'This is the face of war'

In the evening and into the night of 4 November the bombers of KGr. 100, III./KG 26 and I./KG 28 continued to attack Gorky. They appeared singly or in pairs from different directions. At 17.12 two He 111s attacked the 'Molotov' automobile plant from the south-west. In this instance, most of the bombs fell on vacant lots between buildings. Three powerful explosions occurred between Engine Room No. 1, the design department and the wheel shop. Near Woodworking Shop No. 1 nine high-explosive and fragmentation bombs of different calibres exploded. Windows were shattered and the roadway was destroyed for 15m (50ft). The tank with two tons of solvent exploded, destroying three transformers. An SC50 fell next to Machine Shop No. 3. It damaged 3m (10ft) of rails and a steam line, and blew out all the windows on the east side of the building.

At 17.30 the next He 111 flew over the burning plant and dropped three bombs aimed at the assembly shop. Two exploded nearby, blowing out all the windows and destroying part of the railway track, while the third fell into a pile of scrap metal. The bomber then turned around and attacked the 'Engine of the Revolution' factory. One bomb exploded on the railway tracks between the foundry and the power station, and three in the south-western part of the plant near the shelter trenches. Four explosions shook the machine-tool plant on Shosseynaya Street. At 17.50 another plane dropped a 1,000kg (2.205lb) bomb on the GAZ plant, which exploded between the forging shop and the steam hammer shop: 20m (65ft) of railway track was destroyed and the windows were shattered.

There were no serious air defences in Gorky. The only aircraft which took off to challenge the Luftwaffe were those of Major Nikolai Alifanov's unit. These factory pilots, with no combat experience, were little threat to the battle-hardened crews of such elite units as KGr. 100. There were several air battles over the city but no German bombers were damaged. LaGG-3 No. 31217-71 was riddled by defensive fire: when the fighter crash-landed, fifty holes were counted in it, including twenty-two in the fuselage and twelve in the wings! Two other fighters, LaGG-3s No. 31213-44 and No. 31213-75, were also serious damaged.

After a pause between 21.07 and 01.20 air attacks on the 'Molotov' plant continued. Part of No. 2 foundry shop, the office of the gasoline warehouse, the auto-trailer garage, the rubber warehouse, and the eastern half of the Electric power plant. Civilian targets were also damaged: the so-called

'American Village' (where the Ford workers who had helped build the plant had been housed), a kitchen factory and a concert hall. Buildings close to the explosions had all their windows blown out and some walls partially collapsed. Oberleutenant Hans Georg Bätcher participated in this raid on Gorky. His *Fliegerbuch* reports: the He 111 took off from Seschinskaya at 20.23 (Berlin time). From a height of 4,000m (13,123ft) Bätcher dropped one SC1000 and three SC250 bombs. Over the target the anti-aircraft fire was negligible. At 01.17 the He 111 returned to base. The flight lasted about five hours.

That night German bombers not only reached the city of Gorky, but also the small provincial town of Cheboksary, 200km east of Gorky on the right bank of the Volga. There were no important military facilities and factories here, so the purpose of this attack is a mystery. An He 111 dropped nine high-explosive bombs on the central part of the town, destroying the courthouse and seven houses. Two people were killed and eighteen wounded. A local resident said: 'The thunder, not thunder, did not understand. It happened at night, we ran outside. There was a crash twice. Couldn't understand. Never heard that before. People ran out into the street. Nobody understood anything.' After the bomb attack on Cheboksary, the He 111 flew over the northern bank of the Volga and attacked the village of Sosnovka. The target of the bomb attack was a gypsy camp, where fires were burning. In the morning on the Ishlei–Cheboksary road residents found leaflets. They called for the people to help the Wehrmacht and to join the service of Hitler.

Cheboksary became the most distant target in the central sector of the front attacked by German bombers during the war. Between Gorky and Cheboksary a low-level He 111 strafed the village of Yurino (in the delta of the river Vetluga), Kozmodemyansk and the village of Usman. The purpose of this long-range mission also remains unclear . . .

Between 01.40 on 4 November and 02.15 on 5 November 5, KGr. 100, III./ KG 26 and KG 28 dropped on Gorky approximately eighty high-explosive bombs and aerial mines. That was enough to cause a lot of damage to military targets. The 'Lenin' radio plant and the 'Engine of the Revolution' were completely out of action for a long time. Thanks to the Soviet regime's indifference to the deaths of workers, the exact number of those killed is unknown, but the authors have been able to identify at least 300.

Sixteen electric motors, nine generators, eleven transformers, ten compressors, a hydraulic press, three drilling machines, four bridge cranes, four boilers and four steam pumps were destroyed by explosions and fires at 'Engine of the Revolution'. All the drawing files in the department of the chief mechanic were burnt. This made problematic the repair of old German-made equipment (the plant was formerly a factory of the German Felser company). Tens of thousands of components for munitions were destroyed: the total losses of the bomb attack were valued at the huge amount of 4,215 million roubles. After the raid, hundreds of people fled from the plant, 189 of whom never came back. This vital plant could not be fully restored until the end of the war.

Burning the Gorky 'Molotov' automobile plant (GAZ). 6 November. Drawing by the painter Permowski, who was an eyewitness

Fire brigade in Gorky city

On the morning of 5 November, the area of the automobile plant presented a horrible sight. There were corpses and human remains scattered around. Painter I.I. Permowski wrote in his diary:

> Here lies a charred corpse. Instead of a head, some shattered bone with dried blood. Side peeled off, and see the inside. Horrible sight. And yet people do not disperse. Looking to soak up the scary sight of death.
> Is it a woman?
> There is a man!
> But what do you learn from the burnt remains of a man? And that curiosity makes people discover features that distinguish male and female. Try to turn the corpse.
> Do not run away from death!
> Here Hitler caught up with them!
> This is a truck with Moscow refugees. Ridiculous death! 400km from the front and burned up at our factory.
> Bomb has fallen quite near, says a man.
> One tram scattered in all directions. There, behind the tram line is the motor, and here a part of the cabin . . .

There was no trace of the great barracks. It's smashed to pieces. Two other barracks also suffered, one is half-ruined with the roof fallen off, another was leaning on one side, as a house of cards. In the door lies the corpse of a man. He spread his half-bent legs in grey socks. The head is covered with a piece of cardboard . . .

It's terrible, everyone says.

'This is the face of war,' I want to shout.

And tomorrow maybe I'll also be lying around as a bag of crushed bones . . .

'The whole plant was set on fire, burning all around'

On the night of 5/6 November the Luftwaffe repeated its air raid on Gorky. The main target was again the 'Molotov' automobile plant. Tactics consisted of sequential attacks by individual aircraft.

At 23.34, the first He 111 dropped SD70 fragmentation bombs on the power lines leading from the power plant in Balakhna to Gorky. The plan was that the interruption of the electricity supply would paralyze the water pumping stations, making it impossible to extinguish the fires caused by the raid on the plant. And this trick worked. Four electrical high-voltage lines and two electrical substations were knocked out. Electrical line No. 108 suffered particularly badly, with shrapnel breaking six spans and damaging twenty-one. Pylon No. 153 was knocked down by the blast. On line No. 109 the cable was cut in seven places. The Germans were even able to destroy the underground cable! Only 50 per cent of the power supply had been restored after 11½ hours.

At 01.30 Gorky heard the frightening rumble of German aircraft. They flew over the Oka river and the Moscow–Gorky railway. These landmarks were clearly visible in the dark. The first explosions were heard in 01.47 in the village of Admzentr. At 01.50 a large-calibre high-explosive bomb hit the press shop, penetrated the roof, hit a beam and exploded under the ceiling. The next two bombs fell on the main assembly line of the 'Molotov' plant. The planes of KGr. 100 'Wiking' dropped high-powered SC1800 bombs, specially designed for the destruction of concrete structures and industrial facilities. The He 111 of Oberleutnant Hans Bätcher, commander of the 1st *Staffel*, took off from Seschinskaya at 21.24 (Berlin time). Under the fuselage was attached one of the

1,800kg (4,000lb) bombs. After its fall there was a huge explosion, one building was totally destroyed.

The painter I.I. Permovski watched this bombing from the shelter:

> Above us in the sky the fantastic picture of the air battle. The roar of engines. The smooth flight of tracer rounds. The roar of the fighters. Crossed beams of searchlights. Hear the muffled explosions of the bombs. On the horizon the glow of a plant catching fire. Defensive fire increases with every minute.
>
> We hear a cry. Into the trench jump two fighters of the Red Army.
>
> 'Busy in here!' laughs one.
>
> 'Come in, there's enough room,' we answer.
>
> The fear gradually goes away. More people. The feeling of loneliness disappears.
>
> The plane flies at a very low level. Soldiers shoot. There's a constant ringing in my ears.

At 02.07 a large-calibre bomb hit Machine Shop No 2, destroying the north-western corner of the building. The second bomb exploded in the frame shop, destroying the press area, the carpenter's workshop and the paint shop. The next big explosion occurred in the electrical substation of the mechanical repair shop. Then, incendiary bombs fell on the south-western part of the plant, which caused many fires.

The roof of Engine Room No. 3 was made of wood and insulated with various combustible materials. Some of the incendiary bombs struck it and fell to the floor of the shop. Others stuck in the insulation, and the roof quickly caught fire. A few minutes later, the whole roof was engulfed in flames, which were impossible to extinguish. Then the fire spread into the interior, and the whole shop caught fire. Forge No. 2 and the compressor station burned down completely. In the forge building, the fire destroyed eighteen hammers and the entire heating and lighting system.

The roof of the main office of the plant was also covered with incendiary bombs. One of them hit the ventilation shaft and got stuck. The four-storeyed building had wooden floors, the fire in the ventilation shaft spread through the upper floors, and they burned down completely. The grey cast-iron shop was badly damaged. High-explosive bombs punched a hole 10m (33ft) wide in the reinforced concrete roof, the horizontal beams were broken, gates were blown out, the water supply and heating was destroyed, and the warehouse of production was destroyed. The next shop, No. 8, also suffered from blast damage.

A large number of incendiary bombs fell onto the factory garage. The repair shop, the warehouse and the entire fleet of eighty vehicles were destroyed. Residential barracks located at the western end of the plant caught fire. Refugees from Moscow were accommodated there. They had not run for cover, fearing that their property would be looted. During the fire, they were trapped in the buildings. Some jumped out of windows, but many burned alive with their possessions.

'At 3:00 the sky was lit up with a red glow. The street was lit up in pink,' Permovski wrote in his diary.

> People left the shelters, looked at the raging sea of fire. Identified: a burning automotive shop, 1st mechanical, main office, experimental workshops. One side was on fire, throwing flames, next to the workers' school burned the barracks. Giant pillars of fire and smoke. Stopped people coming of the plant. Asked what shops burn. Answered differently, with bitterness, with indifferent stupid despair.
>
> The whole plant was set on fire, burning around.

Nine fire appliances and a fire train, and 1,800 men of different services participated in extinguishing fires and rescue operations. According to the Russian rescue service, during the air attack on the city of Gorky thirty-two high-explosive bombs and several thousand incendiaries were dropped. The exact death toll is again unknown.

The Luftwaffe's air attacks had a great psychological effect. On 6 November a rumour spread at the 'Lenin' radio factory that at 15.00 there would be another air attack. Many workers gave up and ran home. At the next plant, No. 326 'Frunze', there was panic. The head of the Planning Department, Komarov, admitted to everyone that he felt 'animal fear' at the possibility of dying in an air raid. Two hundred students of the factory's vocational school fled the city. In the neighbourhoods around the automobile plant, hundreds of residents left their homes and fled to the villages outside the city. The painter I. I. Permowski wrote:

> People gather in the guard booth. We all think about the terrible events that happened all night. It's decided to dig a dugout.

Suddenly in runs Anatoly Smirnov, the projectionist. He begs me to give him the handcart.

'Somewhere far away from this hell. In a nearby village. Alexei Ivanovich in the morning sends his family over the Oka, I saw . . . I need to send my family away, no stone will be left on top of another here. . .'

People are fleeing of the 'Socialist City' [one of the districts of Gorky], from the barracks near the plant. Running away from work.

'Inform the supervisor, I have gone to the village. I don't want the salary. I don't want to live in this horror,' says the club cleaner.

Out fear of Stalin, the commander of the Russian air defences wanted to hide his complete failure. In such situations, the Russians usually increased the number of bombers that participated in the raid and then claimed that from this huge group only one or two 'broke through' to their target, the rest having been 'driven off' by anti-aircraft fire. This case was no different. On the morning of 6 November, the chief of staff of the Gorky area air defences Lieutenant Colonel Savko produced 'Operational Intelligence Summary No. 72'. It reported: 'From 20.00 5.11.41 to 02.38 6.11.41 enemy made reconnaissance and bombing operations in groups (3 – 15) and single aircraft type He 111, Ju 88, and Ju 86. Of 136 aircraft 14 broke through to the city. Dropped large high-explosive bombs – 16, small – 600, incendiary – 800. Twenty-two bombs fell in the city, the rest on the far and near approaches.' All this was lies and deception.

The OKW reported: 'During the past day, the bombers struck a heavy blow to the city of Gorky – an important industrial centre, which is important in the production of vehicles and aircraft. As a result of direct hits by heavy bombs, significant damage was caused to the 'Molotov' automobile plant, the shipyard on the Volga river bank, and railway communications. There were several large fires.'

The raids on Gorky had pronounced strategic consequences. The work of factories supplying the front with military equipment was disrupted. The 'Engine of the Revolution' plant ceased production of 120mm mortar bombs and 'Katyusha' rockets. At the 'Molotov' plant there were difficulties with the manufacture of trucks, T-60 light tanks, mortars and shells. The damage to these plants affected the work of Artillery Plant No. 92. There wasn't enough metal for the gun barrels. At the 'Engine of the

Poster calling on citizens to fight fires. The inscription reads: 'The Fire helps the enemy to find the target for a bomb attack'

Revolution' plant the production of gearboxes for T-34 tanks was halted and their delivery to Plant No. 112 'Krasnoje Sormovo' stopped. At the same time there were interruptions in the supply of engines from the automobile plant. In the first nineteen days of November, only twenty-two gearboxes and thirty-four engines were delivered. As a result, in November, the plant 'Krasnoje Sormovo' produced an average of only one and a half tanks per day! Thanks to the successful actions of the Luftwaffe, production in Gorky of 82mm and 120mm mortars, 76mm guns, T-34 and T-60 tanks, artillery shells and rockets, radio sets and field telephones was significantly reduced.

For Hans-Georg Bätcher, the air raid on Gorky in the night of 5/6 November was his 90th combat sortie and his last in 1941. A week later of KGr. 100 'Wiking' was withdrawn for rest and refitting at the Hannover-Langenhagen airfield in Germany. This famous pilot would return to the front in the southern sector in January 1942.

Chapter 5

On the Threshold of the Goal

The Russian command also took advantage of the pause in the fighting. At dawn on 7 November, it was decided to hold the traditional military parade in Red Square dedicated to the 24th anniversary of the October Revolution. The event was prepared in strict secrecy. The troops were moved to the square at the end of the night and the distribution of invitations began at 05.00. A plan was developed to evacuate Stalin and his retinue to the nearest shelter as soon as possible. The risk was great: everyone was afraid of an unexpected Luftwaffe air raid.

But the main defence of the parade was the weather. In the morning and afternoon of 6 November the weather in the Moscow area had been clear and frosty, but in the evening the city was enveloped in a cyclone. 'In the afternoon clear, dry, frosty weather,' the staff of the German Second Army reported. 'It snowed in the evening with a strong wind.' At night over Moscow there was continuous cloud cover at an altitude of 50–200m (164–656ft). Visibility in some places was reduced to 50m (54 yards). This allowed the parade to be broadcast openly on the radio. It was a great propaganda success. 'We thought that Moscow was already taken . . .,' recalled Nina Degteva, at that time a resident of the city of Lyskovo in the Gorky region. 'We saw the glow of the Gorky bomb attack. We were afraid, and soon the Germans will be here . . . And suddenly this news: the Red Square parade, Stalin speaks! We were all amazed by this. Many people cried in the streets. Everyone knew that all was not lost.'

In Russia, as in all totalitarian states, military parades have always been loved. The Russians believed (and believe now) that parades scare possible enemies and show everyone 'the power of the country'. In 1941, parades were to show the world that Russia was not broken.

On the same day, the 'reserve' parade in the city of Kuibyshev (the alternative capital if Moscow had fallen) was the most significant in propaganda terms. It was the largest parade in the history of Russia!

ON THE THRESHOLD OF THE GOAL

The show lasted 90 minutes, during which 22,000 elite troops, and hundreds of tanks and armoured vehicles passed through the central square of the city. The main sensation was the aviation part of the parade. The Russian press wrote:

> The distant roar of engines heralds the approach of one of the most powerful types of troops – aviation. The rumble grows, and the eyes of all turn to the winter sky. Rushing one after another in clear calm, the ranks of a combat squadron, ruthless avengers on the Nazis, who destroyed our cities and villages, slaughtered innocent people, in air raids on Moscow and Leningrad.

Seven hundred aircraft flew over Kuibyshev, including many Il-2s and Pe-2 dive bombers! The show was for the benefit of foreign diplomats and journalists. Stalin wanted to show them that the Russian forces were 'countless and inexhaustible'.

A big parade was also held in Voronezh. It was organized by the chief of the Central Office of the Communist Party in Ukraine, Nikita Khrushchev. By the time the Ukrainian territory under his control was seized, Khrushchev focused on the defence of Voronezh. Serious security measures were introduced. Russian fighters were ordered to shoot down all aircraft, even Russian ones, within a 25km (15-mile) radius of the city.

The parade was commanded by Marshal Semyon Tymoshenko, who made sure that the South-Western front, revived after its defeat in September 1941, appeared in good shape. 'Most of the passing fighters are armed with new modern weapons – machine guns, semi-automatic rifles, light machine guns,' journalists wrote.

> After the march of infantry units and cavalry on the square there is artillery. Here's the deadly threat to the armoured Nazi thugs – anti-tank guns. The calibre of the guns is gradually increasing. When huge long-range guns pass by the stands, admiration pours out into loud applause ... Strictly maintaining alignment are detachments of motorcyclists and armoured vehicles. Behind them on the square are the tanks – high-speed powerful machines of the latest designs, formidable steel fortresses, their powerful firepower inflicting heavy blows on the German bandits.

In other major cities, the parade was on a smaller scale. In Tbilisi, 'armed columns of workers' paraded in front of the stands, while in Tashkent the parade was called 'viewing of the armed people'. 'Paramilitary columns' of students with wooden replicas of weapons and sticks marched past! In Ashgabat, the parade was made up a crowd of wounded from the hospital, assembled railway workers and Pioneers (similar to the Nazi *Hitlerjügend*).

On 7 November, storms again delayed the Wehrmacht's attack on Moscow. The roads in Army Group Centre's area became impassable. It was impossible not only to attack, but to carry out the normal delivery of supplies by road. Supply of the Third and Fourth Panzer Armies and the 2nd Panzer Group was only possible by air.

On 8 November Russian Army aviation, despite the snow and rain, carried out air attacks against German troops in the area of Volokolamsk and Maloyaroslavets. Only seventy-four sorties were made, but the Germans noticed this activity. Fourth Army headquarters reported 'In the area of XII Army Corps low-level air raids and bomb attacks. In the areas of LVII and XX Army Corps and the 4th Panzer Group – minor actions of enemy aircraft'. In the Tula region, the positions of the LIII Army Corps, particularly those of the 167th Infantry Division, were hit.

The Luftwaffe acted only in a limited way. II *Fliegerkorps*, which operated in the southern sector of Army Group Centre, delivered supplies to the Second Panzer Army and carried out reconnaissance flights with single fighters. VIII *Fliegerkorps*'s bombers conducted a series of raids on the Bologoe–Rybinsk and Moscow–Yaroslavl railways, while its fighters escorted Ju 52s and cargo gliders delivering fuel and other supplies to the 3rd and 4th Panzer Groups.

On 9 November there was sleet and visibility was 2km (1¼ miles). The Luftwaffe showed considerable activity. Bombers attacked Soviet troop positions in the Tula region, and in the northern sector the Bologoe–Rybinsk and Moscow–Yaroslavl railways again. In the centre of Moscow several airfields were attacked. Starting at 13.50 the Germans launched an air raid on the Russian capital, dropping 67 high-explosive and fragmentation bombs and approximately 1,500 incendiaries. Several businesses and dozens of houses were completely or partially destroyed. According to the Russian rescue service, 26 people were killed and 137 injured. Fires in Moscow continued to burn until the next morning. The 6th IAK PVO made 382 sorties, but the Russian pilots achieved only one victory. West of Serpukhov Lieutenant Gerasim Grigoriev's LaGG-3 of the 178th IAP shot

Pen and Sword Books

c/o Casemate Publishers

1950 Lawrence Road

Havertown, PA 19083

Pen & Sword Books have over 6000 books currently available and we cover all periods of history on land, sea and air.

If you would like to hear more about our other titles sign up now and receive 30% off your next purchase. www.penandswordbooks.com/newsletter/

By signing up to our free discounts, reviews on new releases, previews of forthcoming titles and upcoming competitions, so you will never miss out!

Not online? Return this card to us with your contact details and we will put you on our catalog mailing list.

Mr/Mrs/Ms ....

Address...

Zip Code.................... Email address.....................

Website: www.penandswordbooks.com
Email: Uspen-and-sword@casematepublishers.com · Telephone: (610) 853-9131
Stay in touch: facebook.com/penandswordbooks or follow us on Twitter @penswordbooks

We hope you enjoyed this book!

76mm anti-aircraft gun of the 1931 model on one of the streets of Moscow

down Ju 88 A-5 (pilot Leutnant H. Meier) of I./KG 76, during a mission to attack the Taldom railway station.

On 10 November, German bombers carried out air raids on the railways to the north and south of Moscow, as well as airfields. There were no air battles.

MiG-3 fighter at the winter airfield

On 11 November, in cloudy and snowy weather, German bombers supported the attack of the XLIII Army Corps, which tried to break through to Tula from the north-west on the Aleksin–Tula road. Attacks were carried out against the railway lines around Moscow and on airfields. At 13.00 and 14.19 there were two consecutive raids on the Ramenskoye airfield, in which eighteen high-explosive bombs were dropped. At 13.25 Lyubertsy was attacked (fourteen bombs were dropped, four of which did not explode), and at 14.45 Dubrovitsy (nine fragmentation bombs were dropped). According to the Russians, the attacks did not cause significant damage. At lunchtime, two He 111s raided Moscow (the alarm was given at 12.47), dropping fifteen high-explosive and fragmentation bombs on the city. Russian documents report that they 'caused minor damage', but twenty-two people were killed and seventy-two wounded.

These attacks cost the Luftwaffe three bombers. He 111 H-6 W. Nr. 4409 '1T+?K' of 2./KG 28 failed to return to base. Its exact fate is unknown. Anti-aircraft artillery shot down He 111 H-6 W. Nr. 4100 '1H+DR' of 7./KG 26: the crew were all killed. He 111 H-3 W. Nr. 3207 of 3./KGr. 100 'Wiking' was damaged by ground fire and crashed while attempting an emergency landing. Two of the crew were killed.

Russian aircraft continued to attack ground targets. For example, I-153 and MiG-3 fighters of the 120th IAP, taking off from the Central Airfield of Moscow, attacked German troops near Tula and Serpukhov, firing off seventy-four rockets. Army Group Centre's daily report mentioned 'low-level attacks' on positions of the 17th Panzer Division (Second Panzer Army). On this day, numerous raids on Kalinin were also recorded, in which German troops in the city suffered serious losses.

On the morning of 12 November, the 'Russian winter', of which Hitler and the Wehrmacht command were very much afraid, really began. The air temperature plummeted to -15° Celsius. The Luftwaffe supported the attack of the XLIII and the LIV Army Corps at Tula, bombing railways and airfields. Reconnaissance aircraft operated throughout the gigantic front from Kalinin to Yelets. Transport aviation was engaged in the supply of panzer divisions, but Ju 52s and cargo gliders could not fully replace railways and road transport. 'Tank corps of the army do not have sufficient stock of fuel,' the headquarters of Second Panzer Army reported the next day. 'The current fuel supply is only enough for transportation in order to supply the army. Replenishment of reserves to 5–6 norms of the expense necessary for an advance to the Oka river is impossible without essential increase in receipt of fuel.'

The Russians were also active. The 6th IAK PVO carried out 545 sorties with a total duration of 459 hours. The average duration of a Russian fighter's sortie in cold weather was only 50 minutes. Luftwaffe Bf 109s were in the air twice as long. 'Stalin's Falcons' claimed five air victories (three Hs 126s and two Ju 88s). In fact, the Luftwaffe finished the day without loss. The Russians lost Lieutenant Zorin of the 445th IAP shot down and killed, and the MiG-3 of Lieutenant Goldobin of the 565th IAP was reported missing. The Germans have recorded bombing attacks on Kalinin and its environs. The 10th Luftwaffe Anti-Aircraft Regiment, based in the city, reported shooting down its 50th Russian aircraft.

On 13 November the 6th IAK PVO carried out 409 sorties, covering the troops of the Western Front near Moscow, as well as Yakhroma, Zagorsk, Kashira, Serpukhov and Stalinogorsk. Six Yak-1s of the 43th IAP escorted bombers which carried out another air raid on Kalinin. Russian pilots claimed two enemy aircraft shot down, with four losses (two Yak-1s, one I-153 and one MiG-3). On this day, a German ace, Oberfeldwebel Edmund Wagner of JG 51, was killed near Moscow. At that time, he had fifty-eight victories, twenty-two of which he had won in October 1941. According to one account, his Bf 109 was shot down near Aleksin by a volley of rockets from an I-153, while according to another, Wagner was shot down in a battle with Pe-2 dive bombers. On 17 November 1941, he was posthumously awarded the Knight's Cross. The daily report of Army Group Centre recorded 'lively' action by Russian aviation in the sector of VII and IX Army Corps of Fourth Army and heavy air raids on the Kalinin and Staritsa airfields.

In the evening, I./KG 28 carried out a new raid on Moscow, the main target of which was railway facilities within the city. Air-alarm was declared at 19.55. According to the Russian rescue service, seventeen high-explosive bombs were dropped on the city, badly damaging a station on the Moscow–Tovarnaya line. Eight houses were also destroyed, and six people were killed and thirty-three wounded. On its return to base, He 111 H-6 W. Nr. 4543 crashed on landing.

Russian pilots discuss combat mission

Moscow residents sit in the basement of a house during a bomb attack. Photo By Margaret Burk-Wite

The weather on 14 November was clear with moderate frost, convenient for the operations aviation. Soviet troops went on the offensive against the German Fourth Army, attacking especially strongly in the sector of the XII and XIII Army Corps near of Serpukhov. In several places Russian tanks managed to break through the German defences, and only the arrival of the Ju 87s of StG 1 managed to stop them. Within three hours they bombed Soviet troop concentrations in the woods, overcoming the crisis. The Russians were supported by the I-153 biplanes of the 120th IAP, which carried out two rocket attacks behind German lines west of Serpukhov. The pilots reported twenty-two vehicles and seventeen horse-drawn carts damaged.

Ju 87s of StG 1 with Bf 110 Es of II./SKG 210 attacked the Russians to the south of Alexin, supporting the efforts of the XLII Army Corps. At the same time, Ju 52 dropped containers with food and ammunition to the corps which occupied a deserted wooded area north-west of Tula and was cut off from other troops. For a long time it could only be supplied by air.

The Luftwaffe was active over Moscow. At 13.26 an alarm was declared in the city, then eighteen high-explosive and fragmentation bombs were dropped. According to Russian reports, there was no 'serious' damage, and two people were killed and six injured. At 15.50 six Bf 110 accompanied by single-engine fighters raided the central airport of Moscow, dropping thirteen fragmentation bombs. This was the first time that Bf 109s had appeared over Moscow.

On this day there were several air battles over the heart of the huge city. The air defence pilots reported sixty-two dogfights and thirty-one victories. The greatest number of victories, including directly over Moscow, was registered by the 28th IAP (based at Monino airfield to the east of the city). For example, Lieutenants Konstantin Fedotov and Ivan Kholodov claimed personal victories over 'Me 109s'. The Yak-1 element of Lieutenant Ivan Kalabushkin of the 562nd IAP shot down one Bf 110 and two 'Me 115s'. The pilots of the 562nd IAP claimed ten 'Me 115s' collectively shot down. On two group victories over 'Me 115' Ivan Strukov, Pyotr Sergeev, Evgeny Ivanov and Ivan Sokolov claimed with two shared victories over 'Me 115s'. Lieutenant Fedor Mitrofanov of the 445th IAP in the region of Vysokinichi shot down a Ju 88. Lieutenant Nikolai Tarakanchikov of the 34th IAP claimed an 'Me 109' downed south of Podolsk, and his comrade Lieutenant Viktor Korobov an 'Me 110' in the Vnukovo area. But all these victories are not confirmed by Luftwaffe information. For the Germans this day passed without loss, while the Russians suffered serious losses. Five MiG-3s of the 28th IAP (Lieutenants Poydenco and Chernov, Sergeants Bezgudov and Alekseev), and Lieutenant Glushko and Lieutenant Sergeev of the 233rd IAP and Sergeant Kovalev of the 562nd IAP failed to return to base.

Russian air attacks against ground targets were more effective. Fighters, ground-attack aircraft and light bombers appeared out of the haze and fog at low level, shooting at the soldiers on the march, vehicles and horse-drawn carts, bridges and settlements. Such attacks were terrible because from the moment of visual detection of aircraft to opening fire, dropping bombs and launching rockets was only a few seconds. Soldiers and drivers did not even have time to get off the road and take cover. On 14 November, the Germans suffered considerable losses from attacks by Russian aircraft in the sectors of the Fourth Army and 3rd Panzer Group. The headquarters of the XLI Army Corps reported: 'Continuous air attacks increase our losses in personnel and equipment, threaten transportation and supply.'

The Luftwaffe *Jagdgeschwaderen* operating in the Moscow area in the autumn of 1941 reported only very low and infrequent combat losses. This had been the case since the beginning of the Second World War (even in the skies over Poland in September 1939). From 7 to 27 October IV./ JG 51 was based at Yukhnov airfield. During this period, the group claimed thirty-seven victories (mostly bombers – SBs, Pe-2s and Il-4s), for one loss. From 1 to 8 October III./JG 51 had eighteen victories for one loss. Then, until 22 October the Bf 109 pilots shot down forty-one aircraft, of which twelve were shot down on 10 October, nine on 17 October and eight on 22 October. Their own losses amounted to two Bf 109 F-2. However, on 13 October there was an unprecedented event. Near Medyn a ground-attack Il-2 (of the 215th or 502th SAP) shot down the ace Joachim Hacker of 7./ JG 51, who had thirty-two victories!

On 23 October III./JG 51 moved closer to Moscow, to Maloyaroslavets, and by the end of the month scored thirty-one more victories for three Bf 109s lost. During November, the group chalked up twenty-six victories and lost three fighters and two pilots (the most serious of these was the death of Edmund Wagner).

II./JG 51 had a similar record during Operation 'Typhoon'. In the period 11 – 19 October, operating on the southern flank, its pilots scored thirteen victories for one loss. On 20 October, the group relocated to Orel airfield. In the sector of Guderian's Second Panzer Army they shot down eighteen aircraft (mostly bombers and ground-attack aircraft), with one Bf 109 lost. Between 5 and 8 November the pilots of II./JG 51 recorded fourteen victories and one loss.

From 1 to 12 October I./JG 51 had twenty-four victories for one Bf 109 shot down. Between 12 and 31 October, the group operated from the airfield at Medyn, and shot down another forty-seven Soviet aircraft for one pilot killed and three missing. On 6 November, the group relocated to Staraya Russa in the north.

German fighters were greatly inferior to the enemy in numbers. But they were much more effective. The average duration of a Russian fighter's combat sortie was 50–60 minutes, of which 20–30 minutes was taken up with getting into the air, flying to the target area, returning to base and landing, leaving only 20–25 minutes combat time. In normal conditions German Bf 109 E/F fighters could be in the air for up to two hours, extending to three hours with drop tanks (which Russian fighters did not use because of technical defects and poor reliability). The reason for the short duration of flights was the uneconomical Russian engines (copies of foreign models), which consumed an excessive amount of fuel. Most Soviet fighters of that period were fitted with copies of the old French Hispano Suiza 12Y engine. They were of poor quality and had many defects. Flight time decreased and due to the need to fly at low level, fuel consumption increased. Due to bad weather and constant cloud, the typical operational altitude in the Moscow area was significantly less than the 'classic' one,

4,000m (13,000ft)! Because of these factors, the combat effectiveness of Luftwaffe fighters was 2½–3 times higher than Red Army aviation. German pilots was also much better trained and had more experience than their Russian counterparts. Even when the ratio of the strength was 1:5 and even 1:10, the Luftwaffe fighters were superior to their enemies!

Luftwaffe Phantoms: the 'He-113' and 'Me-115'

Soviet reports and documents often mention German 'Messerschmitt Me 115' and 'Heinkel He 113' fighters. Where did these phantoms come from?

In 1940 Soviet Russia was actively monitoring the aviation production of potential enemies (Britain and the Third Reich). In March 1941, the Intelligence Directorate of the General Staff of the Red Army reported secret information: 'Aircraft in prototype construction . . . single-seat fighter Messerschmitt Me 115, with the Daimler-Benz DV-603 engine capacity 1500-1700 HP.'

On 29 August 1941 there was a dogfight in the Leningrad area. Afterwards, Russian pilots reported encountering Luftwaffe fighters which differed from the Bf 109 E. They had a longer fuselage, more powerful armament and higher speed. These aircraft were identified as 'Me 115s'. The first official victory over it was won by Lieutenant P.T. Tarasov of the 15th IAP. After that, reports of the appearance of 'Me115s' appeared for over a year.

An even more durable phantom, which never existed (even in the form of an experienced machine!), was the 'Heinkel He 113'. They were 'seen' and 'shot down' in large quantities between 1941 and 1944! For all this time no 'He 113' made an emergency landing in Soviet territory or was found abandoned on an airfield. These fighters only appeared in the air. Drawings, silhouettes and scale models of the mythical 'He 113' were widely distributed to the Russian aircraft regiments and the aviation schools. The reason that this fighter was never captured was explained by Russian experts as follows: the machine was very secret and equipped with a self-destruct mechanism . . .

In fact, the Bf 109 F was mistakenly identified as the 'Me 115' and the 'He 113'. When the Russians captured several samples of this fighter and tested them, they identified 'Friedrich' as 'Me 109 F'. But after this the 'Me 115' and 'He 113' still continued to figure in the reports of Russian pilots.

The 'Me 115' didn't have a real prototype. The prototype 'He 113' was the He 100 D fighter, which had not gone into production. On the orders

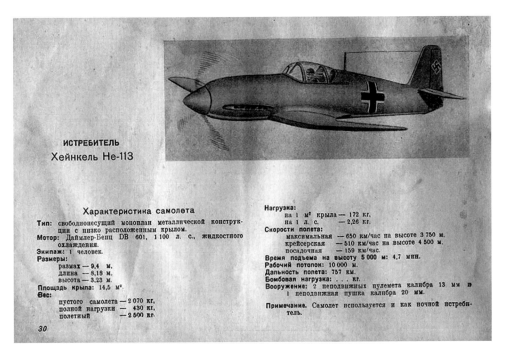

ИСТРЕБИТЕЛЬ
Хейнкель Hе-113

Характеристика самолета

Тип: свободнонесущий моноплан металлической конструк-
ции с низко расположенным крылом.
Мотор: Даймлер-Бенц DB 601, 1 100 л. с., жидкостного
охлаждения.
Экипаж: 1 человек.
Размеры:
размах — 9,4 м,
длина — 8,18 м,
высота — 3,23 м.
Площадь крыла: 14,5 м².
Вес:
пустого самолета — 2 070 кг,
полной нагрузки — 430 кг,
полетный — 2 500 кг.

Нагрузка:
на 1 м² крыла — 172 кг,
на 1 л. с. — 2,26 кг.
Скорости полета:
максимальная — 650 км/час на высоте 3 750 м.
крейсерская — 510 км/час на высоте 4 500 м.
посадочная — 159 км/час.
Время подъема на высоту 5 000 м: 4,7 мин.
Рабочий потолок: 10 000 м.
Дальность полета: 757 км.
Бомбовая нагрузка: . . . кг.
Вооружение: 2 неподвижных пулемета калибра 13 мм и
1 неподвижная пушка калибра 20 мм.

Примечание. Самолет используется и как ночной истребитель.

30

The Russians did not doubt the existence of the He 113 and FW 187 fighters and even made a detailed description of them

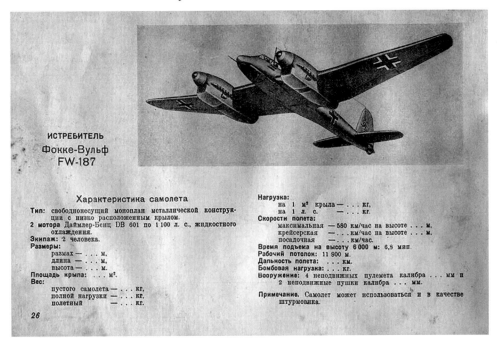

ИСТРЕБИТЕЛЬ
Фокке-Вульф
FW-187

Характеристика самолета

Тип: свободнонесущий моноплан металлической конструк-
ции с низко расположенным крылом.
2 мотора Даймлер-Бенц DB 601 по 1 100 л. с., жидкостного
охлаждения.
Экипаж: 2 человека.
Размеры:
размах — . . . м,
длина — . . . м,
высота — . . . м.
Площадь крыла: . . . м².
Вес:
пустого самолета — . . . кг,
полной нагрузки — . . . кг,
полетный — . . . кг.

Нагрузка:
на 1 м² крыла — . . . кг,
на 1 л. с. — . . . кг.
Скорости полета:
максимальная — 580 км/час на высоте . . . м,
крейсерская — . . . км/час на высоте . . . м,
посадочная — . . . км/час.
Время подъема на высоту 6 000 м: 6,5 мин.
Рабочий потолок: 11 800 м.
Дальность полета: . . . км.
Бомбовая нагрузка: . . . кг.
Вооружение: 4 неподвижных пулемета калибра . . . мм и
2 неподвижные пушки калибра . . . мм.

Примечание. Самолет может использоваться и в качестве
штурмовика.

26

of Göring, in the spring of 1940 a disinformation campaign was launched. Photographs of nine experimental He 100 Ds were printed in magazines and newspapers. They were painted with various emblems and serial numbers and then repainted, creating the illusion of 'mass production'. Then came the misinformation: the new fighter was called the He 113. The British did not believe this 'leak of information', but in Russia they took it seriously.

With the help of such sound collectors Russians learned about the approach of German aircraft

Russian soldiers study the German aircraft Hs 126, which made an emergency landing

Chapter 6

'Last Offensive'

By mid-November, Army Group Centre had finished preparing for a new attack on Moscow, but only to the minimum possible level. Field Marshal Fedor von Bock warned army commanders about the lack of reserves (apart from one division) and advised them 'to rely on existing forces'. In Panzer divisions there was not enough fuel, and some artillery units were without ammunition. A similar situation existed in the Luftwaffe. The main aim of the offensive had not been achieved, but in early November, many units began to be sent to the rear to replenish and reorganize and then move to other countries, such as I./KG 2, KGr. 806 and several tactical and long-range reconnaissance *Staffein*. On 13 November KGr. 100 'Wiking' flew to Germany, and two or three days later KG 54 'Totenkopf' and KG 55 'Greif' followed. In accordance with the plans approved in the summer of 1941, the transfer of *Luftflotte* 2 and II *Fliegerkorps* headquarters and support units to Sicily began.

As a result, only VII *Fliegerkorps* under Generaloberst Wolfram von Richthofen was left in the Moscow area. He too had 'lost weight', having had to share units with other fronts. On 15 November the specialized aviation group III./KG 4 'General Wever' of Major Wolfgang Buring flew to the airfield at Pleskau (Pskov), and earlier I./JG 51 left for Staraya Russa. There was a large gap between the sectors of VIII *Fliegerkorps* and *Luftflotte* 4. To fill it *Führer der Nahkampfverbände* 2 (*Nakfü* 2 – Leader of Close Air Support Units 2) was created, with its headquarters at Orel. The remaining Luftwaffe forces were too small for such a huge front. But Hitler didn't see it as a problem. 'The presence of two air fleets does not change anything in operational and tactical terms, using them in three directions, because a separate aviation corps has been allocated for Army Group Centre,' he said at a meeting.

The Russian command guessed that the Wehrmacht was preparing for a new offensive and decided to launch a pre-emptive strike. On 15 November, the Soviet 16th Army attacked in the area of Volokolamsk, and the 5th, 43rd and 33rd Armies attacked the positions of the German Fourth Army in several places. Fierce fighting took place in the sector of the 12th and 13th Army Corps in the Serpukhov district, where the 415th 'Siberian' Division and the 125th Tank Regiment attacked with the support of 'Katyusha' rocket launchers. The Russians broke into the German lines, but Ju 87s of StG 1 appeared just in time. Their attacks made it possible to hold the line.

At 13.00 the Luftwaffe carried out an air attack on Tushino airfield, dropping eighty high-explosive and fragmentation bombs. The airfield was severely damaged, one MiG-3 and several fighters and ground-attack aircraft of the 47th Aviation Division of the Western Front being destroyed.

The 6th IAK PVO carried out 324 sorties and claimed eight aircraft shot down. Four of its fighters failed to return to base. German data records two losses. North-east of Tula He 111 H-5 W. Nr. 3926 'A1+ES' of 8./KG 53 'Legion Condor' was shot down. Of the five-man crew two were killed and three, including the pilot Feldwebel Franz Grawe, were captured. To the east of Mozhaisk near Dorokhovo Bf 109 F-2 W. Nr. 12913 (Unteroffizier Bernard Wilsky) of 6./JG 52 was shot down. The pilot was killed. The fighter was fell into the hands reasonably intact by the Russians, repaired and tested at the Red Army Air Force Research Institute. This victory was shared between five Yak-1 pilots of the 562nd IAP. The Germans reported heavy air raids on Kalinin (Soviet sources say the target was the bridge across the Volga there) and attacks by single bombers on Bryansk.

On 16 November, fierce fighting continued in the Volokolamsk area. The Russian 316th Infantry Division of General Panfilov and a group under General Dovator took the area of Bortniki–Sofievka–Bludy and reached the milestone of Hrulevo–Davydovo. The German LXVI and V Army Corps captured the hill north-east of Volokolamsk, driving the Russians out. Later, these events became known in Soviet Russia as 'the feat of Panfilov's 28'. Russian propaganda came up with a story about how Panfilov's soldiers repelled the 'powerful tank attack' of the Germans and heroically died like the '300 Spartans'. Later this myth was built into a cult and was used for the indoctrination of young soldiers.

A critical situation arose in the sector of the XIII Army Corps of the Fourth Army. In the fierce battles that took place in the woods, the Germans were able to hold out but at the cost of heavy losses. Once again the decisive role was played by the Ju 87s of StG 1, which from morning to late evening struck at the Soviet troops. 'The continuous raids by the dive bombers of

Trolleybus on one of the streets of Moscow. November 1941. In the background the building of the Manege (central exhibition hall) in a camouflage

Residents of Moscow building barriers against tanks on the main street

Hagens'[5] group were vital in repelling the Russian attacks,' reported the headquarters of the Fourth Army. 'Their premature withdrawal from the battle would significantly weaken the defence front.'

'Enemy aircraft throughout the day showed great activity,' reported the war diary of the Soviet 49th Army. 'At 13.30, a massive raid by dive bombers was carried out on troops and the command post of the right wing of the army.'

In addition, Luftwaffe supported the advancing elements of the LVI Army Corps by the Volga reservoir and attacked the railways. In the evening, a lone bomber raided Moscow, dropped five high-explosive bombs on the Tagansky district, killing two people and wounding sixteen.

The 6th IAK PVO flew 454 sorties and claimed 10 planes shot down (four Me 109s, three Ju 87s, one Ju 88, one Do 215 and one 'Me 110'). But none of these victories was confirmed. On this day, the first Hurricanes appeared in the air defence of Moscow. Eleven of the British-built fighters flew from Kineshma to Lyubertsy airfield. They formed a special 28th (bis) IAP.

On 17 November, Army Group Centre launched an offensive on several fronts. Due to bad weather Luftwaffe activity was limited. Ju 87s of StG 1 supported the defence of the XIII Army Corps in the Serpukhov district, while StG 2 carried out attacks in the northern sector. At 09.45 and 15.31 there were air raids on Moscow. A total of 50 high-explosive and fragmentation bombs and 800 incendiaries was dropped. Explosions and fires did considerable damage in the Sovietsky, Centralny and Pervomaisky districts. Dozens of Muscovites were killed or wounded.

On 18 November aviation became more active despite the bad weather (fog, visibility less than 1km). The Luftwaffe carried out a series of raids on Russian airfields, and attacked Soviet troops' forward positions. At 09.40 ten Ju 88s carried out an attack on Lyubertsy airfield, dropping fifteen bombs. The airfield was severely damaged, one Hurricane of the 28th (bis) IAP was destroyed and five people were injured. At 15.00 three He 111s escorted by Bf 109s attacked Vnukovo airfield, dropping eighteen fragmentation bombs. The airfield was severely damaged, and one I-153 was destroyed. The advanced Klin airfield was subjected to air strikes four times, but without serious consequences.

From early morning until late at night, a single aircraft attacked Moscow from high altitude, dropping seven high-explosive bombs and 450 incendiaries. The air-alarm in the city was sounded four times

---

5. Major Walter Hagen – the commander of StG 1.

LaGG-3 fighter preparing for take off

Anti-aircraft gun 85mm from 732nd ZenAP deployed to fire on German tanks. Tula, November 1941

(at 07.15, 13.59, 19.55 and 23.05). Factories and houses in the Leninsky and Frunzensky districts were damaged.

The 6th IAK PVO carried out 260 sorties, and 12 air battles were recorded. The pilots claimed shooting down nine aircraft (five Me 109s, three He 111s and one Me 110). German data confirms only one victory. In the Serpukhov district He 111 H-4 W. Nr. 6966 of I./KG 28 was shot down by a fighter, most likely that flown by Politruk Nikolai Baskov of the 445th IAP.

Russian losses were significant – six fighters. Lieutenants Shvagirev and Maksimov of the 178th IAP and two pilots of the 27th IAP were killed; Lieutenant Alekseev of the 436th IAP was reported missing. The LaGG-3 of Sergeant Burlakov of the 564th IAP was damaged and made an emergency landing.

In the following days, weather conditions severely limited air operations. On 19 November 19, the Germans bombed Tushino airfield twice, but did not cause serious damage. An air raid on Moscow was also unsuccessful. Most of the bombs were dropped outside the city, and only 10 small incendiary bombs landed in the park of the northern port. Actions of Russian aviation are described in German reports as 'insignificant'.

'Due to unfavourable weather, only a few flights were made for the purpose of meteorological reconnaissance and disruption of railway traffic,' Army Group Centre's daily report for 20 November read. The war diary of the 6th IAK PVO described their operations that day as follows:

> The 436th IAP attacked enemy ground troops in the areas of Vozdvizenskoye, Kopylov and Galoguzovo. 18 sorties with a total duration of 8 hrs 15 mins were made. 10–12 vehicles and 10 motorcycles were destroyed and a company of enemy infantry scattered. A large concentration of enemy troops was observed in the Kopylov-Reshetnikovo area. Reshetnikovo was covered by anti-aircraft artillery.
>
> The 27th IAP attacked enemy ground troops in the New Zavidovo–Gavrilkovo–Bezborodova–Kopylov area. 14 sorties with a total duration of 8 hrs 40 mins were made. 13 – 15 tanks, 40 – 45 vehicles with infantry, and 12 motorcycles were destroyed. Up to 50 infantry and a platoon of cavalry were scattered. 54 rocket shells and 1 ammunition load were spent. The result of observation: the movement of

a motorized column to Turginovo in the south, 12km west of Kopylov – 200–250 vehicles.

The 120th IAP attacked enemy ground troops in the New Zavidovsky, Polovnikova, Galoguzovo and Domnino areas. 6 sorties lasting 4 hrs were made. 36 rockets and 1 ammunition load were expended. Up to 20 vehicles with infantry and 6 – 8 armoured vehicles were destroyed, up to 2 infantry platoons were scattered.'

'Our aircraft did not operate, and the enemy were very active,' reported the headquarters of the 3rd Panzer Group leading the offensive in the above-mentioned Zavidovo and Kopylov areas. Russian aviation tried to halt the advance of the 6th Panzer Division with ground attacks. In the midst of the fighting near the command post of the Soviet 16th Army (near the village of Bryukhovo) a close reconnaissance aircraft, Hs 126 B-1 W. Nr. 3168 '5F+6H' of 1.(H)/14, was shot down. The observer was killed and the pilot Oberfeldwebel A. Borneck, parachuted into Russian territory. After that, the fate of the German pilot was predictable: taken prisoner, the interrogation, and then sent to Siberia. But Borneck really wanted to live and didn't want to be held captive, especially when the victory of the Third Reich seemed to be close. Taking advantage of the confusion he escaped while being transported to the rear and then reached his troops, advancing on Moscow.

On 21 November, the weather conditions were again unfavourable. The Russians complained about the heavy fog and cloud cover, and the Germans about the strong wind. Air operations were limited and only at low level. The Germans recorded numerous air attacks on the troops of the LVI Army Corps and the 3rd Panzer Group. Dive bombers of III./StG 2 'Immelman', in November based at Gorshkovo airfield (100km [62 miles] west of Moscow) attacked Soviet troops in the Solnechnogorsk area, which had been reached by units of the 2nd Panzer Division. Bombers also attacked the Bezhetsk–Bologoye railway. On this day, the Germans reached the city of Klin.

Bf 110 E *Schnell-bombers* of SKG 210 supported the 2nd Panzer Army and carried out low-level attacks on Soviet troops and tanks near the city of Efremov and Uzlovaya station. Bombers of I./KG 28 and KG 53 'Legion Condor' were also active and near Kashira He 111 H-6 W. Nr. 4400 '1T+FK' of 2./KG 28 was shot down. At midnight the city of Stalinogorsk was captured in a sudden armoured attack.

Russian pilots from the 445th IAP posing on the body of the plane He 111 H-6 W. Nr. 4400 '1T+FK'. The plane was shot down south of Moscow

Russian Fanaticism and Cruelty

Civilians in this cold time suffered great hardship. Any houses surviving after the battles and bombardments were occupied by German soldiers wanting to warm up, and at night villages were set on fire by Russian aircraft. Stalin issued the brutal and immoral order, 'Leave the Germans a snowy desert'. All the houses were to be completely destroyed, and the fate of the population did not bother the Russian dictator. Stalin believed that the people (old men, women and children) were obliged to sacrifice themselves for the sake of victory. Those who did not want die of their own free will, would be 'helped' to do so by Russian aviation . . .

In daylight the towns and villages were attacked by Su-2, Pe-2 and Il-2 bombers, and at night U-2s and R-5s deluged them with incendiary bombs. The headquarters of the Soviet 49th Army reported that 'Army aviation bombed enemy troop concentrations and set fire to enemy-occupied settlements.' The war diary of the neighbouring 50th Army also recorded that:

> As a result of the bombardments in Troizkoye, N. Wiazowna, Vysokinichi there were big fires. The commander of a squadron of night bombers, Captain Burov from 20 to 25.11

> on the basis of Order No. 0428 of 16.11.41, was to set fire to all the buildings in the territory occupied by the enemy in the districts Dedilovo, Bogoroditsk. In the first instance to burn all the buildings (houses, outbuildings and all kinds of structures) near Dedilovo, Stoylovo, Panino and Kyreevka. Secondly, Bogoroditsk, Novo-Pokrovka and Ivanovo.

During this period saboteurs, young people brainwashed by Stalinist propaganda, were sent behind German lines to set fires in occupied villages. One of these saboteurs, Zoya Kosmodemyanskaya, was caught by local residents and handed over to the Germans. The fanatical Komsomol member was executed, and Soviet propaganda made her a 'national hero'. Several generations of Soviet citizens were brought up on her example. Later, after the liberation of the burned villages, the Russians took photographs the ruins and published them in newspapers with the caption, 'The village burned by fascists'.

On 22 November, the Luftwaffe was active only on the southern flank. He 111 bombers attacked Soviet troops in the path of the advancing units of the 3rd and 4th Panzer Divisions and the railway lines between Moscow and Serpukhov, and Moscow and Kashira. Bf 110 Es attacked marching columns near Venev. The airfield at Volyntsevo, north-east of Tula, was attacked several times. In this area He 111 H-5 W. Nr. 4495 'A1+CM' of 4./KG 53 'Legion Condor' was shot down. All five crew disappeared in the endless 'white mist' . . .

German bombers were forced to fly at low level to locate and attack their targets, which was very dangerous as the aircraft were not only vulnerable to anti-aircraft artillery, but also small arms fire. On 23 November north-east of Tula He 111 H-5 W. Nr. 3557 'A1+IS' of 8./KG 53 was brought down by ground fire. But this time the crew was lucky. Leutnant Ernst Glasow was able to land the aircraft on the snow 30km (18.6 miles) from the German lines. The five crew members avoided being captured and returned to their unit. On the northern flank the Wehrmacht captured Klin and Solnechnogorsk. The remaining distance to Moscow was 40km (25 miles).

On 24 November fighting began for the city of Venev. The weather in Second Panzer Army's sector was better, so the main Luftwaffe effort was focused there. He 111s bombed trains and railway stations in the Ryazhsk, Ryazan, Kashira and Serpukhov areas, while close-support Hs 123s, Bf 109 E-4/Bs and Bf 110 Es attacked settlements, roads and Soviet troop positions. An air raid on the city of Tambov targeted the major supply base for the Soviet Southwest Front located there. The 10th Motorized Infantry Division achieved great success on this day. Its leading units reached the city of Mikhailov and the airfield located 2km (1¼ miles) from it. The Russian planes that were there managed to take off at the last moment, but a train with eight planes loaded aboard was stopped on the railway. Ahead lay a vast and desolate forest area and the road to Ryazan, 50km (31 miles) away.

The Germans Come to Moscow

On 25 November, the weather conditions remained stable. To the west and north of Moscow there was fog with haze and it was snowing. This impeded the actions of aviation. Near Tula and Ryazan there was frost and 'light snow'. Close-support aircraft and *Schnell-bombers* made low-level attacks on troop concentrations, marching columns and field fortifications along the entire front of the Second Panzer Army. Bombers carried out raids on the airfield near Michurinsk, the Ryazan–Ryazhsk railway, Chemical Plant No. 204 in the city of Kotovsk (Tambov district) and Tambov itself. During a raid in the Ryazhsk district Ju 88 A-4 W. Nr. 2566 '5K+BB', flown by the commander of II./KG 3 'Blitz' Oberleutnant Friedrich Paskay, was shot down. The crew was listed as missing. This victory was claimed by the commander of the 171th IAP Lieutenant Colonel Orlachin.

Thanks to the powerful support of the Luftwaffe, Guderian achieved impressive success in the spirit of Blitzkrieg. Venev had not yet been captured, but units of the 4th Panzer Division reached Serebraniye Prudy. The vanguard of the 17th Panzer Division dashed forward and reached the outskirts of Kashira. German soldiers could the ice-covered Oka river and the railway bridge, from which it was only 100km (62 miles) to the south-eastern outskirts of Moscow. The northern and southern tank 'wedges' of Army Group Centre were only 170km (106 miles) part. All that stood between the Germans and the bridge over the Oka was the 352th Independent Anti-Aircraft Battalion of the Moscow anti-aircraft defences. The gunners opened fire and halted the advance of the German tanks.

In spite of the bad weather, Russian aviation concentrated on attacking ground targets. For example, the 120th IAP jointly with army aviation bombarded German troops near Golovkovo–Strelina, and Dubinino – Solnechnogorsk. I-153 and MiG-3 fighters launched 139 rockets and dropped 8 FAB-50 high-explosive and 40 AO-15 fragmentation bombs. 'Multiple raids on settlements in the areas of the 87th and 252nd Infantry

Divisions against 11th Panzer Division low-level attacks flight on a causeway across the Istra reservoir', reported the staff of the 4th Panzer Group. 'In the corps' sector enemy aircraft carried out low-level attacks,' complained the headquarters of the LVI Army Corps. Russian bombers carried out two air raids on Kalinin, and low-level fighters strafed the Kalinin–Klin highway.

On 26 November, the 6th IAK PVO completed 338 sorties. But the average duration of each flight was 48 minutes. Efficiency was low. Seeing an enemy, the pilots usually tried to shoot it down in the first attack and could not pursue because of their limited range. In twenty-six air battles only two planes were shot down. Near Detchino He 111 H-6 W. Nr. 4975 'A1+VA' of St./KG 53 'Legion Condor' was shot down. Four of the crew were killed, only the pilot, H. Lorenz, bailed out and a few days later was able to reach friendly troops. In the Solnechnogorsk area Bf 109 F-2 W. Nr. 12811 of 6./JG 52 was also lost.

November 27th became one of the climactic days of the battle for Moscow. The German 3rd Panzer Group broke through to the frozen Moscow–Volga canal, and the 4th Panzer Group captured Istra. Simultaneously, the leading units of the V Army Corps reached the area of Kryukovo, little more than 20km (12.4 miles) from Moscow. The frightened Russian command ordered all aircraft to attack the German troops approaching Moscow.

The operation involved eleven aviation regiments of the 6th IAK PVO: the 11th, 27th, 28th, 34th, 120th, 177th, 178th, 233rd, 436th, 445th and 562nd. I-153, I-16, Yak-1, MiG-3 and LaGG-3 fighters carried out low-level attacks on the Germans in the Solnechnogorsk, Mordves and Klin areas, while other fighters covered the Russian forces desperately defending the outskirts of Moscow. Pilots reported sixteen air victories but most of them are not confirmed. The Yak-1 of Lieutenant Ivan Kalabushkin of the 562th IAP shot down He 111 H-5 W. Nr. 3960 '1T+GK' of 2./KG 28. Three of the crew were listed as missing, while the mechanic survived and some days later crossed the front line. The Yak-1 of Lieutenant Ruchkin of the 445th IAP intercepted and damaged He 111 H-6 W. Nr. 3773 'A1+AK' of 2./KG 53 south-east of Olenkovo. The bomber made an emergency landing at the former Soviet airfield near Kalinin. All four of the crew of Leutnant Erwin Fell are to this day unaccounted for.

The Spanish volunteers of 15.(Spain)/JG 27 suffered serious losses on this day. They were sent to Russia by the Spanish dictator Franco in gratitude for the help that Germany gave him in the Civil War of 1936–9. Then many Germans died in the Peninsula, fighting the 'Communists'. Now military fate led the Spaniards deep into snow-covered Russia, where

Hitler was waging the 'final battle' with Bolshevism. Officially, Spain was not at war with the USSR, so all the pilots wore German uniforms and flew under German names. On 27 November, the Spanish squadron lost two experienced pilots, including the unit's commander. While carrying out ground attacks near Istra, Bf 109 E-7/B W. Nr. 3771 was shot down by anti-aircraft fire. Its pilot, Captain Aristides Garcia-Lopez Rengel, was recorded as missing. In the same area Bf 109 E-3 W. Nr. 3185, flown by the experienced pilot and commander of 15.(Spain)/JG 27 Commandante Jose Munyos Pérez Himénez (in German documents designated Major 'Josef Munos') also went missing. What his fate was is unknown. But according to Russian information on this day in Avdeevka anti-aircraft guns shot down an aircraft, which was identified as an Hs 123. In the wreckage was found the body of a Spanish major with two medals on his jacket. Himenez did have two medals ('For Military Merit' and the 'Military Cross'). According to other sources, the Spaniard was able to bail out. An Hs 123 B-1 of 10.(Sch)./LG 2 acting in support of units of the Second Panzer Army was also shot down.

Russian losses amounted to nine fighters (seven Yak-1s, one I-153 and one MiG-3). Most were shot down by anti-aircraft fire when attacking ground targets. Captain Sokun of the 34th IAP, Lieutenant Lepsky, Lieutenant Golovaty and Sergeant Varfolomeev of the 11th IAP, Lieutenant Maxim Kulak of the 120th IAP, Lieutenant Belyaev of the 436th IAP, and Lieutenant Gnatenko and Sergeants Klochkov and Shavelev of the 562nd IAP failed to return to base, although Klochkov, Shavelev and Golovaty made emergency landings on Russian territory and were able to rejoin their units.

At 17.40, a pair of He 111s of I./KG 28 carried out an air raid on Moscow, dropping two high-explosive and twenty incendiary bombs. The 'Tsyurupa' plant in the Sokolniki district was partially destroyed, with serious damage being done to the fine grinding shop.

On 28 November, the 6th IAK PVO carried out 520 sorties, including 171 to attack ground targets. Pe-3s of the 95th and 208th IAPs bombed German forces in the area of Litvinovo–Peshki, Yak-1s of the 11th IAP attacked in the Solnechnogorsk–Istra area, the I-16s of the 445th IAP attacked the positions of the 17th Panzer Division south of Kashira, the MiG-3s and I-16s of the 28th and 177th IAPs attacked ground targets in the Solnechnogorsk area, and I-153s of the 120th IAP scored hits in the Korovino–Cherepanovo–Lytvynovo area. The fighters alone delivered 108 bombs and 488 rockets on different targets. The Germans noted the actions of Russian aviation in the 4th Panzer Group's sector: 'Enemy planes carried out low-level bombing attacks in the area north-east of the town of Istra and on the crossing of the river Istra.' The losses of the 6th IAK PVO amounted to three fighters. The I-16 of Sergeant Bychkov of the 445th IAP was shot down in an air battle, while the Yak-1 of Sergeant Burmistov of the 11th IAP and the I-16 of Lieutenant Katunin of the 445th IAP failed to return to base.

Russian pilots reported thirty-nine air battles and claimed twenty aircraft shot down. But the real success was minimal. At 17.05 a single He 111 of III./KG 26 carried out an air raid on Moscow, dropping a load of incendiary bombs on Aircraft Factory No. 22, starting a fire in Shop No. 5. On its return flight, the bomber was shot down. Three of the crew were missing while one was able to reach his own troops. This victory over the enemy was credited to Lieutenant Fedor Mitrofanov (near Sitnya-Shchelkanovo) and Lieutenant Nicholay Blagodarenko (south of Klimovskoe) of the 445th IAP.

On the night of 28/29 November, the Germans crossed the Moscow-Volga canal south of Yakhroma on the ice, creating a small bridgehead on

A 'Valentine II' tank of English production, camouflaged under the winter landscape

MiG-3 fighters at Vnukovo airfield

the eastern bank. To the south there was fighting in the area of Krasnaya Polyana, and individual reconnaissance units were closer to Khimki, a suburb of Moscow. But the climax of the offensive of Army Group Centre had passed. On this day, the commander of the Western Front, General Georgi Zhukov, asked Stalin's permission for a counter-attack.

On 29 November bad weather again plagued air operations. Only a few crews tried to support their troops fighting in the snow-covered forests. Five Pe-3s of the 208th IAP flew through snow and fog to the Istra area. With great difficulty, the crews managed to find suitable targets north-west of the city. The low-flying aircraft dropped six FAB-100 and FAB-50 bombs. 'Scattered two companies of infantry and a few vehicles,' said the brief report about the mission. But only three aircraft returned to their base at Ramenskoye, located east of Moscow. The crews of Lieutenant Filonov and Lieutenant Bas disappeared in the white haze . . .It also swallowed up He 111 H-6 W. Nr. 4403 '1T+DC' of 2./KG 28 in the Kashira area. The entire crew of the bomber was listed as missing.

On 30 November the weather was a bit better. In the Moscow area the temperature had risen to only -3° Celsius and visibility had increased to 3.2km (2 miles). German bombers, fighter-bombers, *Schnell-bombers* and close-support aircraft began intensive low-level attacks on the positions of Soviet troops in the Kryukovo, Krasnaya Polyana and Zvenigorod area, villages and towns in the front line, and railway lines to the south and south-east of Moscow. At 15.28, a powerful air raid was carried out on the capital, during which fifty high-explosive and fragmentation bombs were dropped. Many targets in the Krasnaya Presnya, Leninsky and Pervomaisky districts were damaged by explosions and fire. According to the Russian rescue service, thirty-seven people were killed and eighty-six wounded. Ju 87s did not fly on this day due to heavy cloud cover.

The 6th IAK PVO carried out 564 sorties, but the average duration of the fighters' flights was only 40–55 minutes, due to the short distance from the airfields to the target areas. Fighters of six aviation regiments attacked various ground targets to the south-east of Solnechnogorsk, expending 538 rockets, 5,500 cannon shells and 144 high-explosive bombs. The actions of the Russian aviation was marked by the German command. '20th Army Corps: high explosive and incendiary bombs are dropped. 5th Army Corps: active air operations, especially on the forward advancing units. Some air attacks involved up to 20 aircraft,' reported the headquarters of the 4th Panzer Group. 'Brisk actions of enemy aircraft in the areas of both corps,' reported the headquarters of the 3rd Panzer Group.

Russian pilots claimed sixteen victories on the 30th. But these successes are once again not confirmed by German information. The Germans reported only one loss. In the area of Solnechnogorsk Bf 109 F-2 W. Nr. 12765 flown by Unteroffizier Otto Millbauer of 3./JG 52 was shot down. Two weeks earlier, this pilot had been shot down over Russian territory but was found and evacuated by a rescue Fi 156. This time he was not so lucky, and was killed. On this day II./JG 52 moved to the airfield at Klin, located 70km (43 miles) from the outskirts of Moscow.

As usual, Russian losses were higher than those of the Luftwaffe. The 6th IAK PVO lost five aircraft (two Yak-1s, two Pe-3s and one MiG-3). Ground fire and fighters shot down Politruk Cazakov of the 11th IAP, and Lieutenant Pozhidaev and Starschina Aleshin of the 208th IAP; Lieutenant Golovaty of the 11th IAP and Sergeant Borodin of the 428th IAP were reported missing.

The Luftwaffe flew to airfields near Moscow, and Russian aviation regiments were preparing for evacuation. At the end of October, a plan was prepared to move the fighters to the airfields east of Moscow, such as Shatura, Orekhovo-Zuyevo, Noginsk, Kolchugino, Vladimir and others. In case of an immediate threat of encirclement of the capital, the Russian command wanted to leave five or six aviation regiments in the city, the rest to be transferred to the east to continue operations in the Moscow area from there.

Statistics for November

During this month the 6th IAK PVO carried out 8,262 sorties, including 4,683 to cover Soviet troops, 1,418 to attack ground targets and 2,000 for air defence. The pilots reported 190 downed aircraft, and 660 trucks, 156 tanks, 47 motorcycles, 22 armoured vehicles and so on destroyed. In fact, in November, 'Stalin's Falcons' record exaggerated their successes. The reliably established losses of the Germans in the Moscow area were thirty aircraft (thirteen He 111s, ten Bf 109s, three Ju 88s, two Bf 110s, one Hs 123 and one Hs 126), only some of which could be claimed by the 6th IAK PVO, as some would have been shot down by the anti-aircraft artillery, ground forces and the fighters covering the front-line troops.

After each raid Russian pilots reported large quantities of enemy military equipment destroyed. Between 27 and 30 November alone, the 6th IAK PVO reported 105 tanks destroyed. In general, the Russians believed that in November they destroyed at least 1,500 German tanks. But accurate assessment of the results of attacks was not carried out: all vehicles close to the explosions of bombs and rockets, or shrouded in smoke, were considered 'destroyed'. In fact, the destruction or damaging of a tank by a direct hit or near miss was a happy accident. Furthermore, it is obvious that the Germans simply did not have that many tanks. On 30 November the 3th Panzer Group had only seventy-five serviceable tanks (an average of twenty-five tanks per division), and the neighbouring 4th Panzer Group and Guderian's panzer army were in a similar situation.

Fighter Aircraft in the 6th IAK PVO on 1 December 1941

Type	Number	Serviceable
MiG-3	212	175
I-16	94	66
Yak-1	60	50
Pe-3	31	28
I-153	28	26
LaGG-3	26	13
Tomahawk	11	7
Hurricane	10	9
Total	472	374

In early December, the overall strategic position of the Third Reich looked stable and encouraging. The Nazis controlled a vast territory stretching from Brittany on the west coast of France to the outskirts of Moscow in the east. Most of Europe was under Hitler's control. In Africa, German and Italian troops were successful. Therefore, the first crisis on the Eastern Front, which arose at the end of November, did not cause serious alarm. Army Group North could not link up with the Finnish army and solve the problem of Leningrad. And in the south on 21 November the Russians unexpectedly repulsed the Germans. In the Moscow area Wehrmacht still continued to advance slowly, although in some sectors their troops had to retreat. They still retained footholds on the eastern bank of the Moscow–Volga canal and on the Oka near Kashira.

Some German generals suggested halting the advance and going over to the defensive but Hitler ordered the attack to continue. The commander of Army Group Centre, Feldmarschall von Bock, ordered the Fourth Army to begin its long-planned offensive in the central front. The attack began on the morning of 1 December on both sides of Naro-Fominsk. The Luftwaffe tried to support this attack. They operated single aircraft and small groups, flying mainly at low level. Three times, at 10.00, 12.10 and 14.30, Vnukovo airfield, located south-west of Moscow, was attacked but the twenty-two high-explosive and fragmentation bombs dropped did not cause serious damage. At 11.30 over the airfield Khimki of the clouds, an unidentified plane dropped eight bombs on Khimki airfield. The airfield was damaged, but Russian fighters were unharmed. At 10.00 the first air attack on Moscow was carried out by Bf 110s. They dropped twenty-nine high-explosive bombs on the 'Voykov' factory, located in the north-western part of the city. The foundry was destroyed, and twenty-eight workers were killed and ninety-three injured.

The air defence regiments performed thirty-eight short sorties to cover their airfields and troops. The average duration of the fighter's flights was only 34 minutes! No aerial victories were claimed on this day. The Croatian 10.(Croat)/KG 3 lost two Do 17 Z-2s (W. Nr. 1200 and W. Nr. 2666) together with the crews. In one of them perished the commander of a squadron, Bojnik (Major) Vladimir Gravats. Ju 88 A-4 W. Nr. 3578 of 5./KG 3 was reported missing in the Golosino area.

In the severe cold air operations experienced serious difficulties. The Germans had to dilute aviation fuel and oil with special additives, and warm up the engines for 4–5 hours. The aircraft consumed an increased amount of fuel, which reduced flight time and range. But the Russian aircraft were even less ready for winter. For example, the nominal radius of action of an LaGG-3 was 483–563km (300–350 miles) but in practice, it did not exceed 150–200km (93–124 miles). The flight time of the aircraft with a full tank of fuel was no more than an hour.

The oil system of the LaGG-3 and Yak-1 fighters had a volume of 38 litres. It consisted of two oil tanks, several oil filters, a C-shaped honeycomb air-oil radiator with a thermostat and an aerothermometer for incoming oil. In cold weather, the oil had to be completely drained after each flight through three holes: a special neck at the bottom of one of the oil filters, the radiator and the pipeline plug. If the oil was not drained, in the cold it froze and the engine failed. Before the flight, the oil needed to be heated and poured into the tanks at a temperature of 75–85° Celsius. The Russian engines had water cooling, and the capacity of the fighter's water system was 90 litres. At the end of the flight, all this water had to be drained out.

On 2 December, German troops advancing along the Minsk highway reached the area of Golitsyno and Aprelevka. The distance to Vnukovo airfield was 18km (11 miles), and to Moscow 30km (19 miles). But the Germans ran into an impassable jungle of forest debris, obstacles and minefields. The assault was supported by Ju 87s of StG 2 'Immelmann' and *Zerstorers* of II./ZG 26 'Horst Wessel'. At 15.00 there was an air raid on Vnukovo airfield, in which twenty-five high-explosive and fragmentation bombs were dropped, putting the airfield out of action. There were sporadic air battles over the area of the fighting. The 6th IAK PVO carried out 652 sorties, claiming 36 air battles and 15 victories.

In reality, the Germans lost five planes that day. In the Vyazma area a MiG-3 of the 428th IAP shot down Do 17 Z-2 W. Nr. 2904 of 9./KG 3 'Blitz'. This was the last *Staffel* in the Luftwaffe that used these old aircraft as bombers. In the Golitsyno area two Ju 87 R-4s (W. Nr. 6208 '6G+NR' and W. Nr. 6288 '6G+FN') of II./StG 1 were shot down. In one of them perished the commander of the 5th *Staffel* Oberleutnant Joachim Riger, who had carried out 257 missions. According to one account, the Stukas were shot down by ground fire, but another claims that Riger collided in the air with the Ju 87 of his wingman Unteroffizier Hans Frick. On 19 March 1942, Riger was posthumously awarded the Knight's Cross.

Over Kubinka a Russian fighter shot down Hs 126 B-1 W. Nr. 4289 'H1+6R' of 7.(H)/12. Both of the crew were killed, and at Rublevo a Bf 109 F-2 W. Nr. 12745 of 4./JG 52 was downed, the pilot also being killed. The victory was claimed by a large number of pilots of the 11th, 16th, 19th and 564th IAPs. Sergeant Vsevolod Alexandrov in an LaGG-3 shot down an

'Me 109', but then the Russian pilot himself was shot down in the Dedovsk district and was killed.

The losses of the 6th IAK PVO were once again more than those of the Germans. The corps lost seven fighters, including Alexandrov's LaGG-3. Lieutenant Potapov of the 34th IAP, Sergeant Polanski of the 562nd IAP, and Lieutenants Danilenko and Bogdanov of the 177th IAP. The MiG-3 of Lieutenant Poyasov of the 565th IAP suffered engine failure and he crash-landed in the Vnukovo area.

On the night of 2/3 December, the Luftwaffe carried out an air raid on Moscow, dropping forty-seven high explosive and fragmentation bombs but the targets of the attack were not hit. Most of the bombs exploded on open ground and in the woods between the Mikhailovsky highway and the 'Timiryazev' Academy. The Russian rescue service recorded no casualties. But this was no thanks to the air defences. Weather conditions again changed dramatically. The next day only a single aircraft took off, but there was no air combat. And the Russians hit a new low. The average flight time of the fighters was 30 minutes.

On 4 December hard frosts hit, which Russian civilians called the 'Anti-Fascist'. The temperature dropped to -17° Celsius. But for aviation, on the contrary, conditions were favourable, visibility increasing to 8–10km (5–6 miles). The 6th IAK PVO carried out 660 sorties, 186 of which were to attack ground targets in the Yakhroma, Krasnaya Polyana, Chernaya Gryaz and Kryukovo areas. The fighters fired 615 rockets and dropped 160 bombs, reporting the destruction of 15 tanks, 125 vehicles, and 42 trucks with troops. Losses amounted to five fighters, most due to ground fire. Two Yak-1s of the 562th IAP (Sergeants Ivanov and Levin), the Pe-3 of Lieutenants Chirkov and Goncharov of the 95th IAP, the MiG-3 of Sergeant Chepikov of the 423th IAP and the LaGG-3 of Sergeant Piontkovsky of the 178th IAP were lost. In the operational summary of Army Group Centre only the actions of Soviet aircraft in the sector of the 3rd Panzer Group were noted: 'Enemy aircraft bombed our artillery positions.'

The Luftwaffe was active also, the pilots of the 6th IAK PVO reporting thirty-three air battles and shooting down nineteen aircraft but German data confirms only two of these victories. Over the Moscow-Volga canal Politruk Nikolay Baskov of the 445th IAP shot down Bf 109 E-7/B W. Nr. 4086 flown by Spanish volunteer Lieutenant Ricardo Bartolomeo Calvaria of 15.(Spain)/JG 27. His fate is still unknown. In the same area the Yak-1 of Lieutenant Ivan Kalabushkin of the 562th IAP was shot down He 111 H-6 W. Nr. 4479 '1T+KK' of 2./KG 28. The bomber made a belly landing in a street in the city of Dmitrov to the amazement of local residents. The pilot carried out the landing brilliantly, not even clipping the fences lining the street, although on impact the left wing of the aircraft was torn off.

On this day the Germans achieved some success in the attack. The 3rd Panzer Division, moving to the east, captured Revyakino station and cut the Moscow-Tula railway and the parallel highway. The German troops were supported by Bf 110 E-2 *Schnell-bombers* of SKG 210. In the Naro-Fominsk area, however, the troops of the Fourth Army failed to break through to Moscow from the south-west and began to retreat back over the Nara river.

On the night of 4/5 December He 111 H-6s of I./KG 28 carried out an air raid on Moscow, dropping thirty-two high-explosive bombs and eighty incendiaries. The Izmailovo electric substation and several facilities in Stalinsky district were damaged. Two people were killed and twenty-four wounded.

On 5 December, the German attack finally fizzled out. Two days earlier, the commander of the 4th Panzer Group, Generaloberst Erich Hoepner, honestly told the command that, exhausted by continuous battles, his troops were not able to advance. He asked politely: 'Is not it time to make a retreat?' Two days later, the headquarters of the 3rd Panzer Group told von Bock that it was impossible to continue the offensive in the current conditions and 'no improvement in this regard is expected.' The commanders of the forward units had realized that the Russians had assembled fresh forces and were

He 111 H-6 W.Nr. 4479 '1T+KK' from 2./KG 28, made an emergency landing on the streets of the city Dmitrov

preparing to attack. This information was confirmed by air reconnaissance (the crews of Hs 123s, and Bf 110s reported the concentration of troops near the front, and the crews of Ju 88 Ds the continuous movement of military trains with troops and equipment via Yaroslavl, Gorky and Tambov towards the west). But the leadership dismissed these 'pessimistic' messages.

On 5–6 December the Russians dealt powerful blows in the Kalinin, Yelets and Dmitrov sectors. In the north the German garrison in the city of Tihvin was attacked. This important point, which ensured the blockade of Leningrad, had to be evacuated two days later. Problems arose elsewhere for the Third Reich and in other regions. On 7 December, Erwin Rommel began a large-scale withdrawal in North Africa. On the same day, Japan attacked on Pearl Harbor, bringing the USA into the war. On 10 December, in his '*Wolfschanze*' HQ, Hitler declared to his retinue: 'The War is coming to an end'!

In December 1941, the NKVD in Moscow region, which controlled all aspects of life, including the aftermath of air attacks, produced a secret report. In the period 22 July to 6 December 1,732 high-explosive and about 60,000 incendiary bombs were dropped on the city. As a result of explosions and

Russian tankers preparing to attack

143

fires 132 enterprises suffered damage. Of this number, three plants, twelve factories and seven municipal buildings and railway facilities were totally destroyed. During the air attacks were completely or partially destroyed 1,291 residential buildings, 86 warehouses, 85 cultural, educational, scientific, medical and public institutions, including Moscow University, the Pushkin Museum of Fine Arts, Lenin's Library, the Conservatory, the offices of the newspapers *Pravda* and *Izvestia* and the magazines *Moscow Bolshevik* and *Ogonek* were damaged to varying degrees. Casualties were 1,404 killed, 2,037 seriously injured and 3,301 slightly injured.

The results of air raids on Moscow were proportional to the number of bombers involved in them. Many attacks took place in bad weather, and most of them involved small groups of aircraft or even single machines. Large-scale attacks were rare and only three involved more than 100 bombers. Luftwaffe losses were minimal and significantly lower than during air attacks on other targets (railway stations, naval bases, bridges, crossings). The air defences of Moscow were of low effectiveness.

To the present day, false information is given in Russia about how 'thousands of German aircraft' raided Moscow. Historians write about the 'effective work of anti-aircraft artillery and pilots', which 'did not allow' most of the 'vultures' into the sky above the capital. Official figures report that 5,000 He 111s and Ju 88s 'tried to break through to Moscow' and only a few dozen of them reached the target. Historians who refute these false figures are declared 'unpatriotic' and 'russophobes'. Stalin's propaganda lives on in Russia.

Chapter 7

Flying Through the White Haze

The Last Do 17 Z Lost and the First Attack by Russian Hurricanes

When the Russians began their offensive, the air forces was ordered to throw all forces into battle to support their troops. On 6 December 1941 twelve of the twenty-five regiments of the 6th IAK PVO took part in attacks on ground targets. The fighters fired almost 500 rockets and dropped 142 bombs. In air battles four aircraft were claimed to have been shot down, but German data confirms only one victory. In the Juratino area Hs 126 B-1 W. Nr. 4047 of 2.(H)/41 was shot down. The navigator Leutnant A. Emet was killed but the pilot escaped and managed to cross the front line. On this day the Luftwaffe made attacks on the Moscow orbital railway. Trains were hit and the tracks damaged in several places.

On 7 December, in heavy frost, the 6th IAK PVO carried out 446 sorties, of which one third were ground attacks. They were carried out on the northern flank of the front and in the south in the Mordves area. The fighters dropped 130 bombs and fired 551 rockets. The pilots claimed five victories, but these are not confirmed by German information.

It was warmer on 8 December and the weather was cloudy. Air operations were limited. The main action of the Luftwaffe was an air raid on railway facilities in the Michurinsk region to slow down the delivery of Russian troops to the Moscow front. During the raid, He 111 H-3 W. Nr. 5632 of 3./KG 53 'Legion Condor' was shot down. The crew was able to make it 150km (93 miles) through the snow to get back to their squadron! On this day after heavy fighting the Russian partly recaptured Yakhroma and Krasnaya Polyana. The immediate threat to Moscow was lifted.

Between 9–12 December the weather remained bad for aviation. The Russians almost did not fly but the Luftwaffe continued to operate at full capacity and suffered serious losses. The bombers were flying at very

Soviet cavalrymen in the village of Kryukovo. A German tank is visible, which stopped 25 kilometres from Moscow. December 1941

Destroyed German equipment in the vicinity of Moscow

low level and were vulnerable even to infantry weapons. On 9 December Ju 88 A-4 W. Nr. 1368 of St./KG 3 'Blitz' was lost in the Moscow area, and He 111 H-5 W. Nr. 3815 '1T+CL' of 3./KG 28 was reported missing in the Stalinogorsk area the next day. On the same day in the Klin district anti-aircraft fire brought down Hs 123 B-1 W. Nr. 2254 of 10.(Sch)/LG 2 and Do 17 Z-3 W. Nr. 2633 of 9./KG 3. This was the last combat loss of the Do 17 Z as a bomber by the Luftwaffe. Soon afterwards III./KG 3 'Blitz' returned to Germany. The outdated Do 17 then only served as a bomber in the air forces of the Third Reich's allies, the Luftwaffe only using it as a reconnaissance aircraft. On 11 December Bf 110 E-1 W. Nr. 3984 of 4./ZG 26 'Horst Wessel' crashed due to icing in the Skniatino area.

On 13 December there was another cold snap, which allowed aviation operations to intensify. The 6th IAK PVO carried out 195 sorties, forty-four Yak-1, MiG-3 and Pe-3 fighters of the 11th, 28th, 208th and 562nd IAPs supporting the advancing troops with strafing and bomb attacks. A pair of MiG-3s (Lieutenant Konstantin Fedotov and Sergeant Vishnyakov) of the 28th IAP got lost and made an emergency landing near Zvenigorod. Such cases were common in bad weather. Low-level flying hampered orientation in the featureless snow-covered landscape. The Luftwaffe suffered considerable losses. South-west of Kashira Bf 109 F-2 W. Nr. 12932 of 6./JG 51 was lost. In other areas He 111 H-6 W. Nr. 4346 of III./KG 26 and He 111 H-6 W. Nr. 4573 '1T+LL' of 3./KG 28 disappeared. Details about their fate have not been found, but it is known that all the crews of these bombers were killed.

On 14 December, the 6th IAK PVO carried out 531 sorties and engaged in 11 air battles. A group of Yak-1s of the 11th IAP attacked German troops near Novo-Petrovskoye and Teryaeva Sloboda. Lieutenant Venedikt Kovalev's fighter was damaged by ground fire. According to the testimony of his comrades, the pilot did not bail out but deliberately crashed his burning aircraft into the anti-aircraft battery. Pilots who sacrificed themselves like Japanese kamikazes were declared national heroes, examples of fanaticism and self-sacrifice.

In addition to Kovalev's Yak-1 the Soviets lost four fighters (three Yak-1s and one LaGG-3). On this day for the first time in the Moscow area Russians used Hurricanes and Tomahawks of the 28th and 126th IAP. Before the counter-attack, foreign-built aircraft were kept in reserve. But the success of Russian aviation was modest. On this day, the Luftwaffe lost only Ju 88 A-4 W. Nr. 2605 of 4./KG 3 'Blitz'. The crew was listed as missing.

Above: Pilots from 129th IAP near the fighter LaGG-3. Kalinin front, December

Left: Charging 12.7mm machine gun BS on LaGG-3 fighter

On 15 December, air defence pilots carried out 100 sorties to attack ground targets and 344 to patrol. The pilots reported about sixteen air battles and five victories. The most distinguished was Sergeant Ivan Golubin of the 16th IAP. First, in the area of Vorontsovo, he shot down two 'Me 109s', then during another flight in the same area a Ju 87. The top ace of his regiment, he had ten solo and two shared victories. But these three victories are not confirmed. In the last battle Golubin was shot down by a group of Bf 109s (the victory was credited to the commander of III./JG 51, Hauptmann R. Leppla). The P-40B of Lieutenant Stepan Ridny of the 126th IAP shot down an He 111 in the Mytischi district. On this day the Germans lost two such aircraft: He 111 H-6 W. Nr. 4412 '1T+NK' and He 111 H-6 W. Nr. 4575 '1T+MK', both of 2./KG 28. One crew was missing, the second was all killed. The losses of the 6th IAK PVO amounted to four aircraft. In addition to Golubin, Captain Durnikin of the 34th IAP, Sergeant Kondratyev of the 564th IAP and Lieutenants Smirnov and Pighin, the crew of a Pe-3 of the 208th IAP, also failed to return to base.

Christmas Slaughter of the Luftwaffe

On 16 December German troops evacuated Kalinin. Two months of heavy fighting had reduced this city to rubble. In the near future, the German troops would gain useful experience of long battles in isolation. Units of the Ninth Army retreated in the direction of Rzhev. Soon this city on the right bank of the Volga would become a 'fortress', of which all Germany will hear . . .

On this day, because of snow, Russian aircraft did not operate, but the Luftwaffe provided support to their troops, waging brutal battles. A sense of duty to their comrades forced the pilots to risk it. They flew at a low level, breaking through the snow and firing at the Russian troops. For many, these risky missions were deadly. In Tula ground fire hit another 'torpedo-plane', He 111 H-6 W. Nr. 4408 '1T+FL' of 3./KG 28, and near Rusa Bf 109 F-2 W. Nr. 12626 of 2./JG 52 (the pilot was killed). In the Krasnaya Zarya area Bf 110 E-2 W.Nr. 4418 'S9+VM' of 4./SKG 210 was shot down, as was Bf 110 E-6 W. Nr. 2152 'S9+MN' of 5./SKG 210 in the Verkhov'e area.

From 17 to 23 December it was cloudy and snowing in the Moscow area. Russian fighters limited themselves to short flights lasting 40–50 minutes at low level. But these conditions did not stop the Luftwaffe, and in those days VIII *Fliegerkorps* suffered its heaviest losses since the beginning of the campaign.

On the 17th He 111 P-2 W. Nr. 2623 of St.I/KG 28 crashed, killing the group commander, Oberstleutnant Heckmann. The next day He 111 H-6 W. Nr. 4557 of I./KG 28 was shot down and He 111 H-6 of III./KG 26 was damaged by ground fire, but was able to return to base with one dead and one wounded crew man aboard. Near Dubrovo-Ruza a Russian tank (!) shot down Ju 87 R-4 W. Nr. 6264 'T6+ER' of 7./StG 2 'Immelmann'.

On 19 December near Bogoroditsk He 111 H-6 W. Nr. 4499 of 5./KG 53 'Legion Condor' went missing. Over Gorbachev station the Russian air defences simultaneously shot down two He 111 H-6s (W. Nr. 4299 and W. Nr. 4608) of II./KG 53. In the Dyat'kovo area another He 111 H-6 W. Nr. 4503, again of II./KG 53, was also hit. In one day the unit lost four bombers.

There was a tragic incident on 20 December. While transferring from Gorstkova airfield to Dugino seven Ju 87s of different types (B-1, B-2, R-2 and R-4) from III./StG 2 'Immelman' crashed in a snowstorm! Six men were killed and two seriously injured.

On 21 December, three German planes went missing at once: in the Tula district Ju 88 A-4 W. Nr. 1360 '5K+AC' of St.II/KG 3 'Blitz' (along with the crew, the group commander Hauptmann Kurt Peters was lost), in the Zavidovo area a reconnaissance Do 17 P W. Nr. 3591 of 2.(F)/11, and in the Novo-Petrovsky region Ju 88 A-5 W. Nr. 6407 of 9./KG 76. Over Mashkino (in the Kolomna district) Bf 109 F-2 W. Nr. 8304 of 9./JG 51 was shot down.

On 22 December He 111 H-6 W. Nr. 4694 of II./KG 4 'General Wever' was reported missing in the Tula-Aleksin district, and Ju 88 A-4 W. Nr. 3640 of 5./KG 3 'Blitz' in the Krapivna-Odoev district. Over Shaykovka Bf 109 F-2 W. Nr. 12894 of 5./JG 51 was shot down. The pilot was killed.

On 23 December, the Luftwaffe suffered its most catastrophic losses. In the Kozelsk district Bf 110 E-2 W. Nr. 4001 'S9+DP' of 6./SKG 210 disappeared, as did two He 111 H-6s (W. Nr. 4599 '5J+MN' and W. Nr. 4640 '5J+GN') of 5./KG 4 'General Wever' in the Tula–Odoev-Aleksin district. Ju 88 A-4 W. Nr. 1466 of St.II/KG 3 'Blitz' was lost without trace in the Kaluga-Odoev area. The fate of all the crews of these aircraft remains a mystery. Over Timoshevo He 111 H-6 W. Nr. 4605 of II./KG 53 'Legion Condor' was shot down by ground fire.

The deployment of the Luftwaffe's first squadron of land-based torpedo bombers, I./KG 28, which had spent five months serving as a specialized bomber group and then as the usual 'flying artillery' in the snow-covered Moscow region, came to an end. In early August, it had arrived on the Eastern Front with fourteen combat-ready torpedo-bombers. Before Christmas in the Moscow area 2./KG 28 and 3./KG 28 lost twenty-two aircraft, ten experienced crews and their commander. The rest of the group combined with III./KG 26 (also badly battered), which had also had a maritime role before Operation 'Barbarossa'. The group remained in Seschinskaya until mid-January, then left for Germany.

Model sends Richthofen 'To The Devil'

There were several reasons for the Luftwaffe's heavy losses. The weather conditions were severe and often changed during the day. Previously, German pilots did not have to operate in harsh climates, and pilots and mechanics had no experience of flying and maintaining equipment in severe frost, icing and snowfall. There was also a negative 'human factor'. Since November, all power over the Luftwaffe near Moscow was in the hands of Generaloberst von Richthofen. This cruel commander sought to obey Hitler's order to 'hold at all costs' literally. The bloodthirsty Richthofen never considered the opinions of his subordinates, considered the 'maximum concentration of effort' the means of success and tried to squeeze every last effort out of his units. Reconnaissance aircraft, courier and transport planes (even Fi 156s!) were ordered to take bombs on board and attack the enemy while simultaneously carrying out their main tasks. The bombers were used for low-level attacks on the advancing Russian troops, were constantly under ground fire and suffered heavy losses.

Richthofen mercilessly criticised (while informing on them to Hitler) the commanders of the ground forces, calling them 'fools', 'cowards' and 'defeatists'. At the end of December, the situation in VI Army Corps' sector north of Rzhev was critical. Richthofen declared directly to Hitler that the 'idiot General Ferster' (the corps commander) was to blame. The Chief of the General Staff, Generaloberst Halder, tired of Richthofen's constant complaints and tantrums, proposed that the *Führer* appoint him 'part-time' commander of VI Corps. If you want to try it, go ahead! Soon there was an unprecedented event. Richthofen landed in his Storch near VI Corp's headquarters and to the amazement of the staff announced that he was now in command of the corps and was taking matters into his own hands.

When 'the chief specialist of the *Führer*', as he called himself, studied the situation ('on the ground' it did not looked as easy as from the cockpit of a Fi 156!), he saw that the front had completely collapsed, and the soldiers of the Soviet 39th Army had reached the outskirts of Rzhev. Soon General Walter Model, whose character was similar to Richthofen, was appointed commander of the Ninth Army. Model quickly and rudely ('. . . and go to the devil, Herr General of Aviation! Command your planes!') dismissed the hyperactive meddler from interfering in the affairs of ground troops.

On 24 December the weather was a bit better (in the afternoon 6–10 points of cloud at 100–300m [328–984ft]), and Russian aircraft returned to the sky. The 6th IAK PVO carried out 542 sorties, mostly covering their troops in the Ruza, Dmitrov, Kaluga, Serpukhov, Tarusa and Maloyaroslavets areas. Russian pilots claimed seven victories. German data confirms only one of them: Ju 88 A-4 W. Nr. 1364 of 6./KG 30 'Adler'. The crew was reported missing. At Christmas this *Staffel* had been transferred to the Moscow area from northern Norway. During this period in that region it was the polar night, which made it impossible to fly. KG 30's pilots had extensive experience of flying in harsh, cold conditions, so acclimatization was not required. The 'Polar explorers' were transferred to the snow-covered airfield at Orsha. Probably, the aircraft was shot down by the LaGG-3 of Lieutenant Gerasim Grigoriev of the 178th IAP.

The Russians lost six fighters: two MiG-3s (Politruk Chepurenko and Lieutenant Rodionov) of the 428th IAP, one I-16 (Lieutenant Davydenko) of the 233rd IAP, one Yak-1 (Lieutenant Puzanov) of the 163rd IAP, one Pe-3 (pilot Lieutenant Kirikov and navigator Captain Smirnov) of the 95th IAP and one LaGG-3 (Lieutenant Rassadkin) of the 438th IAP. It turned

Refuelling the fighter with compressed air

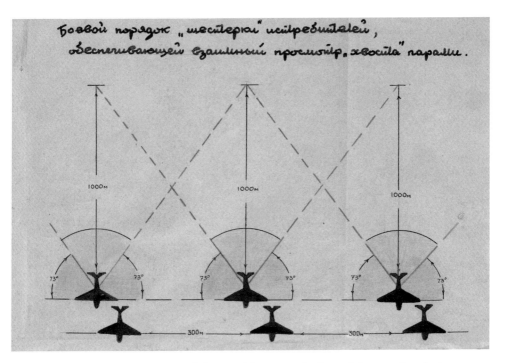

Scheme of flight of Russian fighters with a mutual view of the rear hemisphere. Such tactics helped pilots to avoid sudden attacks of German fighters

out later that Rassadkin had crash-landed due to engine failure, suffered multiple injuries and had been taken to hospital, while due to poor visibility Chepurenko, Kirikov and Smirnov made emergency landings in the area of Podolsk. Davydenko ran out of fuel during the flight, after which the pilot made an emergency landing. Rodionov similarly landed near Lake Senezh, then reached 'home' after a long walk through the snow.

On Christmas Day, the Germans retreated along the whole front, but especially quickly on the southern flank. The commander of the Second Panzer Army Generaloberst Heinz Guderian refused to comply with Hitler's categorical order 'to hold at any cost' and 'not retreat'. He rapidly withdrew all his troops 100–120km, abandoning all the heavy weapons and a significant part of their other equipment. It allowed to keep army efficient, to avoid 'cauldrons' and to hold the extended front. The *Führer* had tolerated such 'tricks' for a long time, but on 25 December ordered Guderian to resign. On the northern flank, on 20 December the Russians had occupied Volokolamsk.

Between 25 and 27 December there were snowstorms in the Moscow area which severely restricted air operations. On the 28th, however, it was clear and frosty, and the 6th IAK PVO carried out 424 sorties, of which 126 were ground attacks. Fighters attacked German troops to the south-west of Moscow in the Maloyaroslavets and Borovsk areas, and on the Belousov–Vologda–Medyn highway, dropping 168 high-explosive bombs and launching 272 rockets on a variety of targets. Besides tanks, motor vehicles and horse-drawn wagons, the pilots also reported the destruction of two bridges to the south-west of Maloyaroslavets. In the air four victories were recorded. Lieutenant Rubtsov of the 120th IAP claimed one 'Me 109' shot down, and Lieutenant Ivan Lozowoy of the 126th IAP a Ju 88. Seven Hurricanes of the recently-arrived 736th IAP shot down two Ju 87s in the Ostashkovo-Volokolamsk district (each pilots was credited with two-sevenths of a victory). During the battle the first Hurricane, flown by Lieutenant Ratnikov, was lost. According to German information, on this day only Hs 123 B-1 W. Nr. 2328 of 10.(Sch)/LG 2 was downed in the Moscow area.

December 29th was the last day of 1941 when aviation region was active in the Moscow. The war diary of the 6th IAK PVO recorded:

Weather Conditions: 10 points of cloud, altitude of 400–3000m visibility of 1 to 6km. Temperature -17°C.

The pilots of the corps covered the city of Moscow, those of the Western Front the areas of: Spas-Ostashewo, Nedelnoe, Prudki, Kaluga, Ryazan, Shakhovskaya station, Dyatlovo-Sereda.

28th, 177th, 16th, 208th and 95th IAP attacked enemy ground troops in the areas: Yakshino-Ostashewo, Dubosekovo-Kalinino–Shakhovskaya, Dyatlowo–Sereda.

Total corps elements carried out 421 sorties with a total flight time of 328 hours. 56 min., 111 of them to attack enemy ground forces.

Expended: 221 rocket, 74 FAB-100, 50 FAB-50, 25 AO-25, 8,160 cannon shells, 13,670 cartridges.

In the result of attack delayed the movement of convoys, between Repino and Chernevo, suspended loading and unloading at the Shakhovskaya station. 164 trucks with cargo and infantry, 2 fuel trucks, 17 vans, 23 horse-drawn carts, 3 antiaircraft guns destroyed and damaged, 2 batteries of anti-aircraft artillery were suppressed, up to 4–5 battalions of infantry are scattered. Enemy troop concentrations in the villages of Dubosekovo, Klishina, Chernovo and Vnukovo were dispersed.

On the last two days of the year, the Russian aviation regiments did not operate due to dense fog. But the Luftwaffe (wanting to 'congratulate' the residents of Moscow at New Year) on the personal orders of Richthofen carried out two air raid on major cities. At 23.00 on 30 December, a single Ju 88 A-4 of 6./KG 30 'Adler' dropped three high-explosive bombs on Moscow. Two houses in Bruhlov Street were destroyed and seven residents injured. On New Year's Eve, the Ju 88 A flown by Oberleutnant Kopack of the same squadron carried out a long-range raid on the city of Gorky, dropping bombs on an unspecified 'plant'. No details of this raid could be found in Soviet records. The Germans were still taking losses: on 30 December Bf 110 D-3 W. Nr. 4369 '3U+DM' of 4./ZG 26 'Horst Wessel' was shot down in the Velykoselye-Kumanovo area, and on 31 December He 111 H-6 W. Nr. 4502 of 5./KG 53 'Legion Condor' and Ju 88 A-4 W. Nr. 8601 of 4./KG 76 were reported missing in the Kalinin district.

Statistics for December

In December 1941 the 6th IAK PVO carried out 6,324 sorties: 2,810 to cover Soviet troops, 1,605 ground attacks and 64 patrols. The pilots reported 132 air battles and shooting down 82 aircraft.

These successes were again exaggerated. But VIII *Fliegerkorps* really did suffer heavy damage. The loss of fifty-eight aircraft to ground fire, Soviet fighters and the weather can be established. The greatest losses were in twin-engine bombers (nineteen He 111s and nine Ju 88s). The Luftwaffe also lost ten Ju 87s, six Bf 109s, five Do 17s, five Bf 110s, two Hs 126s and two Hs 123s. But only part of them can be confidently ascribed to Russian fighters. In many cases, the exact causes of the aircraft's loss cannot be established.

A Russian report about the actions of the 6th IAK PVO in June–December 1941 reads as follows:

> In October, when the front line approached the city of Moscow, the enemy aircraft had greater opportunities, but the largest number of aircraft operating during the day did not exceed 60–70. In December in district Moscow for a day appeared 30– 20–5 enemy aircraft.
>
> In the second half of October, the Germans put into action Ju 87 bombers, and a little later Ju 86. This was an indication of the lack of the main types of combat aircraft . . . For these

reasons and due to the large losses suffered by the enemy from Russian anti-aircraft artillery and fighters, by the end of the year, the number of air raids and the number of aircraft participating in them had decreased dramatically . . ..

During the 6 months of the war, it was established that bombers and reconnaissance aircraft did not engage in combat with our fighters. The enemy fighters engaged in battle only when they had numerical superiority. It is established that the German pilots did not make frontal attacks, except for the Me 110, which had a strong frontal armament. When they encountered fighters, bombers randomly dropped their bombs and headed west at high speed. The effectiveness of the German bomber force is low, especially for small targets.

Already in 1941, Russian pilots considered the Ju 87 'obsolete! But this did not prevent the Luftwaffe using them successfully on the Eastern Front until 1944.

The fighter air defence of Moscow reported 1,575 air battles and 646 planes brought down (18 of them by intentional ramming) between June and December 1941. These figures were exaggerated by a factor of 7 to 8. The 6th IAK PVO's losses amounted to 289 fighters and 147 pilots killed. Several dozen aircraft and pilots were lost for technical reasons.

Combat Losses of the 6th IAK PVO, 22 June–31 December 1941

Cause of Loss	Aircraft	Pilots
Shot down in air battles	125	66
Shot down by anti-aircraft artillery	30	21
Missing	134	60
Total	289	147

Operations in Early January 1942

In early 1942, the 6th IAK PVO was still the most powerful group in Stalin's air force. It consisted of 29 regiments and almost 500 fighters (191 MiG-3s, 95 I-16s, 73 LaGG-3s, 55 Yak-1s, 27 Pe-3s, 20 P-40s and 19 Hurricanes). Most of the regiments were based to the east and south-east of Moscow. The furthest from Moscow was the 309th IAP at Gridino, 60km (37 miles) east of the city.

FLYING THROUGH THE WHITE HAZE

As the Wehrmacht retreated, the Russians returned to the airbases they had lost. On 3 January the 27th IAP moved from Zagorsk to the airfield at Klin (from 30 November to 14 December 1941 it had been occupied by II./JG 52). 'When examining the airfield at Klin, which was liberated by our troops from the Germans, it is clear that the refuelling was carried out manually, synthetic gasoline at low temperature turned into an oily liquid with the presence of grains (partial crystallization),' reported the survey of the base.

On the night of 1/2 January Luftwaffe had carried out an air raid on Moscow with a couple of aircraft. They dropped two high-explosive bombs, and three canisters of flammable liquid. Military Warehouse No. 312 was completely destroyed. The attack was a surprise, and there was no air-raid warning sounded in the city.

On 2 January, at 20.08 Moscow time, a group of bombers carried out another attack on Moscow, dropping twenty high-explosive bombs on the Frunzensky and Zelesnodorozny districts of the city. Several houses were destroyed, fourteen people were killed and fifty-nine wounded. No Russian fighters took off.

During this period in the Moscow area the weather was very cold: - 31°C, with fog and haze.

On the night of 2/3 January the Luftwaffe again attacked Moscow, dropping eleven high-explosive bombs on the Sovietsky district. Three houses were destroyed, two people were killed and ten were wounded. Again, no warning was sounded. The bombers approached the target at high altitude with muted engines in continuous clouds. So they weren't seen. The Russian radar stations also failed to pick them up.

But the main blow that night was dealt to the cracking-electrolyte plant in Podolsk, which was the largest enterprise of this type in the country. According to the Russian rescue service, 105 high-explosive and incendiary bombs were dropped at the plant, which led to widespread destruction and a major fire in the warehouse full of finished batteries. The plant was put out of action for a long time.

On 3 January, Russian aviation became more active. During a patrol departure to the south of Yukhnov a MiG-3 flown by Lieutenant Fyodor Mitrofanov of 445th IAP encountered an He 111 at an altitude of 800m (2,625ft) out of the haze. Mitrofanov attacked the bomber at close range. The He 111 dropped to a height of 200m (650ft) and tried to escape at low level. The Russian pilot claimed that he overtook it and shot it down near the village of Domanovo. This was Mitrofanov's fourth personal victory, making him one of the best aces of the 445th IAP. The victory has a high degree of probability. In that area He 111 H-6 W. Nr. 4501 of 4./KG 53 'Legion Condor' was damaged and crashed while attempting an emergency landing.

On this day, the 178th IAP was engaged in aerial reconnaissance behind enemy lines. The Soviet air force lacked special reconnaissance aircraft and squadrons dedicated to this role. Therefore, conventional bombers and fighters were often employed.These aircraft did not have cameras, the pilots making reports on their return to base. Often several fighters were sent to the same area, the reports of multiple pilots allowing a relatively accurate picture of the situation to be formed. In 1941–2 most of the flights the famous ace Alexandr Pokryshkin made in his MiG-3 were for reconnaissance. That day the commander of the 178th IAP Lieutenant Colonel R.I. Rakov never return from a reconnaissance mission. In the Maloyaroslavets area his I-16 ran into three Bf 109s, which shot him down near the Ugodsky plant.

I-16s and MiG-3s of the 28th, 176th and 233rd IAPs carried out weather reconnaissance in the Dmitrov–Kimry–Volokolamsk area. In the Moscow area it was very frosty, but visibility was low. Everywhere there was fog and haze, limiting visibility to 200–2,000m (200–2,000 yards). Flights took place at low level, in many cases at treetop height.

On 4 January, large numbers of German aircraft were seen in the air for the first time in the New Year. The I-16 element of Lieutenants Finogenov, Mikhailov and Chernavsky, while attacking German infantry in the Rylovo–Yuryevskoye area, ran into a Ju 88 accompanied by a pair of Bf 109s at an altitude of 1,600m (5,250ft). The Germans climbed rapidly. The Russian pilots attacked the bomber three times and considered it to have been shot down. Similarly, the MiG-3 element of Lieutenants Fyodor Mitrofanov and Vasily Rozhkov and Schapovalov of the 445th IAP encountered a pair of bombers at 1,000m (3,280ft) during a patrol in the Kaluga district. Seeing the Russians, the pilots turned in the direction of Vyazma, dropping to low level. According to the MiG-3 pilots, they managed to catch up with and shoot down both enemy aircraft. The commander Mitrofanov claimed an He 111 and Rozhkov a Ju 88. Shapovalov's MiG-3 was reported missing. In the Maloyaroslavets area Lieutenant K.A. Kryukov of the 428th IAP claimed to have shot down Do 215. But none of these victories are confirmed by German sources. That day the Luftwaffe lost only the Croatian Do 17 Z-2 W. Nr. 2700 of 10.(Croat)/KG 3, which after an attack by a Soviet fighter made an emergency landing near Staritsa. But it was the victim of the fighters of the Kalinin Front air force.

FLYING THROUGH THE WHITE HAZE

Pe-3 heavy fighters of the 95th and 208th IAPs made two consecutive raids on the airfield at Yukhnov. The pilots reported five 'Me 110s' destroyed on the ground. In repulsing one of the air attacks, the commander of III./ JG 51 Hauptmann R. Leppla attempted to take off, but because of the rush crashed into Ju 52 standing on the runway and wrecked his Bf 109 F-2 W. Nr. 8185. The pilot was injured. This was all the damage caused by the Russian raids.

Russian losses were again greater than those of the Germans –five fighters. Two were shot down by ground fire and three failed to return from missions. Among them were Lieutenants Ivan Zabolotny and Ivan Shumilov of the 16th IAP. Shumilov returned to his regiment the next night, but Zabolotny was lost. At that time, the Soviet ace has completed 110 combat missions and had ten personal victories. On 27 June 1942 he was posthumously awarded the title of Hero of the Soviet Union.

'The limited actions of enemy aircraft were due to low temperatures (- 20, - 35°C) and the inability to operate equipment in winter conditions,' was how the headquarters of the 6th IAK PVO explained the lack of Luftwaffe activity. But Russian aviation also suffered great difficulties because of the cold. To ensure each take-off, the ground crews at the airfields had to run the engines two or three times a night and prepare the machines long before dawn. In the bitter cold, the mechanics used a blowtorch which took a long time to warm up the oil radiators. Aircraft with air-cooled engines were better suited for such conditions. 'The great advantage of the Su-2 aircraft was the air-cooled engine chosen for it by the designer,' recalled Grigory Shalupkin, a mechanic of the 135th Bomber Regiment.

> This made it possible in the harsh winter of 1941/42 to fly in the most severe frosts, which sometimes reached minus 30° Celsius. We got up early, in severe cold, and were on duty directly at the planes, warming up motors with special heating lamps, and started them for warming up. You see, our planes are already returning from the job, and the Germans still have not been seen or heard.

Heavy snow made it difficult for the pilot to land, and to navigate even over-familiar terrain. 'The winter was extremely cold and persistent this year,' recalled Anatoly Samochkin, a pilot of an Su-2 bomber. 'In flight overalls, boots, plus a lot of warm clothes. However, all this wasn't enough in strong,

strong frosts. We set up dugouts at the airfield with stoves, and we warmed up in them waiting for missions.

In severe frosts the sky was constantly covered with haze. Because of the windless weather, the smoke of the many fires did not dissipate in the atmosphere, forming a thick veil, which greatly limited visibility. In such circumstances, a lot of time and effort was spent on searching for the target area, locating ground targets, the return flight, searching for the airfield and landing in poor visibility. Encountering the enemy in the air was a matter of chance only.

On 6 January, because of a sharp deterioration in the weather, Russian aviation was not active. But on the contrary the Luftwaffe was. At 11.25 a single German aircraft was spotted in the Moscow area, which (in a rare case) was shot down by a direct hit from anti-aircraft artillery. The Moscow residents watched as the Ju 88 fell engulfed in smoke on Tushino airfield. According to German records, it was a reconnaissance Ju 88 D-1 W. Nr. 1133 '5F+BM' of 4.(F)/14. The crew was reported missing. Two He 111 H-5s (W. Nr. 3341 and W. Nr. 4887) of St./KG 53 'Legion Condor' and an He 111 H-4 W. Nr. 3224 of III./KG 26 were attacked by fighters over the front line, were hit and made emergency landings in German-held territory. According to Soviet records Lieutenant Evgeniy Gorbatyuk of the 28th IAP shot down

Christmas in Moscow

Automatic 37mm cannons '61-K' on the position

an He 111 in the Mytyajevo district, and near Maloyaroslavets another was brought down by Lieutenant N.M. Sorkin of the same regiment. On 7–10 January, the weather deteriorated further and it began to snow. In three days there was only one air battle.

After the Soviet troops' major successes in December 1941, the Germans were pushed back 145–193km (90–120 miles) from the furthest limit of their advance on 5 December. Stalin and his retinue hoped to repeat the scenario of 1812. Then, the 'Grand Armée' of Napoleon quickly captured Moscow, but then also soon ran to the west on snow-covered roads. In June 1812 the French entered Russian territory, and by early 1813 the survivors were back in Poland. 'The Ghost of Napoleon' evoked fear in German officers and men. They were afraid to freeze and die in Russia, repeating the fate of thousands of Frenchmen (in the campaign of Napoleon Germans also participated). Stalin's propaganda urged the population to believe in this scenario. But the Wehrmacht suddenly turned out to be stronger than the 'Grand Armée'!

In the first week of January, the Russian offensive slowed down and even stalled in some sectors. The German high command recovered from the shock, and famous commanders, who had called for a retreat to (Guderian, Hoepner, von Bock, and others) were replaced by Hitler with more 'stable'ones (ready to fight to the death), who fanatically obeyed the 'halt order'. As a result of the reduction in the length of the front, it was possible to consolidate combat formations and secure several strongholds. The Soviet command still had no experience of large-scale offensive operations (for half a year Russians had been only fighting in defence or making tactical 'pin pricks'). Zhukov, who led the offensive, made several mistakes. He stubbornly tried to break through the German defence in the same places. The Russians had insufficient intelligence information, and aircraft were unable to obtain it. Cruel and bloody battles were waged on all fronts, but Germans didn't want to give way.

The air war in the Moscow region intensified on 13 January. The pilots of the 28th IAP alone conducted five fights with fighters and reconnaissance aircraft. But in all cases the Germans immediately flew into the sun, the Russian pilots were blinded and they lost sight of the enemy. At 12.40 in the Afanasievo area, the MiG-3 element of Lieutenant Finogenov of the 177th IAP met three 'Me 109s', which after the first attack dropped to low level and headed west. They were Bf 109 E ground-attack aircraft of I./Sch.G 1, which flew in threes, not pairs. A direct ground-support unit, Sch.G1 had been formed on that day, from the former II./(Sch)/LG 2. After these battles, the headquarters of the 6th IAK PVO correctly concluded that German pilots on reconnaissance missions were to avoid contact with enemy aircraft and head for their own lines at the first sign of danger. This allowed them to carry out limited operations while preserving the small number of aircraft still remaining to them. By January 1942, the Germans no longer cared about air victories!

On 15 January a Yak-1 element of the 27th IAP attacked a single Ju 88 in the Volokolamsk district, which after the first attack jettisoned its bombs and disappeared in the clouds. In the same area a couple of MiG-3s (Lieutenants Ivanov and Alexander Chilikin) at an altitude of 400m (1,312ft) encountered a Ju 88 dropping bombs on Soviet troops. At the time of the attack, the engine of Ivanov's fighter failed. Chilikin alone shot down the bomber, which fell in the area of Volokolamsk. But the loss of a Ju 88 by the Germans on this day is not confirmed. In the Moscow area only He 111 H-5 W. Nr. 3751 'A1+HT' of 9./KG 53 'Legion Condor' was lost, and this was credited to a pair of P-40Bs (Lieutenants Stepan Ridnyi and Peter Belasnik) of the 126th IAP.

On 16 January, air defence fighters conducted ten air battles and reported four aircraft shot down. During a patrol in the Medovniki area the MiG-3

Russian soldiers examine He 111 littered with snow

Burnt fighter LaGG-3 from the 33rd IAP

element of Lieutenant Evgeniy Gorbatyuk of the 28th IAP met a single He 111 on a collision course, at an altitude of 100m (328ft). The bomber immediately went into the clouds. The Russian fighters split up: two went into the clouds, while one remained under them. When the crew of the bomber above the clouds saw the pursuers, the pilot dived through the clouds and again went to low level flight. But there he was suddenly attacked and shot down by the third MiG-3. At 13.35 in the Borovsk district a pair of MiG-3s (Lieutenant Kryukov and Sergeant Kryukov) of the 428th IAP shot down a Ju 88. Another group victory was won by the pilots of MiG-3s of the 28th IAP (Lieutenants Sorokin and Fedorov), and Sergeant Yefim Goldberg of the 562nd IAP. They were credited with an He 111 shot down in the Volokolamsk area. A pair of P-40B Lieutenants Stepan Ridnyi and Peter Belasnik of the 126th IAP in the area of Nazar'yevo shot down another bomber. All these air battles took place at extremely low level in conditions of thick haze and fog with limited visibility.

According to German information four aircraft were lost on this day:

- Ju 88 D-1 W. Nr. 1485 '8H+GL' of 4.(F)/11 went missing in the Naro-Fominsk–Kaluga region;
- Ju 88 A-4 W. Nr. 2562 '5K+KP' and Ju 88 A-4 W. Nr. 3564 '5K+CH' of 5./KG 3 and 6./KG 3 went missing in the Zubovo–Kaluga area;
- The damaged Ju 88 A-4 W. Nr. 1174 of 5./KG 30 was destroyed during an emergency landing near Tarasovo.

This was a bad day for the Ju 88 on the Eastern Front. In the Valdai hills in the Ostashkov district the reconnaissance Ju 88 E-1 W. Nr. 1263 '5F+EM' of 4.(F)/14 went missing. The Ju 88 E was a very rare type in this region. For the 6th IAK PVO it was quite a successful day. Their losses amounted to only one MiG-3 of the 28th IAP. It was brought down by the Bf 110 *Zerstorer* of Feldwebel Tamm of II./ZG 1. He was counted a victory over the 'I-18'.

On 17 January, the air defence pilots carried out 444 sorties, of which 196 were for covering troops and 248 to cover rail transport. Four meetings with enemy aircraft and two effective fights were recorded. Lieutenant Alexander Chilikin of the 27th IAP shot down a Ju 88. Probably it was Ju 88 E-1 W. Nr. 1239 '6M+AM' of 4.(F)/14, reported missing in the Kaluga–Mozhaisk area. Lieutenant Minaev of the 736th IAP (in a Hurricane) shot down an 'Me 110' in the Istra district. This may have been Bf 110 E-1 W. Nr. 3822 of 6./ZG 1, which was lost for an unknown reason in the 'Polyudov' area. The crew survived.

Russian Units Behind German Lines

On 18 January the 6th IAK PVO carried out 571 sorties, engaged in 10 dogfights and reported three planes. Near Rzhev the 126th IAP shot down two 'Me 109s', one of which was attacked and shot down by Lieutenant

Matyushin during take-off from Rzhev airfield. German data confirms the loss of one Bf 109 F-2, W. Nr. 9182 of 1./JG 52. The pilot, Oberfeldwebel Robert Potz, who had ten victories, was killed. Lieutenant Maksimov of the 428th IAP in a MiG-3 attacked and shot down an Hs 126 50km (31 miles) north-west of Medyn. But this is not confirmed.

On 19 January, the air defence fighters carried out 388 sorties and fought 7 air battles. The pilots of the Kaluga group intercepted an He 111 (the damaged He 111 H-6 W. Nr. 4696 of II./KG 4 'General Wever' reached German territory but was destroyed during a crash landing), losing one fighter (at 11.30 the Oberleutnant R. Josten of 3./JG 51 recorded downing an 'I-61'). Sergeants Nikolenko and Borodin of the 428th IAP reported downing a Do 215 in the Iznoski district. In fact, it was the Croatian Do 17 Z-3 W. Nr. 2529 '5K+BT' of 10.(Croat)/KG 3, which according to German data went missing with its crew in the Voznesenskoye area. Lieutenant Semyon Levin of the 126th IAP was credited with a victory over an 'Me 109' (not confirmed).

A consolidated air group was formed by the Russians at the Kaluga-Grabtsevo airfield. Its mission was to support the attack on the city of Yukhnov and airborne operations in the Vyazma area. The vast expanse of Russia meant that the Germans could not occupy all the territory they nominally controlled. Many areas weren't occupied at all, guerrillas and local 'self-government' being in control. In many settlements, the German authorities were represented only by 'elders' selected from the local population. This created a favourable environment for landing Russian troops.

At dawn on 18 January, sixteen PS-84 transport aircraft took off from Vnukovo. They dropped the first 462 paratroopers of the 5th Airborne Corps in the area south-west of Vyazma. In the evening four aircraft with a 65-strong group of specialists landed there. They prepared an airfield near Znamenka, which was occupied by the partisans. Three PS-84s managed to take off and return, but the fourth plane got stuck in the snow. On the morning of 19 January it was discovered by German reconnaissance aircraft and destroyed in an attack by Bf 109s. On that day, another twenty transport aircraft with paratroopers flew from Vnukovo (including huge TB-3 aircraft), but due to bad weather, only eleven of them reached the objective.

On 20 January the Luftwaffe began air attacks against the landings. Two PS-84 were destroyed on the ground, and another shot down in the air. Despite the difficulties, by 22 January the Russians managed to deliver onto German-held territory more than 1,000 soldiers with guns and mortars. Soviet fighters were ordered to support the paratroopers from the air.

On 22 January the 6th IAK PVO completed 297 sorties, but there was only one air battle. In the Yakovlevo area Lieutenant Nikolay Samokhvalov of the 126th IAP shot down a Ju 88. It was probably Ju 88 A-4 'B3+GN' of 5./KG 54 'Totenkopf'. This *Staffel* had recently been transferred to the Moscow area.

On 24 January, there were only two air combats. The MiG-3 of Lieutenant Simonov of the 436th IAP in the district of Mosalsk knocked shot down an 'Me 109' (Bf 109 F-2 W. Nr. 9204 of St.II./JG 51) in the Mosalsk district and Lieutenant Levin of the 126th IAP an He 111 (not confirmed).

By this time, the German troops had left the Mozhaisk ledge and moved to a straight defensive line. It ran east of the Rzhev–Gzhatsk line. To the south, the Germans kept the hills in the area of Yukhnov, and strongpoints in the area of Kirov, Lyudinovo and Zhizdra. But the Wehrmacht was losing control of its rear areas and lines of communication. Soldiers of the Soviet 39th Army and the 11th Cavalry Corps broke through the weak German defences at Rzhev. The Russians tried to act in the spirit of 'blitzkrieg'. They bypassed strongpoints and the city, rushing south parallel to the Rzhev–Sychevka–Vyazma railway. Simultaneously, a Russian offensive began on the Valdai hills, aiming at the rear of Army Group Centre, towards Velikiye Luki, Vitebsk and Smolensk. In the east the task force of General Belov, consisting of five cavalry and two infantry divisions, broke through the German defences to the south-west of Yukhnov and reached the area to the south of Vyazma.

Since October, there had been guerrilla units operating in these areas formed by Russian troops surrounded and isolated in the forest. Just behind the German lines there was a separate front, threatening the Fourth and Ninth Armies with complete disaster.

Not only were German ground units and garrisons often partially surrounded, but also Luftwaffe airfields of the Luftwaffe. III./StG 2, until mid-February based at Dugino (17km [10.5 miles] south of Sychevka), repeatedly repelled attacks by Russian tanks and cavalry. The direct approaches to the airfield were defended by anti-aircraft guns and machine guns manned by ground personnel, and Ju 87s performed between five and seven, sometimes as many as ten flights a day, attacking the enemy on the distant approaches. The total duration of such flights was 15 minutes, including take-off, landing and loading bombs! During this period, there were an average of 30 combat-ready aircraft in III./StG 2, and this small unit carried out between 150 to 300 flights per day. In several cases, some Russian tanks reached the outskirts of the airfield, but each time they were stopped by anti-aircraft guns or urgently-scrambled Ju 87s. As a result, the Germans managed to keep an important air base, as well as other key strongholds. In addition to Stukas, other units were also based at Dugino, for example, II./JG 52 (from 14 December 1941 to 20 January 1942), Bf 110 *Zerstorer* and nearby Hs 126 reconnaissance aircraft.

On 26 January the 6th IAK PVO carried out 305 missions. A significant part of the flights of the Yak-1s, MiG-3s, I-16s, P-40s and Hurricanes took place in the German rear in the area of Vyazma and Sychevka. In the Rzhev area, a pair of MiG-3s (Captain Fyodor Chuikin and Lieutenant Alexandr Chilikin) of the 27th IAP encountered four Bf 109s at an altitude of 1,000m (3,280ft), which were covering German troops. The war diary described this the episode:

> The pair of MiG-3s had dropped to 200m, and undetected got onto the tail of the Me 109s. Captain Chuikin attacked the wingman of the second pair at a distance of 200m and damaged the engine of a German aircraft, after the second attack the Me 109 fell burning 10km north of Rzhev. Then the Me 109s noticed the MiG-3 and got on their tail; the MiG-3 started to climb at full speed, then abruptly decelerated, resulting in the Me 109s overshooting the MiG-3s, exposing themselves to attack. One Me 109 began to get on the tail of Captain Chuikin, but was attacked by Chilikin (hit in the cockpit and the engine) caught fire and crashed in the same area. The remaining two Me 109s escaped from the battle at a low level. During the air battle the Me 109s tried to draw the MiG-3s into their territory and into the fire of anti-aircraft artillery.

According to German reports, in this battle Bf 109 F-2 W. Nr. 12909 of 9./ JG 51 was shot down and its pilot killed.

The MiG-3 pilot Lieutenant Nikolay Miroshnichenko of the 34th IAP brought down an He 111 in the Gusevo area. Another victory over an He 111 was claimed in the Gusevo-Peerovo area by a group of MiG-3s also from the 34th IAP (one-third of a victory was credited to Lieutenants Tarakanchikov and Korobov). In fact Ju 88 A-4 W. Nr. 1378 '4D+ HN' of 5./KG 30 'Adler' was shot down in this area. On this day nine MiG-3s of the 120th IAP took part in filming. The propaganda film was to show the Russian population the heroic actions of 'Stalin's Falcons'.

On 27 January, Russian fighters again supported the troops that had broken into the German rear. Near Rzhev a Tomahawks element of the

126th IAP attacked a group of four Ju 88s, which were escorted by five Bf 109s. With no losses on their side, two 'Me 109s' were claimed to have been shot down (one-third of the victory went to Lieutenant Belasnik and two-thirds to Lieutenant Yefim Lozovoy). The German data confirms the loss of only one Bf 109 F-2 W. Nr. 12894 of 5./JG 51, the pilot being killed. On the southern flank in the Yukhnov area Lieutenant Samsonov of the 436 IAP shot down an 'Me 109', and Politruk Rudenko of the 28the IAP an He 111 in the Sazhino area. However, the Russian pilot made a mistake in identifying his target. In fact, he damaged Ju 88 A-4 W. Nr. 8669 of 6./KG 76, which crashed during an emergency landing in the Mishukovo area.

At the airfield at Grabtsevo Bf 110 night fighters of I./NJG 4 destroyed nine TB-3s of the 3rd TBAP, one Yak-1 and one I-16 of the 436th IAP in two attacks. Another thirteen TB-3s sustained serious damage. The four-engined aircraft were intended to deliver cargo and paratroopers to the south-west of Vyazma. I./NJG 4 was the first night fighter unit to be formed on the Eastern Front, but they were frequently not used in their intended role but as *Zerstorer*.

'Klim Voroshilov' Heavy tank (KV-1) in the winter forest

Russian paratroopers with skis moving in the German rear

On 28 January the MiG-3 element of Captain Fedor Chuikin of the 27th IAP attacked and shot down a Ju 52 15km (9 miles) west of Rzhev (not confirmed by German sources), and Lieutenant Polozenko shot down a Ju 88 north-east of Rzhev. That day Luftwaffe lost the reconnaissance aircraft Ju 88 D-1 W. Nr. 1199 '5F+FM' of 4.(F)/14 in the Moscow area.

The last days of January passed without air battles. But German pilots continued to die. On 30 January four He 111s of KG 4 'General Wever' and KG 53 'Legion Condor' and three Ju 88 A/Ds of KG 3 'Blitz' and 4.(F)/11 were lost in the Moscow region. These were KG 3's last losses during this period. From July 1941 to January 1942 it had lost thirty-three aircraft (twenty-one Ju 88 A-4/A-5s and twelve Do 17 Zs) in the Moscow area. Soon II./KG 3 was sent to rest and reform.

The Russian continued landings of airborne troops behind German lines. From 28 to 31 January 175 transport aircraft sorties were carried out in the area south-west of Vyazma. Of these, 148 reached the target area, and 2,500 paratroopers and 34 tons of equipment were dropped. But because of the bad weather and the actions of the Luftwaffe, the operation was not going according to plan. A significant proportion of the paratroopers were scattered over a wide area, and many of the cargo containers could not be found. Losses of Russian transport aircraft for four days amounted to fourteen destroyed and eighteen damaged.

Statistics for January

During January the 6th IAK PVO carried out 6,753 sorties with a total duration of 6,414 hours. The average duration of a fighter's flight was about one hour. This was the standard figure for Red aviation. Of the sorties, 3,684 were performed to cover troops, 2,173 to protect railway infrastructure and transportation, 507 to attack ground targets, 160 to defend cities (including Moscow), 140 to protect the landing of troops, 115 for weather reconnaissance, 107 to defend airfields, 85 to defend road transport, 46 to defend the movement and loading of troops, 31 to attack airfields, 25 for photographic reconnaissance, 18 to protect bridges, 9 for filming, 8 to intercept reconnaissance aircraft and 5 to escort transport aircraft.

The Luftwaffe in January was inactive. In the vast air defence zone of Moscow only 187 flights of German aircraft were recorded! The pilots of the 6th IAK PVO reported shooting down forty-six aircraft (sixteen 'Me 109s', nine Ju 88s, eight He 111s, six 'Me 110s', three Hs 126s, two Ju 52s and two Do 215s). The greatest success was achieved by the 126th IAP, equipped with American P-40 fighters (the Russians called them 'Curtiss'), with seven victories. Five victories each were recorded for the 27th IAP (MiG-3s), the 95th IAP (Pe-3s), the 177th IAP (MiG-3s, I-16s) and the 428th IAP (MiG-3s). The 736th IAP (Hurricanes) had four victories, and the 28th IAP (MiG-3s), the 176th IAP (MiG-3s, I-16s) and the 445 the IAP (MiG-3s, I-16s) each had three victories. On average, there was one victory claimed for every 147 sorties.

The actual losses of the Luftwaffe, which can attributed to the air defence fighters, were approximately thirty aircraft (twelve Ju 88s, ten He 111s, four Bf 109s, two Do 17s and two Bf 110s). The heaviest losses were to twin-engined bombers, which had to operate at low level, striking advancing Soviet troops, railway stations and tracks, airfields and supply bases.

The combat losses of the 6th IAK PVO amounted to seventeen fighters, nine of them were shot down in air battles and three by anti-aircraft artillery. Two were destroyed at airfields and three were missing. Types lost: eight MiG-3s, three I-16s, two Yak-1s, two P-40s, one Hurricane and one I-153.

The Composition of the 6th IAK PVO on 1 February 1942

Regiment	Airfield	Aircraft	Total	Serviceable
11th IAP	Kaluga	Yak-1	11	8
16th IAP	Lyubertsy	MiG-3	27	20
27th IAP	Starisha	MiG-3 I-16	20 3	9 0
28th IAP	Kubinka	MiG-3	15	6
34th IAP	Vnukovo	MiG-3	16	15
95th IAP	Chkalovsk	Pe-3	25	11
120th IAP	The Central Airfield of Moscow	MiG-3	21	12
121st IAP	Noginsk	MiG-3	8	7
126th IAP	Chkalovsk	P-40	18	6
171st IAP	Tula	MiG-3 I-16	11 7	1 2
176th IAP	Yurkino	MiG-3 I-16	12 7	6 6
177th IAP	Podolsk	MiG-3 I-16	10 12	7 6
178th IAP	Lipitsy	LaGG-3 I-16	9 9	2 3
233rd IAP	Tushino	MiG-3 I-16	6 13	5 12
287th IAP	Khimki	Hurricane	18	5
291st IAP	Monino	LaGG-3	16	11
309th IAP	Gridino	I-16 I-153	2 14	2 13
423rd IAP	Tula	MiG-3 I-16	10 10	4 3
428th IAP	Sukovo	MiG-3	17	6
438th IAP	Lyubertsy	LaGG-3	14	8
441st IAP	Kalinin	MiG-3 LaGG-3	7 4	7 1
445th IAP	Kashira	MiG-3 I-16	11 11	9 5

Regiment	Airfield	Aircraft	Total	Serviceable
488th IAP	Monino	Hurricane	18	4
495th IAP	Alferovo	MiG-3	8	3
		I-16	18	6
562nd IAP	Khimki	Yak-1	8	3
564th IAP	Ostafievo	LaGG-3	11	2
565th IAP	Ramenskoe	MiG-3	15	11
736th IAP	Khimki	Hurricane	22	8
Headquarters 6th IAK	Moscow	MiG-3	2	2
		Total	496	257

Operations in the First Week of February

On 1 February 1942 the 6th IAK PVO was composed of 28 regiments with 496 fighters, but only 257 of these were considered serviceable. On 2 February the corps received reinforcements in the form of forty-five British Hurricane fighters, which were assigned to the 67th and 429th IAPs. The 67th was an elite unit, of near-legendary status in Russian aviation history. In June–October 1941, it fought in Moldova and the Odessa region, where it inflicted heavy losses on Romanian aircraft. After the battle the 67th IAP was withdrawn to the rear and re equipped with Hurricanes. The 429th IAP was a new unit formed in early 1942.

On 2 February, the 6th IAK PVO carried out 323 sorties, including 188 to protect troops and 90 to cover rail transport. The main attention was paid to railway traffic between Klin–Kalinin and Kalinin–Vyshniy Volochek. The most distant areas were patrolled by the twin-engined Pe-3 heavy fighters of the 95th IAP. They were also used for long-range aerial reconnaissance, five Pe-3s conducting a survey of the German airfield at Smolensk. Near Rzhev Lieutenant Dobrohotov's Hurricane element of the 736th IAP shot down a Ju 52. According to the pilots, they managed to set fire to the aircraft's central engine, but under the protection of Bf 109s was able to escape in the direction of Sychevka. According to German data, no loss of a Ju 52 was recorded in this area on this day.

In the Vyazma area Lieutenants Zupanov and Kunava of the 177th IAP shot down a Ju 88. On this day the Luftwaffe lost two Ju 88 A-4s of 6./KG 54 'Totenkopf', but both were brought down by ground fire.

An LaGG-3 element of the 178th IAP reported an inconclusive dogfight with nine 'Me 109s' in the Uruhin area.

On the night of 3 February, the Luftwaffe carried out an attack on Myasnovo airfield, where the Kaluga group of fighters was based, dropping 11 high-explosive bombs and 500 incendiaries. Two MiG-3s were damaged. On 3 February nine Bf 110 Es of I./ZG 1 made a raid on the Kaluga-Grabtsevo airfield. There the Kaluga group lost two Yak-1s and a U-2, and one Yak-1 was damaged. After the attack the *Zerstorers* were attacked by Politruk Nikolay Baskov and Lieutenant Fedor Mitrofanov of the 445th IAP. They claimed two victories. In fact, only one Bf 110 E-1 W. Nr. 3960, was shot down, both of the crew being killed. This day on the Eastern Front was not a good one for I./ZG 1: three of its aircraft were shot down (two in the Toropets district) and its commander, Hauptmann R. Kaldrath was killed.

Tomahawks of the 126th IAP carried out a raid in the German rear near the city of Rzhev. Chkalovskaya airfield, where the P-40s and Pe-3s were based, was located to the east of Moscow, 170km (106 miles) from the front line. Tomahawks had longer range than Russian-produced fighters as they were able to use drop tanks. In this episode Lieutenant Stepan Ridniy scored several successes. With other fighters, he shot down Hs 126 B-1 W. Nr. 4128

Dive bombers Ju 87 flying at low level over a Russian village

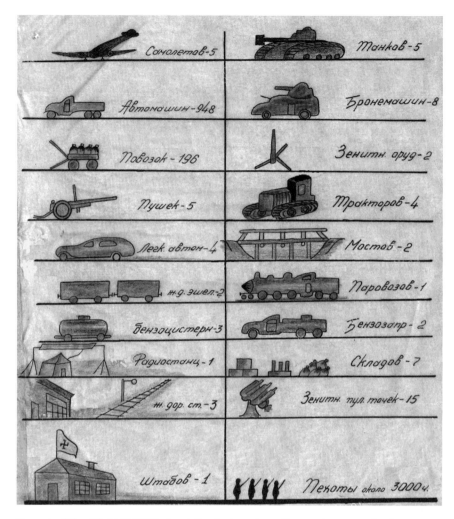

Report of the 6th IAK PVO about the destruction of ground targets. Soviet reports resembled infantile children's drawings

3.(H)/21 near Sychevka, then in Nikitye personally brought down an 'Me 109' (Bf 109 F-2 W. Nr. 11869 of 10./JG 51, pilot killed). The pilots of 34th IAP claimed three victories north-west of Yukhnov (two He 111s and one Ju 88). One of these victories, at 14.40, was won by Lieutenant Nikolai Tarakanchikov. Another two air victories claimed by the pilots of the 177th IAP. The group, composed of Lieutenants Zupanov, Frolov and Phuntov, shot down two Ju 88. But these victories are not confirmed, no Luftwaffe bombers were lost or damaged that day. In total, on this clear day (visibility was 15–20km [9–12 miles]), the fighters of the 6th IAK PVO reported nine victories (three are confirmed).

The Raid on Gorky and the Rage of the Dictator

In order to complicate the landing of troops behind their lines and the work of the air bridge in the Vyazma area, the Germans continued to periodically strike at Soviet airfields. On the night of 4 February, a raid was made on the air base in Tula, in which 50 high-explosive bombs and 200 incendiaries were dropped. As a result, the airfield was damaged, but of the aircraft on it only one MiG-3 of the 423rd IAP was damaged. During the war, both sides actively attacked airfields, believing that it was easier to destroy planes on the ground than intercept them in the air. Very often, pilots greatly exaggerated their success during such raids, which lead to their endless repetition. In fact, most of these attacks were ineffective. In many case, the attackers lost more planes than were destroyed on the ground. At the same time, along with the attacking machines, pilots were killed, but only equipment was destroyed on the airfields.

In early February, the Luftwaffe resumed its long-range raids against Russian industrial centres. The night of 3/4 February in the Moscow area and to the east of it was frosty, clear and moonlit. About midnight a Russian observation post (VNOS), located near the village of Vyazniki, spotted a single plane, which flew to the east. The observers identified it as a 'passenger' or 'transport' aircraft. A few days before there was a case when a Russian transport plane with paratroops aboard got lost its course and instead of the Vyazma area dropped them near the city of Gorky! Down on the ground the Russian paratroopers were sure that they were behind German lines. They prepared to liberate the villages and blow up the railways. But the next morning the soldiers met surprised locals who told them: this is the Gorky region, the Germans are not here . . .

So when four days later the headquarters of the Gorky district air defence division received a report about the approach of a strange aircraft, it did not sound the alarm. Perhaps it was their own paratroopers again? The officer on duty, Captain Korobitsky, considered the information unimportant and did not report it to his commander. The anti-aircraft batteries located around the city of Gorky were silent, and all was quiet at the airfields of the 142nd Fighter Division, which was to protect the numerous military plants located there. In the freezing factory shops the tired workers continued to work all night, with only occasional rests during '*perekur*' ('smoke breaks'). At the 'Molotov' automobile plant (GAZ) work was still in full swing at this late hour. Trucks, tanks and armoured vehicles regularly rolled off the production line. All of the vehicles quickly went to the front in the centre of Moscow . . .

At 01.30 the rhythmical sound of the machines was suddenly pierced by an eerie howl, followed by two powerful explosions. Initially, many workers thought that there had been an accident. When reports of explosions at the GAZ plant reached air defence headquarters, it was decided to sound the alarm. At 01.55 the sirens wailed in Gorky and the anti-aircraft batteries were ordered to open fire. But no-one knew where and what to shoot at. The crews ran out of their dugouts to their guns and began blazing away into sky, where nothing could be seen apart from the full moon. The fire crews were also in complete confusion.

Soon it became clear that there had been an air raid. One high explosive bomb had hit Engine Room No. 2 while the other had hit the wheel shop. A large fire broke out and burned for seven hours. The shop was severely damaged. Seventeen night-shift workers were killed in the explosions and forty were injured.

When dawn broke over Gorky, residents could see large clouds of smoke rising above the car factory. On the streets the most fantastic rumours rapidly spread. Some people spoke of hundreds of signal rockets that were fired by German agents in different parts of the city. Other people described the terrible details of the bombing. The Soviet press and radio did not report any information about Luftwaffe air raids. People got the news only from conversations in shops and trams. But even there it was difficult to find out what had happened. In the USSR there was mass surveillance, and anyone who spoke about air raids, or listened to someone who did, could be accused of being a 'Hitler agent'. In all factories employed hundreds of agents of the NKVD were employed to regularly report on the sentiments of the population. Most Soviet citizens preferred to remain silent for fear of arrest . . .

The short February day quickly came to an end, and darkness fell over the agitated city once more. At 02.35 the people first heard the air-raid warning, then the popping shots of anti-aircraft guns. The dark winter sky was pierced by multi-coloured signal rockets, illuminating entire quarters of the darkened city. It was difficult to see where they were being fired from, but it could be seen that they were coming from many different areas, independently of one another. Everyone who saw then had a terrible thought: in Gorky there are tens, maybe hundreds, of enemy agents. Their signals were guiding the bombers.

Soon the city heard the roar of the plane. Two high-explosive bombs were dropped on the 'Molotov' automobile plant. They exploded near the building in which T-60 tanks were made. Windows were broken and feeder number 104 was damaged. On the 8th tram line the blast wave damaged three pylons and broke the power cables. One person was killed and two were injured. Three more powerful explosions shook the village of Stakhanovsky, near the automobile plant. Three houses were damaged, one person was killed and three were injured. At 02.40 the rescue service began clearing up the bomb sites. During the night the anti-aircraft batteries put up an intense barrage, but without visible results.

On the morning of 5 February, there was an emergency meeting of the Gorky Defence Committee. It was an extraordinarily high-level meeting, which included the local Communist Party Chief, the head of the local NKVD branch and the Chairman of the Regional Council of People's Deputies (the formal head of the region). After emotional speeches and criticism of the anti-aircraft defence command, resolution No. 165 was adopted, which stated: 'As a result of criminal carelessness and inaction of Captain Korobitsky on duty in the division area of air defence and the failure of vigilance of posts in the night of 3 to 4 February, enemy aircraft managed to sneak unnoticed to the city and drop bombs on the 'Molotov' automobile plant.'

Stalin was made aware of the air raid on the most important industrial centre. The dictator was angry and ordered that the guilty be punished. On 6 February Order No. 129 of the People's Commissariat of Defence, 'About the unpunished admission of the opponent's bomber to Gorky', was issued. The commander of the division area of air defence Vladimir Dobryansky, Battalion Commissar D.P. Egorov and chief of staff Lieutenant Colonel V. Savko were sentenced to 10 days' detention with a 50 per cent reduction in pay (no more punishment than they might have received for a drunken brawl). Captain Korobitsky, who had been on duty at the headquarters and 'slept through' the air attack, suffered the most. He was court-martialled and executed. The commander of the air defence of the USSR, Lieutenant General Mikhail Gromadin, received a disciplinary warning.

In addition to punishing those guilty of negligence, numerous cases of 'air hooliganism' were noted. Russian planes flew over their territory, failing to follow the prescribed routes, without clearance and approval. The flight regime was violated by both civil and military aircraft. For this reason, German bombers easily disguised themselves as Russians and flew freely over enemy territory.

Order No. 129 allowed violators and 'hooligans' to be brought to court and severely punished. From 15 March, the chief of communications of the Red Army established for each day a single radio frequency for contacts between military aircraft and ground air defence. Lost pilots were required to report it and find out their location. Air defence fighters were ordered to intercept all violators and force them to land. In reality, such cases continued in the years that followed. Especially at night, Russian airspace was a mess. Many of the aircraft flying through restricted areas broke the rules and signals. Communications worked poorly. This Russian 'confusion' was periodically used by the crews of Luftwaffe bombers and night fighters. Having studied the Russian flight system and signals, they disguised themselves as Russian planes and flew freely over Soviet territory.

Chapter 8

The Rzhev–Vyazma Line

The main events at this time occurred to the west of Moscow. On 4 February 1942, the pilots of the 6th IAK PVO fought eight air battles and reported eight victories. Again the pilots of the 126th IAP distinguished themselves, making a long-distance raid to the Rzhev and Sychevka areas. The Tomahawk element of Lieutenants Stepan Ridniy, Shumilov and Mikhail Matiushin claimed two Ju 52s shot down in the Sychevka area. German data confirms only one of these victories: Ju 52/3m W. Nr. 5129 'TD+AE' of KGr.z.b.V 800 was reported missing in that area. The four crew disappeared in the frosty mist . . . In the same area the Hurricane of Lieutenant Grobovoy of the 287th IAP shot down an 'Me 109'.

The greatest number of battles occurred around the airfield at Grabtsevo. A Yak-1 element of the 11th IAP, patrolling near the objective, saw four Bf 109s heading towards the airfield. The Russians attacked them head on, then in the ensuing dogfight Lieutenants Lapochkin and Sergei Katseval together shot down one 'Me 109'. The third pilot, Lieutenant Britikov, caught up and shot down another 'Messer' (as the Russians called the Bf 109) in the Yukhnov area. Four MiG-3s of the 445th IAP, operating from Kashira, engaged six Bf 109s in the Grabtsevo area, claiming three victories. These were credited to Politruk Nikolai Baskov and Lieutenant Mitrofanov. Of all these claims, only one is confirmed. The direct support Bf 109 E-7 W. Nr. 0681, piloted by Unteroffizier Kornelius Einedert of I./Sch.G 1, was probably shot down by Mitrofanov south of Grabtsevo airfield. The pilot was killed, and Mitrofanov recorded his seventh personal victory.

On 5 February the weather was clear, favourable for air combat. The Tomahawk pilots of the 126th IAP reported three victories around Rzhev. Lieutenant Vladimir Kamenshchikov's flight was credited with group victories over an 'Me 109' and a Ju 88, and Lieutenants Stepan Ridniy and Mikhail Mikhaylin shared a victory over another 'Me 109'. In the same area (Osuga station) Hurricanes of the 736th IAP shot down a Ju 52/3m

Hurricane from the 6th IAK PVO.

P-40B Tomahawk from the 126-th IAP at the Chkalovsky airfield

W. Nr. 5072 of KGr.z.b.V 600. According to German information, it and its five crew were reported missing in that area. A pair of MiG-3s from the 34th IAP (Lieutenants Victor Korobov and Bikov) shot down an 'Me 110', near Ugryumovo. According to German information, the night fighter Bf 110 D-3 W. Nr. 3682 '3N+JL' of 3./NJG 4 (operating as a *Zerstorer*) was lost north-west of Ugryumovo station.

The MiG-3 pilots Lieutenant Sorokin and Sergeant Pechenevsky of the 177th IAP reported jointly shooting down a Ju 88. It was probably Ju 88 A-4 W. Nr. 8593 'F1+AC' from the headquarters flight of II./KG 76. A pair of fighters flown by Lieutenants Ivan Tikunov and Gaydamak of the 178 IAP were patrolling over their troops in the Vasilevka–Krokowa–V'yazovka–Morozovka areas. There they intercepted and shot down a twin-engined aircraft identified as an 'Fw 187' . . .

In early 1942, Russian pilots began to report the appearance in the sky of a mysterious plane, the 'Fw 187' (Focke-Wulf Fw 187). According to them, these aircraft operated singly, acting as fighters and as *Zerstorer*. Unlike the fictional 'Me 115' such a plane really existed. It was a twin-engined heavy fighter, the Fw 187 'Falke', nine of which built before the Second World War (three prototypes and six production). But the machine was not outperformed by the Bf 110 and was not adopted into service. All the aircraft that had been built were formed into a defence squadron for the Focke-Wulf factory in Bremen. As in the case of the He 100, RLM decided to use the Fw 187 to mislead the enemy. In 1940, the aircraft was actively 'advertised' as the Luftwaffe's 'new heavy fighter'. In the Soviet Union, this misinformation was believed. Drawings of the 'Fw 187' were published in reference books and tables, and hung on the walls of the aviation schools. Russian intelligence could not get detailed information about the plane, so in the columns for 'wingspan', 'length', 'mass' were only dashes. Russian pilots were informed that the 'secret aircraft' was equipped with DB-601 engines, had a maximum speed of 580km/h (360 mph) and can be used as a ground-attack aircraft. Fw 187 was similar to the Hs 129, which was usually confused with this plane.

On the night of 5/6 February the Luftwaffe carried out an air raid on Myasnovo airfield, where the fighters of the Kaluga group were based. The raid was successful: two MiG-3s were destroyed and two I-16s and a MiG-3 were damaged. One of the ground personnel was killed and two were wounded. At 10.53 on the same night eleven Bf 110s attacked the airfield at Tula but there no planes were damaged.

During the day, the regiments of the 6th IAK PVO had carried out 382 sorties, including 196 to cover of their troops, 103 to protect rail transportation and 83 to protect airfields. Six air battles and six victories were recorded. A pair of MiG-3s from the 34th IAP shot down an He 111 in the Il'inka area, and Lieutenants Mikhailov and Cherniavsky shot down an 'Me 110' 10km (6 miles) north-east of Kaluga. The most distinguished were the Hurricane pilots of the 287th IAP. Captain Nicholay Khramov's flight in the area the Sychevka claimed two 'Me 109s' and one 'Me 110', and Lieutenants Chistyakov and Borisov claimed a joint victory over an Hs 126. But all these victories are not confirmed by German information. The Luftwaffe's only casualty that day was an Hs 126 A-1 W. Nr. 3102 of 7.(H)./32 damaged by ground fire in the Yukhnov area. The pilot was wounded.

On 7 February, the weather became cloudier and visibility decreased again. During the next raid in the Sychevka-Rzhev area the P-40 element of Lieutenant Stepan Ridniy of the 126th IAP shot down an Hs 126. The loss

Shot down in battle P-40B after landing on the fuselage

Soviet soldiers with T-40 tanks in the woods

of a 'Crutch' (as the Hs 126 was called for its characteristic appearance) on this day is not recorded. But in the Okrokowo area was Hs 123 A-1 W. Nr. 0794 of 8./Sch.G 1 was shot down. Its pilot was Lieutenant Rudolf von Zahradnichek (son of an Austrian marshal of the First World War, a Slovak by birth). This Austrian nobleman disappeared forever in the 'vast Russian expanse' . . . In the Medyn region two bombers – He 111 H-6 W. Nr. 4637 '5J+JM' of 4./KG 4 and He 111 H-6 W. Nr. 4811 'A1+HP' of 6./KG 53 – and their crews were reported missing.

In the following days, due to bad weather, there was little air activity in the Moscow area. On 8 February, the 6th IAK PVO carried out only 58 sorties, on the 9th 71, on the 10th 158, on the 11th 33, on the 12th none, on the 13th 49, and on the 14th 61. The Luftwaffe also flew little, but suffered losses. On 10 February He 111 H-6 W. Nr. 4561 '5J+DP' went missing in the Mosalsk district and He 111 H-6 W. Nr. 4679 in the Zubovo area. Both bombers belonged to 6./KG 4 'General Wever'.

On 11 February a rare event took place. During a sortie to protect trains on the Povarovo–Klin and Klin–Zavidovo railway lines a Pe-3 heavy fighter of the 95th IAP (crew Lieutenants Stepanov and Kornienko) shot down a Ju 88 30km (18.6 miles) south of Kalinin. According to German data two

Destroyed a He 111 bomber of KG 53

Ju 88 D-1 of 4.(F)/14 before takeoff in the Moscow area

bombers of 1./KG 77 were lost in this area: Ju 88 A-4 W. Nr. 3667 '3Z+CH' and Ju 88 A-4 W. Nr. 2626 '3Z+BH'. At 16.10 on 13 February, five Bf 110s attacked the airfield at Staritsa through the snow, destroying one MiG-3 there.

On 16 February, the 6th IAK PVO carried out 280 sorties. A group of six P-40Bs of the 126th IAP under the command of Captain Arsenin conducted two air battles during a patrol in the area Molchanovo–Orrokowo, claiming victories over a Ju 88 and an He 111. Another Ju 88 was credited to Lieutenant Semyon Levin of the 126th IAP. The Tomahawk group of the 126th IAP also claimed one He 111 and two Ju 88s downed as shared victories (for example, Lieutenant Samokhvalov recorded one-sixth of an He 111 and two-sixths of a Ju 88). In fact, on this day, the Luftwaffe lost only a Ju 88 C-6 heavy fighter W. Nr. 3615 'F1+YM' of 4./KG 76.

On 17 February Hurricanes of the 736th IAP in the area of Monchanovo and Panovo shot down a Ju 88 and an 'Me 109' (credited to Lieutenant Alexei Ryazanov), and the Tomahawks of the 126th IAP shot down a Do 17 22km (13.6m miles) north-west of Rzhev. But none of these victories are confirmed.

The Germans did not show much activity in the Moscow area. At 11.00 nine Bf 110s attacked the airfield at Myasnovo, where the 423rd IAP was based. One MiG-3 was damaged and one mechanic was injured.

The Russians suffered a tragic incident in the 126th IAP. During take-off Tomahawk Mk IIB 'AK-325' crashed due to engine failure, killing one of the best aces of the Moscow air defences, Lieutenant Stepan Ridniy. He had completed 172 sorties, and had eleven personal and six shared victories. He was posthumously awarded the title of Hero of the Soviet Union.

February 18th was successful for the pilots of the 67th IAP. When returning from the mission to protect their troops, a group of Hurricanes was suddenly attacked from out of the sun by a pair of Bf 109s, which shot down one of the machines. During the dogfight, one of the attackers was itself shot down, probably Bf 109 F-2 W. Nr. 12929 of 4./JG 51.

On 19 February, MiG-3s of the 11th, 28th, 34th and 176th IAP, and Hurricanes of the 67th, 287th, 429th and 736th IAP defended the troops of the Russian 39th Army, which were engaged in fierce fighting to the west of Rzhev. In harsh conditions, of German soldiers in snow-covered strongpoints repulsed endless frontal attacks by fanatical Soviet infantry and tanks. To their great surprise, during the day over this small section of forty to fifty Hurricanes could be seen! This happened almost every day, demonstrating the role of the Soviet Union's allies in supplying aircraft. Such a number of Hurricanes could only be seen over England!

MiG-3 from the 27th IAP at the Klin airfield

The British-built fighters escorted transport aircraft that dropped supplies to the troops of the 33rd Army south of Vyazma.

There was little Luftwaffe activity, and only three air battles involving air defence fighters were recorded during the day. In the Rzhev area, a pair of MiG-3s (Lieutenant Viktor Kiselev and Lieutenant Bukvarev) from the 34th IAP shot down an 'Me 110'. On this day in the Gzhatsk area Bf 110 E-1 W. Nr. 4086 '3U+GM' (pilot Feldwebel F. Bergmann, observer Unteroffizier A. Lidecker) of 4./ZG 26 'Horst Wessel' was reported missing. In the same area the element of Lieutenant Platov shot down a Ju 88. The element of Captain Mikhail Naidenko of the same regiment also reported shooting down a Ju 88. The German data confirms the loss of Ju 88 A-4 W. Nr. 2630 'B3+EC' of St.II/KG 54 and Ju 88 A-4 W. Nr. 6649 'B3+HP' of 6./KG 54 with their crews. In the Ostritsa area three I-16s of 728th IAP shot down another bomber, Ju 88 A-4 W. Nr. 1274 of 4./KG 3 'Blitz'.

In the days that followed, things were much the same. The Russians flew a lot, but rarely encountered the Germans. On 21 February, a pair of Tomahawks of the 126th IAP shot down an 'Me 109' to the south-east of Afanasievo. Lieutenant Mikhail Mikhaylin was credited with half victory. German information does not confirm this incident.

The tactics for protecting troops by Russian fighters were as follows. The first element flew in a 'wedge' at 50m (54-yard) intervals, and the second element flew in a wedge 200–300m (219–328 yards) behind and 200–400m (656–1,312ft) above the first. This system prevented Luftwaffe attacks on ground targets and protected the 'lower' elements. In cloud, the wedges flew over the target area in one after the other, each pilot having his own sector of observation.

By this time the 6th IAK PVO had established the following system of warning and guidance of fighters. On the likely enemy approach routes were individual observation posts (VNOS), which had to report the course, height and destination of enemy aircraft, then direct their planes to them. All posts were numbered on a degree scale to make it easy for pilots to remember them. The posts were equipped with arrow panels, radio sets and direct telephone communication to the command posts of the nearby aviation regiments and the command post of the corps. In Klin and Serpukhov radar stations (ERS) with RUS-2 sets were set up and in Moscow, Vnukovo and Lyubertsy stations with British MRU-105 sets. Each station was allocated its own detection sector.

After receiving messages from observation posts about the target, the control officer ordered the appropriate radar station to track it. Commanders of aviation regiments received accurate data on the course of the target, then decided to order fighters into the air and send them to the appropriate waiting area. Then the IAP command posts, using the data received, plotted the targets and directly guided the fighters on to them.

'Blood of Communist' and 'Bloody Rampant Hitler's Fanatics'

On 23 February 1942 the Soviet Union celebrated the anniversary of the Red Army. After heavy defeats in 1941, the authority of the Stalinist regime was weakened. Before the Nazi invasion, Soviet propaganda had claimed that Stalin was infallible, the army he created was invincible, all the decisions of the leader were ingeniousand correct. But by the end of 1941, many people had become disillusioned with Bolshevism and openly rejoiced in its apparently imminent defeat. Opposition sentiments and discontent grew in the country. Therefore, after the first victories of the Red Army in late 1941 – early 1942 all the forces of propaganda were thrown into the restoration of the shaky ideology.

Before the holiday the Bolshevik newspaper *Pravda* published an article about one of the soldiers who had been killed at the front:

> Preparing for battle, the Red Army soldier Stepan Nikolayevich Volkov wrote a note entitled: 'My testament'. Volkov wrote: 'Comrade soldiers, commanders and political workers! Going on the attack, I pledge to fight to the last breath for the honour and independence of Motherland. I'm nonpartisan myself. But if the battle will spill my blood, think of it as a blood of a communist. Death and universal contempt for the fascist executioners who desecrated our sacred land! Dear brothers in arms! If I die in this battle, call me a Communist-Stalinist. Glory to the great Soviet people led by the leader of the world's first socialist state Comrade Stalin . . .'
>
> Volkov was killed in battle. Our people will preserve the memory of this humble hero. He showed the world the image of a non-partisan Soviet patriot. He calls himself non-party, because he was not a member of the great Lenin-Stalin party. But he was the son of his Party. The Party raised him. He gave his young life for the cause of our Party, for freedom, happiness

and honour of his homeland. In his last fight Volkov walked side by side with the communists. He was a real Bolshevik . . .

Propaganda described the death of the hero as a confirmation of the correctness of the political model of Stalin's dictatorship. The press wrote that the Soviet Union was a 'democracy' and the people chose Stalin and his party!

> An impressive picture of the unity of communists and non-Party members was shown to the world by the elections to the Supreme Soviet of the USSR. 98.6 percent of the voters cast their votes for the candidates of the Stalin bloc of communists and non-party, and the elections to the Supreme Soviet of the Union Republics, when 99.4 percent of the voters voted for this bloc . . . The invaders expected to crush the forces of the Soviet people, to divide the Soviet people, to set them against each other. Hitler was wrong! His predatory impact broke on the monolithic unity of the Soviet people, the strength of the Soviet system, the strongest in the world.

In addition to articles about fallen Bolshevik heroes, the press published stories about the crimes of the Nazis in the occupied territories. But real and terrible crimes of Nazism (the murders of Jews) were hidden from the Russian population, and fantastic stories were composed instead for the them. 'In the village of Borisovo, intimidate the farmers the Germans organized brutal torture of the 66-year-old collective farmer Olga Gusenkova,' said the article 'Bloody Hitler's Rampant Fanatics'. 'Having built a gallows on the street and driven the entire population to it, the German inquisitors began to torture an innocent woman. They put a noose around Gusenkova's neck, pulled and released and pulled again. This torture lasted for several hours. The fascist barbarians threw the distraught and unconscious woman into snow. Gusenkova's house was lootedby the Germans, who took everything down to the last thread . . .'

'200 defenceless old men, women and children were shot in this small village by the Nazi monsters,' the article 'Ukrainian land burns under the feet of fascist bandits' read.

> 50-year-old Maxim Kalyada, was killed by the Germans when he was getting water from the well. One fascist wanted to shoot

the dog of the local paramedic Yegor Petrov. The old man asked him not to kill the dog. The German laughed, and the second bullet was fired into Petrov. The son of Petrov, Viktor, came out at the shots. The Germans killed him. Petrov's neighbour Yegor Shulika could not restrain himself, expressed his indignation and at the same moment fell dead under the bullet of a German bandit . . .

Russian propaganda portrayed the Wehrmacht as a gang of looters and robbers. Stealing children's dresses. These stories had to convince the starving Russian people that under the Germans life would be even worse than under the Bolsheviks. The Germans will take off your last pair of underpants!

On 23 February the weather was clear, air temperature was –7°C. The 6th IAK PVO carried out a record number of sorties in this month – 525. But there were only five air battles, and only one was recorded as being successful. A pair of MiG-3s (lead by Captain Naidenko) of the 34th IAP shot down an 'Me 110' near Nekrasovo. On this day Bf 110 D-2 W. Nr. 3815 of I./NJG 4 was damaged in combat and crash-landed at the airfield at Shatalovo. The pilot Feldwebel S. Dickneit subsequently died of his injuries, while the flight engineer W. Schmidt was also wounded but survived.

Near Uvarovo a Bf 110 was shot down by a Yak-1 flown by Sergeant Yefim Goldberg of the 562 IAP. The pilot was seriously injured and was out military of service for a long time.

On 24 February, the Russians made many flights, but only encountered the Luftwaffe once. This episode is illiterately described in the Russian combat diary as follows:

> Unit the Yak-1 11 IAP, leading captain Kuryshev, while patrolling in the area of Nekrasovo-Rogatino led air battle with 4 Me 109. In the area of patrolling of behind on 200 – 300m and above 2 Me 109 were found. Link stood up in turn, but a couple of Me 109 battle on the bends did not accept and went above the link is also on the bends. After 5 minutes, came suddenly in the clouds and a couple of Me 109, attacking the leading, which turn went into a frontal attack on the front pair, then breaking the thin layer of clouds, stood in a bend, where he was attacked by the first pair of Me 109, but having little fuel, re-entered the cloud and returned to their base. The pair

Yak-1, remaining under the clouds, continued to fight with the second pair of Me 109, as a result of which Lieutenant Glazov, damaging Me 109 and then, being hit by anti-aircraft machine-guns and anti-aircraft artillery, made an emergency landing in the field. Lieutenant Goshko at the beginning of combat broke away of the group and landed on their base.

In Russian documents it is often possible to see such stupid and ignorant descriptions of the fighting. According to German information in this battle Bf 109 E-3 W. Nr. 1570 of 4./Sch.G 1 was shot down.

He 111 Night Fighters

On the night of 18/19 February, the Russians began a second airborne operation in the Moscow area. The drop zone was behind the German lines west of Yukhnov (the city continued to hold out against Wehrmacht). Transport aircraft carried out 89 sorties and dropped 528 paratroopers, but 59 aircraft did not find the specified drop zone and returned. The next night 153 sorties were carried (134 aircraft reached the objective), and 2,551 parachutists were dropped. On the night of 20/21 February, sixty-five transport aircraft took off, and thirty-seven of them reached the objective. Some of the aircraft landed and unloaded their troops rather than dropping them by parachute. Due to bad weather and poor organization, many pilots could not find the target area. On the night of 21/22 February 112 transport aircraft flew behind German lines and 100 reached the objective (delivering 296 troops).

The Germans soon noticed the landings, but were unable to take effective countermeasures immediately. Only on the night of 22/23 February, west of Yukhnov, did a night fighter shoot down two huge TB-3 aircraft. 'The plane, from which our comrades had just jumped out, caught fire and fell to the ground like a fiery meteor,' recalled I.I. Gromov and V.N. Pigunov who participated in the landing.

A second TB-3 caught fire. From it through the fire leapt black figures, above which the canopies of parachutes opened, some of them instantly catching fire. Against the background of the sky and the burning giant aircraft parachutes clearly stood out. They were struck by the fire of a fascist fighter. The plane in flames, like the first one, plummeted to the ground and was destroyed. The tragic fate of the TB-3 was shared by the paratroopers who did not have time to leave it.

A third transport received numerous hits, but was able to land in the target area. On board this aircraft the commander of the 4th Airborne Corps, General F.F. Levashov, was killed.

The 'night fighter' was the He 111 of Oberfeldwebel W. Teige of KG 53 'Legion Condor'! During the battle in the Moscow area the Luftwaffe began to use He 111 bombers as night fighters. Although slow, these aircraft had powerful armament and were suitable for such missions. The main targets of theses improvised hunters were Russian transport planes delivering reinforcements and cargo to paratroopers fighting in the German rear. Teige's two victories were the only significant successes in this operation to disrupt the delivery of Russian troops. Between 18 and 24 February in the target area west of Yukhnov, 6,779 paratroopers and 1,431 loads of cargo were dropped. Russian transport planes made 555 sorties and lost only three aircraft.

Simultaneously with the landing operation, Russian bombers conducted a series of attacks on the Smolensk–Vyazma railway line. They were carried out both in the daytime and at night with the aim of paralyzing the supply of German troops in the Rzhev salient. At the same time, there were air raids on Luftwaffe airfields at Seshchinskaya, Shatalovka, Borovskoye and Balbasovo. But these Russian attacks were ineffective due to the lack of aircraft and experienced crews. Large numbers of Red Army bombers had been lost in the summer of 1941, along with most of the pilots trained in the 1930s. It was not possible to restore the bomber regiments in the winter of 1941/42. Typically, raids were carried out by groups of three to five Db-3 and Pe-2 bombers which dropped bombs from high altitude, often overshooting the target. The most effective raids were on the railway junction and airfield in Orsha on 27 and 28 February. 'During the air attacks on Orsha on February 27 and 28, several aircraft and many vehicles of the supply base were damaged,' Army Group Centre reported. '11 people were killed, 21 wounded. One enemy bomber was shot down.'

Participating in the air raid on Orsha on 28 February, Lieutenant Vasily Reshetnikov recalled how over the target his Db-3F was attacked by a night fighter:

> Suddenly, the German anti-aircraft guns stopped firing. On the intercom, I immediately ordered the crew to strengthen

surveillance. Looked behind me to the left and saw the black silhouette of the twin-engine Me 110. Gunner Chernov opened fire, but the German managed to release a powerful stream of bullets and shells from all his forward cannon and machine guns, which hit our aircraft with a roar. I'm doing a sharp left turn. Increased engine speed to reduce the turning radius. The control panel is torn to shreds, there are many holes on the centre section. When the ground was very close, I pressed the throttle of both engines, the left did not give full speed, but the plane went up.

Vasily Reshetnikov managed to reach Russian territory and make an emergency landing. Later, the pilot became a Hero of the Soviet Union, and after the war, the commander of strategic aviation of the Soviet Union. In 2005 one of the authors of this book personally communicated with Reshetnikov who is still alive at the time of writing.

On 26 February, in heavy snowfalls, the 6th IAK PVO completed sixty-four sorties, but only the MiG-3s of Lieutenants Ivan Kholodov and Vorobyov of the 28th IAP encountered the enemy. The pilots intercepted a biplane flying at low level 23km (14.25 miles) south-east of Gzhatsk, identified as an Hs 126. The fighters immediately attacked it and saw it go down. No losses of 'Crutches' were recorded on this day, but in this area the Hs 123 B-1 ground-attack aircraft W. Nr. 2345 of 8./Sch.G 1 was lost.

On 27 February, the weather improved and the air defence fighters carried out 307 sorties, including 205 to protect troops and 83 to cover rail traffic. The Pe-3 heavy fighters of the 95th IAP carried out reconnaissance missions in the Orel, Bryansk, Zhizdra and Roslavl areas. There were ten air battles in which only the Hurricane pilots distinguished themselves. Lieutenant Konovalov of the 488th IAP shot down an 'Me 109' in the Yukhnov area, and Lieutenant Kuznetsov an 'Me 110' in the Gorodnya area. Captain Zadvorny of the 736th IAP was counted aerial victory over 'Me 109' in the area of Izvolski. On this day in the Moscow area the Luftwaffe lost only *Zerstorer* Bf 110 C-6 W. Nr. 2249 of 6./ZG 1, but this was hit by anti-aircraft fire near Glazovo. Russian fighters damaged Bf 109 E-7 W. Nr. 6522 of 4./JG 51, which made an emergency landing in German territory.

At 23.00 the Luftwaffe carried out an air raid on the airfield at Tula, dropping twelve high-explosive bombs. The guard room was destroyed by a direct hit, two guards being killed.

On 28 February the 6th IAK PVO carried out 427 sorties and recorded 10 air battles. Russian pilots reported seven victories, four by MiG-3 pilots of the 120th IAP. Captain Tomilin shot down an 'Me 110' in the Medyn area, Lieutenant Bogachev a Do 215 in Vyasische, Lieutenant Sergey Rubtsov another Do 215 in the Voskresensk area, and Lieutenant Sorokin an 'Me 110' in the Dubrovka area. Lieutenant Baikov of the 34th IAP shot down an He 111 in the Vyazma area, and Group Captain Naidenko another in the Rusinovca area. The MiG-3 pilots Major Sidorov and Sergeant Melnikov of the 428th IAP got an 'Me 109' in the Beliy Kamen area.

On this day, the Luftwaffe suffered serious losses in the Moscow area. Bf 110 E-2 W. Nr. 4495 'S9+FN' (pilot Unteroffizier H. Rohde, mechanic Obergefreiter E. Pohz) of 5./ZG 1 was reported missing in the Yukhnov–Medyn. Another *Zerstorer*, Bf 110 E-1 W. Nr. 4053 of II./ZG 1, was damaged, but was able to fly to the Bryansk airfield and make an emergency landing. The pilot, Oberfeldwebel Gunter Wittig, was wounded. During daylight in the Costovici area, Russian fighters shot down a Bf 110 D night fighter, W. Nr. 3325 of 3./NJG 3. The pilot Oberleutnant G. Bohmel was killed, but the other crew member was unharmed. In the Vyazishche area fighters shot down He 111 H-6 W. Nr. 4497 of II./KG 53 'Legion Condor'.

Statistics for February

In February the 6th IAK PVO carried out 6,176 sorties with a total duration of 6,603 hours. In January, the average duration of a Russian fighter's combat flight was 0.95 hours, but in February it increased to 1.05 hours. This fact was explained by the increased share of foreign-built aircraft, which could stay in the air longer. The air defence fighters carried 2,743 sorties to protect troops, 2,222 to cover railway facilities and transportation, 811 to protect airfields, 135 to protect the unloading of troops from trains, 126 to protect cities and Moscow, 62 for reconnaissance and special missions, 48 for meteorological reconnaissance, 23 to support transport aircraft and 6 to intercept enemy reconnaissance aircraft.

The activity of the Luftwaffe in the Moscow area in February increased by a factor of 4.5. Russian observation posts recorded 850 flights of German aircraft, including 708 during the day and 142 at night.

The 6th IAK PVO claimed fifty-eight air victories (seventeen 'Me 109s', twelve Ju 88s, ten 'Me 110s', seven He 111s, five Ju 52s, three Hs 126s, two Do 215s, one 'Fw 187' and one Do 17). The greatest success was achieved by the 34th IAP, equipped with MiG-3 fighters, with eleven victories. In second place was the 126th IAP (P-40s), withten victories. Seven victories were recorded for the 736th IAP (Hurricanes), six for the 287th IAP (Hurricanes), and five for the 177th IAP (MiG-3s, I-16s) and the 445th IAP (MiG-3s, I-16s). The 120th IAP (MiG-3s) had four victories and the 11th IAP (Yak-1s) three. Several aviation regiments scored one victory each. In the consumption of ammunition foreign Colt-Browning was in the lead with 81,586 rounds. In second place were the 7.6mm ShKAS machine guns with 55,340 rounds, and in third the 12.7mm BS machine guns with 12,140 rounds. Hurricanes shot at the enemy the most!

The real losses of the Luftwaffe from Russian fighters in the Moscow area remained at the level of January, totalling thirty aircraft lost in combat, including nine Ju 88s, eight Bf 110s, four Bf 109s, three He 111s, two Hs 126s, two Hs 123s and two Ju 52s. This number includes losses from front-line fighters and from ground fire.

The 6th IAK PVO lost twenty-five fighters in combat in February. Five of them were shot down in air battles, three by anti-aircraft artillery, five were destroyed on airfields and thirteen were missing. Hurricanes suffered the heaviest losses, at twelve aircraft, followed by five MiG-3s and four Pe-3s. Two Yak-1s, one Tomahawk and a U-2 biplane were also lost.

Hurricanes Battle

At the beginning of the calendar spring (in Central Russia winter lasts until the end of March, if snow cover is presentuntil the beginning of April) fierce fighting continued on the Eastern Front. Russians strained all forces, trying to break through the German defences. But 1812 was not repeated. The Wehrmacht managed to hold the front and defend many strongpoints. The Russian troops perished in whole armies, but the brutal dictator continued to drive the poorly-armed soldiers to the slaughterhouse.

In the area of the Valdai hills Soviet troops advanced deep into the remote forest areas around Andreapol and Toropets. In early March, the offensive halted on the line desperately held by the Germans strongholds: Staraya Russa – Holm – Velikie Luki – Veliz – Demidov – Beliy. The huge Andreapol salient was formed, its right flank twisted around the Demyansk 'fortress' (held since 7 February by cut-off elements of the Sixteenth Army), its left around another German strongpoint at Olenino. In the area of Rzhev, Sychevka, Gzhatsk and Vyazma the German Ninth Army continued to defend in a semi-circle, beating off the endless Russian attacks from the east, north and west. In the German rear, to the south-west of Vyazma and to the east of Smolensk, elements of the Soviet 33rd Army, the 1st Guards Cavalry Corps, the 4th Airborne Corps and numerous guerrilla groups were active. But the most important railway line, Smolensk–Yartsevo–Vyazma–Sychevka–Rzhev–Olenino, was controlled by German mobile units and garrisons.

To the south the troops of the Soviet 10th Army cut the Bryansk–Vyazma railway and reached Kirov. At this time 61st Army units almost cut off another of Hitler's 'winter fortresses', Bolkhov. In March, fierce battles for Rzhev, Vyazma, Yukhnov and the Warsaw highway south-west of Yukhnov began.

On 1 March the 6th IAK PVO had 492 fighters, 290 of which were considered serviceable. In a more favourable condition were the regiments equipped with MiG-3s and Yak-1s (thanks to the manufacturers being nearby), and I-16s and I-153s (the 'old types', as they were called in Russian, which were easier to repair). At this time, more than half of the Hurricanes and Tomahawks were out of action because of a shortage of foreign spare parts. In the spring of 1942, to replace Tomahawks in the Soviet Union, a new modification, the P-40E Kittyhawk, began to be delivered. In March, the first such machines arrived with the 126th IAP. In Russian combat magazines, both types of aircraft were called the 'Curtiss' or P-40.

The wooden Russian LaGG-3 fighters showed themselves to be poorly suited for winter conditions, and very complicated to maintain. As a result, only a quarter of the available fighters of this type could be kept in good condition. Serial production of the MiG-3 was discontinued at this time. The aircraft had been created as a high-altitude interceptor for action at altitudes of 8,000–10,000m (26,250–32,800ft). But the air war on the Eastern Front was conducted at low and medium altitudes: 90 per cent of flights took place at 300–3,000m (984–9,840ft). In such circumstances, the MiG-3 expended too much fuel, and its endurance was extremely low (the fighter could only be in the air for a maximum of 45–50 minutes). The MiG-3 had a weak armament (one 12.7mm machine gun and two 7.6mm ShKAS), and was poorly suited to attacking ground targets. The decisive reason for its cancellation was the shortage of AM-38 engines for the Il-2 (the AM-35 engine of the MiG-3 was almost an exact copy). In addition, the Soviet leadership decided that having three different types of fighter aircraft (the MiG-3, LaGG-3 and Yak-1/Yak-7) in service was not rational. This made it difficult to maintain and train pilots.

On 23 December 1941 Stalin ordered production of the MiG-3 to cease and for Aviation Plant No. 1 to switch to his favourite 'flying tank', the Il-2. In the Soviet Union there was a vicious practice of making all key decisions by one person, a typical feature of all totalitarian regimes. The 'Great Leader' personally chose which aircraft were needed and which were not needed. The role of the retinue and the military was reduced only to 'prompting' and hints. The country had a huge bureaucratic system and many departments. In this the USSR was similar to the Third Reich. The adoption of new weapons and equipment did not take place in competition, but through intrigue, corruption and cunning. The final decision in all cases was by the 'wisest of the wise', Joseph Stalin.

But, having gone into production before the war, the MiG-3, Yak-1 and LaGG-3 did not meet expectations. Therefore, in the spring of 1942, the share of 'obsolete' I-153 and I-16 fighters in many aviation units was greater than the new ones. The Pe-3 heavy fighter, created by Russian designers as an equivalent to the German Bf 110, also did not meet expectations. The Russian *Zerstorer* was not used in its designed role, but for long-range reconnaissance and bombing attacks. In early March, the 95th IAP was transferred from the 6th IAK PVO to naval aviation.

Aircraft in the 6th IAK PVO on 1 March 1942

Type	Total	Serviceable
MiG-3	199	133
Hurricane	112	52
I-16	67	46
LaGG-3	39	11
Yak-1	22	15
Pe-3	22	13
P-40	16	5
I-153	15	15
Total	492	290

On 1 March, the 6th IAK PVO carried out 340 sorties, but there was only one contact with the Luftwaffe. At 17.05 in the Medyn area a group of nine MiG-3s of the 120th IAP met a group of eight Ju 88s, which were escorted by fifteen 'Me 109s'. During the big dogfight Lieutenant Rubtsov damaged one 'Messer', and one more was brought down by Lieutenant Sorokin. But these victories are not confirmed by German information.

In the following days, due to thaws and snowfalls, the number of flights decreased, and no encounters with the enemy were recorded. On 4 March in the Yukhnov area Lieutenant Tchemodanov of the 429th IAP in a Hurricane downed an 'Me 109'. This victory is not confirmed.

On the night of 5/6 March after a long pause Luftwaffe resumed air raids on Moscow. At 00.56 the air alarm was declared in the city, and shortly afterwards came the first group of bombers. The raid, which involved seventeen aircraft, lasted until 03.25. In total, sixteen high-explosive and eighty heavy incendiary bombs were dropped. The consequences of this air attack were very serious. A textile factory, the three-storey No. 32 Gorky Street and the four-storey No 18 Korovinskoye Street were destroyed. One of the targets of the attack was again the Kremlin. Three high-explosive bombs fell in the grounds of the ancient fortress. One exploded near the Nabatnaya tower, near the Spassky gate, destroying the shelter which hid eight soldiers of the guard regiment. The second bomb exploded in the square near the commandant's office, and the third at the Archangel Cathedral. Many buildings in the Kremlin were damaged, window frames and doors flew out, and plaster fell. Twelve people were killed and thirty-two were wounded. In total, 30 people were killed and 102 wounded in the city. Ten fighters (MiG-3s and Hurricanes) of the 16th, 34th and 429th IAP took off to intercept but the hunt was fruitless. This raid was carried out on the personal orders of the commander of VIII *Fliegerkorps* Generaloberst von Richthofen, largely for propaganda purposes. German newspapers and radio could report: the Luftwaffe has again bombed the Russian capital and the Kremlin.

By the afternoon of 6 March the fighters of the 6th IAK PVO has completed 232 sorties. Hurricanes of the 67th, 287th, 429th and 736th IAP, MiG-3s of the 27th and 233th IAP, Yak-1s of the 562nd IAP and Kittihawks of the 126th IAP operated on the distant frontiers, protecting their troops in the Danilino, Emel'yanovka, Bykovo, Kostrovo, Akatovka and Gryaznaya areas (126 sorties). At this time, the Yak-1s, I-16s, MiG-3s and I-153s of the 11th, 177th, 445th, 564th and 565th IAP were engaged in covering the railway traffic on the Maloyaroslavets–Tikhonova Pustyn and Maloyaroslavets–Kaluga lines (seventy-six sorties). The MiG-3s, I-16s and LaGG-3s of the 34th, 171st, 176th, 178th and 423rd IAP defended airfields Lipitsy, Kubinka, Klin and Tula (38 sorties).

Ten air battles and four victories were registered. The P-40 pilot Lieutenant Nikolai Samokhvalov shot down an He 111 in the Bolschoye Ustye area, while the other five Tomahawks led by Captain Arsenin shot

The Krasnaya Presnya district of Moscow, victim of bomb attacks in early 1942

down a Ju 88 in the same area. The third group of P-40s shot down an 'Me 109' north-west of Yukhnov (Lieutenant Efim Lozovoy was credited with one-quarter of a victory).

The war diary of the 445th IAP described a battle as follows:

> 2 I-16 – the pilots, Lieutenant Ruchkin and Sergeant Elagin 445th IAP while on patrol in the area of Tikhonova Pustyn met 10 Me 110. After two attacks of a distance of 300–400 metres of the group leader of the enemy, the Me110 went in a westerly direction, and the group disbanded on 2–3 aircraft. Sergeant Elagin in that time led the air combat on a collision course with another Me110, hit him with the second attack, but was himself attacked by three Me 110s – imitated disorderly fall and came out of the battle. Lieutenant Ruchkin came out of the battle, manoeuvring in height and direction.

According to German sources, only one Bf 110 E-3, of Stab./StG 2, was lost on the entire Eastern Front on that day. But it was destroyed in the night of 5/6 March at the airfield at Vyazma as a result of an air raid by Soviet aircraft. This attack was carried out by aircraft of the Western Front, which managed to destroy or damage eleven German aircraft: four Do 17s and five Fw 189 As of 2.(F)/11, one Bf 110 E-3 and one Fi 156.

Russian aviation also suffered losses. For example, over Yukhnov in combat with a Bf 109 the Hurricane of Lieutenant Pavel Leontiev of 67th IAP. He bailed out but was seriously injured. He was one of the veterans of the regiment, having fought since the first day of the war. Flying the I-16 above Moldova, from 22 June to 23 July 1941 Leontiev won three personal and two group victories, shooting down one 'Me 109', an 'Me 110', a PZL-24, an Hs 126 and a Ju 88. By the time of his fatal fight on 6 March, Leontiev had carried out 175 combat missions. After treatment, the pilot was no longer involved in the fighting, and became an inspector of piloting techniques.

The Combat Strength of the 6th IAK PVO on 5 March 1942

Regiment	Airfield	Aircraft	Total	Serviceable
11th IAP	The Central Airfield of Moscow, Edrovo	Yak-1	16	13
16th IAP	Lyubertsy	MiG-3	32	25
27th IAP	Starisha	MiG-3 I-16	20 1	13 1
34th IAP	Vnukovo	MiG-3	20	19
67th IAP	Kubinka	Hurricane	19	7
120th IAP	The Central airfield of Moscow	MiG-3	28	20
126th IAP	Chkalovsk	P-40	16	5
171st IAP	Tula	MiG-3 I-16	10 5	5 3
176th IAP	Yurkino	MiG-3 I-16	12 4	9 4
177th IAP	Podolsk	MiG-3 I-16	10 10	5 7
178th IAP	Lipids	LaGG-3 I-16	13 11	4 7
233rd IAP	Tushino	MiG-3 I-16	11 4	6 4

Regiment	Airfield	Aircraft	Total	Serviceable
287th IAP	Khimki	Hurricane	19	8
291st IAP	Monino	LaGG-3	9	2
309th IAP	Gridino	Hurricane	16	11
423rd IAP	Tula	MiG-3	10	5
		I-16	6	4
428th IAP	Dubrovitsy	MiG-3	17	8
429th IAP	Cubinka	Hurricane	18	4
445th IAP	Kashira	MiG-3	9	5
		I-16	11	7
488th IAP	Monino	Hurricane	18	8
455th IAP	Ryazan	I-16	14	9
562th IAP	Khimki	Yak-1	8	3
564th IAP	Philly	LaGG-3	13	5
		I-153	6	6
565th IAP	Ramenskoe	MiG-3	10	5
		I-16	4	3
736th IAP	Khimki	Hurricane	20	6
Headquarters 6th IAK	Moscow	MiG-3	2	2
		Total	452	258

On 7 March the pilots of the 287th IAP again excelled themselves. Six Hurricanes led by Captain Nicholay Khramov engaged in battle with four Bf 109s in Yukhnov area, which resulted in Khramov and his lead pilot shooting down one German fighter. In the same area Lieutenant Bychkov brought down an 'He 113'. The German data confirm the loss of one Bf 109 F-2 W. Nr. 8325 of 4./JG 51.

At 12.27 the MRU-105 radar in the city of Klin detected a Ju 88 flying at high altitude. Three MiG-3s of the 27th IAP took off to intercept it. Soon Lieutenant Arkady Kovachevich, with the help of radio navigation, spotted the enemy, flying at an altitude of 6,000m (19,685ft). Seeing the interceptor, the pilot of the Ju 88 turned 180° and began to head west, while gaining altitude. According to Kovachevich's report, he managed to overtake the reconnaissance aircraft at a height of 8,000m (2,625ft). During the first attack, Kovachevich, as required in the instructions, killed the rear gunner, then began to shoot at the engines. Soon they caught fire and the Ju 88 crashed in flames near the village of Subbotniki.

In fact, Ju 88 D-5 W. Nr. 1719 of 4.(F)/14 was damaged, and then received further damage in an emergency landing at the airport at Smolensk. Aboard Ju 88s there was a special device called a 'smoker', designed to mislead enemy pilots. At the right time, a portion of engine oil was injected into the combustion chambers of the engines. This created a highly visible smoke trail, stretching behind the aircraft for a few minutes (until the oil was burnt up). Seeing the smoke, the Russian pilots believed that the engine was on fire and prematurely broke off the pursuit. The short endurance of the fighter contributed to this. The pilots did not want get caught up in a long chase and risk being left with insufficient fuel. Particularly once over German territory, they sought to quickly return to base.

On 9 March, air defence fighters performed 333 sorties and conducted five air battles. Kittihawks of the 126th IAP shot down two 'Me 109s' in the Yukhnov area, and another German fighter shot down near Kalynovka was credited to Lieutenant Vladimir Kamenschikov. A group of five MiG-3s of the 34th IAP, led by Captain Michael Naidenko, shot down a Ju 88 in the Dobroye area (credited to all five pilots). The Hurricane pilot Lieutenant

UTI-4 training aircraft, used as a light bomber

Russian propaganda poster showing the defeat of the Luftwaffe over Moscow

Grobovoy of the 287th IAP was credited with an aerial victory over an 'Me 109' in the Morozovo area. But in this case, all the victories of Russian pilots are not confirmed.

On 10–11 March heavy snowfall hampered aviation operations. On the 12th, the 6th IAK PVO carried out 300 sorties, but only one aerial combat was recorded. In the Gzhatsk area Lieutenant Sergey Rubtsov of the 12th Guards IAPshot down an Hs 126 reconnaissance aircraft. It was Hs 126 B-1 W. Nr. 4054 of 3.(H)/13. One crew member was killed and the other seriously injured. Between 13–15 March the weather in the Moscow area was again inclement, and the aircraft did not operate.

In the second half of March, the employment of Russian fighters changed. To cover their troops near the front lines mainly Hurricanes of the 67th, 287th, 429th and 736th IAP and Kittihawks of the 126th IAP were mainly used, also periodically MiG-3s of the 27th and 34th IAP. Patrols over Moscow, Tula and other important targets were basically carried out by the MiG-3s of the 12th Guards, 16th, 171st, 233rd and 423rd IAP. The I-16, I-153 and LaGG-3 fighters were withdrawn to the 'third line', being assigned a supporting role (protection of airfields, weather reconnaissance and patrolling over railways). Often the mission of fighters was be seen in the sky and raise the morale of railway workers and the local population.

Most of the fighters' sorties did not see contact with the Luftwaffe. On 17 March, Lieutenant Krukov of 428 IAP tried to intercept a single Do 215 in the Kamenka area, but after the first attack his MiG-3 suffered engine failure. On 18 March despite 251 sorties only one aerial combat was recorded. In the Krasny Holm area six Hurricanes of the 429th IAP shot down a Ju 88 (not confirmed).

On the morning of 19 March, two Bf 110s carried out a sudden air raid on Kubinka airfield, dropping ten high-explosive and eleven fragmentation bombs on it. A Hurricane of the 67th IAP was destroyed, with three mechanics being killed and one injured.

Despite the snowfall, haze and heavy clouds the day was full of air battles. The pilots of the 6th IAK PVO claimed five air victories. Four MiG-3s of the 34th IAP and two MiG-3 of the 1st IAP PV NKVD shot down an 'Me 110' near Staritsa. Four MiG-3s of the 34th IAP in the Uvarovka area met a group of fifteen 'Me 110' and hit one of them (six pilots shared the victory, including Lieutenant Korobov). While covering troops near Rzhev, a group of eight Hurricanes of the 287th and 736th IAP met a large group of Ju 87s and Ju 88s at an altitude of 700m (2,297ft), which was accompanied by a pair of *Zerstorers* and four 'Me 109s'. The Russians reported that the battle ended with the complete defeat of the Luftwaffe. The element of Lieutenant Grobovoy shot down two bombers, after which the rest jettisoned their bombs and disappeared. During the battle with the fighters, the Hurricane of Lieutenant Bychkov shot down another 'Me 109'.

In fact, the Germans lost four aircraft in the Moscow area:

- Ju 88 A-5 W. Nr. 3655 'B3+BP' of 6./KG 54 was missing near Rzhev along with the crew;
- Bf 109 E-7 W. Nr. 2805 (white 'R') of 4./Sch.G 1 was shot down by a fighter, its pilot Unteroffizier W. Broddem still listed as missing;
- Bf 110 E-3 W. Nr. 2456 'T6+FA' of St./StG 2 'Immelmann' was missing in the Staritsa area The crew of three Feldwebels: A. Buchholz, W. Hahn and K. Doerr disappeared forever in the white haze...;
- Bf 110 C-7 W. Nr. 3635 of I./NJG 4 was shot down by anti-aircraft artillery in the area of Gzhatsk. The crew, Leutnant R. Kottmann and Unteroffizier W. Braun, were killed.

At 10.30 on 20 March eight Ju 88 As has carried out an air raid on the city of Klin, including the local airfield. Only one MiG-3 of the 27th IAP was damaged. Taking off to intercept, Lieutenants Matakov and Alexander Chilikin claimed two air victories, but they are not confirmed by the German data. In the Yagodino Hurricane pilot Lieutenant Glazunov shot down an 'Me 109'. In fact he damaged Bf 109 F-2 W. Nr. 9229 of St.III./JG 51 which crashed during an emergency landing at Dugino airfield.

The number of serviceable British fighters had by this time been greatly reduced, so they began to send on missions mixed groups from several aviation regiments. Hurricanes went to the most dangerous part of the front near Rzhev, where German planes often appeared.

At 13.55 on 21 March, above Panino railway station nine Hurricanes of the 287th, 488th and 736th IAP entered into a dogfight with a group of 'He 113s' and 'Me 109s'. As a result, Captain Nikolai Khramov and Lieutenant Bychkov were each credited with one personal victory, but these are not confirmed by Luftwaffe information.

On 22 March in the same area (the village of Dengino) an element of Kittihawks led by Lieutenant Ivan Lozowoy of the 126th IAP shot down two 'Me 109s'. In fact the ground-attack Bf 109 E-7 W. Nr. 6142 Unteroffizier F. Wolf of 4./Sch.G1 was shot down, which according to German data went missing in the Rzhev area.

On 23–27 March the weather in the Moscow area was once again cloudy and snowy. Aircraft operations were limited and without result.

On 26 March at both 11.21 and 14. 27 the Luftwaffe bombed the city of Klin, but all bombs fell wide of the target. A similarly inaccurate air raid on Moscow took place on the night of 26/27 March.

The Luftwaffe Angers Stalin Again

On 28 March, the weather remained inclement. The 6th IAK PVO carried out only 101 sorties, the majority to cover rail transport. After dark, at 20.00 there was a mysterious episode. A group of Russian bombers returned from a mission to the airfield at Klin. Three unidentified twin-engined aircraft joined them from behind, dropping red flares, the current signal for friendly aircraft. But the 'behaviour' of these 'UFOs' seemed suspicious to those on the ground, and the signal for permission to land was not given. After that, the three unidentified aircraft dived and dropped fifteen high-explosive bombs. A U-2 communication plane was damaged. One house was destroyed and two soldiers of the 601st Airfield Battalion were killed in the village of Maidanovo adjacent to the base. It is unknown whether the aircraft were Russian or German. Simultaneously with this a single aircraft dropped three high-explosive bombs on Moscow. Air-raid alert was declared in 19.53 and continued until 21.10. The bombs exploded in a park near the 'Dynamo' stadium. No one was hurt.

By the end of March, the area of combat work of air defence fighters decreased. At the beginning of the month they operated to the line Rzhev – Gzhatsk – Vyazma – Yukhnov, now flights reached to the line Volokolamsk – Mozhaisk - Maloyaroslavets – Kaluga.

On 29 March, the 6th IAK PVO completed 223 sorties. Two air battles and one air victory were recorded. Lieutenant Arkady Kovachevich of the 27th IAP shot down a Ju 88 in the Gzhatsk district of. It was in fact probably He 111 H-6 W. Nr. 4975 'A1+BA' of the Stab./KG 53 'Legion Condor'.

At 20.20 the Luftwaffe carried out a massive attack on the airfield at Klin (according to Soviet information, fifty aircraft were involved), dropping thirty-eight high-explosive bombs. Many buildings, hangars and nearby houses were damaged, and the runway was completely put out of action.

Simultaneously with this, an air raid was carried out on Moscow, eight high-explosive bombs being dropped. The Rostokinsky district was seriously damaged, several houses being destroyed there. An eight-storey house on Myasnitskaya Street completely collapsed. One of the bombs again fell near the Kremlin – in the Tainitsky garden opposite the Nameless Tower. A truck loaded with ammunition exploded, killing the two people standing next to it. In all, fifteen people were killed and ninety-six injured.

On 30 March, the Luftwaffe carried out a raid on Serpukhov, three aircraft dropping five high-explosive bombs, which exploded in the city centre. The city water supply, power lines, railway tracks and three houses were destroyed. Many people were killed and injured.

On this day the 6th IAK PVO completed 324 sortied. Two air combats and one victory were recorded. A group of Yak-1s of the 11th IAP, headed by Lieutenant Zuyev, shot down an 'Me 109' in the Presnetsovo area (not confirmed).

On the night of 30/31 March, a single German plane again dropped three high-explosive bombs on Moscow, which fell on the warehouse of the fruit and vegetable plant on the Nagatinsky highway. Four people were killed and three were injured. Fighters of the 6th IAK PVO carried out nineteen sorties (involving only the MiG-3s of the 16th, 34th, 177th and 428th IAP), but they were to no avail. According to German information, Bf 110 night fighters of I./NJG 4 carried out these raids on Moscow. The Russian capital was bombed by the new commander of this aviation group, Hauptmann W. Tierfelder.

On the afternoon of 31 March, air defence pilots reported five air battles and three victories. Lieutenant Sorokin of the 12th Guards IAP in the Koloch district shot down an 'Me 109 F'. A pair of MiG-3s of the 27th IAP in the area of the 'Moscow Sea' (the Ivankovo Reservoir), after ten attacks hit a Ju 88 at an altitude of 4,000m (13,123ft). Lieutenant Arkady Kovachevich intercepted another Ju 88 in the Uvarovo area at an altitude of 8,000m (26,246ft). According to the pilot's report, after eight attacks, the enemy plane, with burning engines, came down near the village of Sloboda (30km [19 miles] south of Gzhatsk). In fact, the Do 17 M W. Nr. 2306 of 2.(F)/Nacht damaged by Kovachevich crashed during an emergency landing at the airfield at Smolensk. Two crew members were seriously injured.

This was the last victory of the ace Arkady Kovachevich in the 6th IAK PVO. From 18 October 1941 to 31 March 1942 he won eight personal and one group victory, at least four of which appear to be confirmed by German information. Later, Kovachevich fought at Stalingrad in the 27th IAP, then in the 9th Guard IAP. By the end of the war, the Hero of the Soviet Union Captain Kovachevich had nineteen personal and five group victories.

Order on 'April Fool's Day'

The air attacks on Moscow, Serpukhov and Klin carried out in late March did not lead to much damage, but made a lot of noise. And they greatly frightened Stalin. Sitting in his Kremlin office, the leader heard explosions only 200m (219 yards) away from him. One of the bombs dropped by I./NJG 4 could have killed the Bolshevik dictator and changed the course of history! So, a minorair raid had serious consequences.

On 1 April, 'April Fool's Day' Stalin wrote a note, in which there was no hint of humour, and addressed it at once to all his trembling servants, namely to the chief of NKVD, Lavrenty Beria, the commander of the air defence of the USSR General Mikhail Gromadin and the Procurator of the USSR Bochkov. In the note, Stalin pointed out:

> As you can see, Moscow peveo [Stalin wrote anti-aircraft defence with a Caucasian accent!] was not working properly:
>
> 1. The gunners in Klin were not at their positions; peveo slept through the raid on Moscow.
> 2. Comrades Beria, Gromadin and Bochkov are instructed to urgently investigate the matter and report back.

Such an order did not imply a thorough investigation of the circumstances and an honest investigation. He meant: quickly find the guilty and punish them. In two days the Commission finished its work and found all the culprits! They were the 'systematically drunk' Military Commissar of the Main Directorate of Air Defence of the USSR Brigade Commissar Kurganov, the chronic alcoholic Chief of the Main Directorate of Air Defence Major General Alexei Osipov, the 'soundly' and permanently drunk Commissar of the 745th Anti-Aircraft Artillery Regiment Zakharov. Kurganov and Zakharov were convicted by the tribunal, and Osipov was dismissed from his post.[6]

The Commission found that the surveillance and warning service (VNOS) worked poorly, and the observers were poorly trained in aircraft recognition. They confused enemy planes with their own (the Bf 110 with the and the Bf 109 with the Hurricane), and were slow to raise the alarm.

---

6. In May 1942, Osipov was forgiven and appointed commander of the air defences of the city of Gorky.

The 6th IAK PVO also came in for criticism. A special order said that too many fighters were under repair, radio communication to guide aircraft from the ground was badly used, etc.

The Moscow Air Defence Front (MF PVO) was created, and ordered to strengthen its anti-aircraft guns, including 272 guns taken from various fronts. Stalin ordered that the air defence of Moscow be made 'completely impenetrable'.

Statistics for March

In this month the 6th IAK PVO performed 5,552 sorties. The average flight duration of Russian fighters increased from 1.05 hours to 1.15 hours. This was due to a significant number of British and American aircraft being employed. Of the total sorties, 2,674 were from the protection of railway facilities and transport, 1,589 for the protection of troops, 535 to cover airfields, 291 to cover airborne assault forces, 163 for interception, 121 for protection of the cities, 76 to cover the loading and unloading of troops, 48 for patrolling searchlight fields, 29 for exercises and flying around observation posts 28 to support transport aircraft, and 22 for aerial reconnaissance. The activity of the Luftwaffe increased significantly in March, in fact almost doubling. During the month in the Moscow area 1,501 flights of German aircraft were recorded in the Moscow area.

The huge number of flights of Russian fighters did not correspond to the number of air battles and victories. The vast majority of flights took place without result. The 6th IAK PVO reported forty-three aircraft shot down, including twenty-six 'Me 109s'. The greatest success was achieved by the 287th IAP, equipped Hurricanes, which scored fourteen aerial victories. The 12th Guards IAP and 27th IAP were each credited with six aircraft shot down. Losses were proportionate to the declared success – fourteen aircraft (eleven Hurricanes and three MiG-3s) shot down in aerial combat or missing. In the consumption of ammunition, in first place again were Lend-Lease Colt-Browning cartridges – 84,052 rounds. Hurricanes again fired the most!

In March the Luftwaffe carried out six air raids on Moscow. According to the Russian rescue service, 37 residents were killed and 169 wounded. No German bombers were lost or damaged during these raids.

The real losses of Luftwaffe in the Moscow area were much less than the victories declared by the air defence pilots. A total only thirteen aircraft can be established, including four Bf 109s, four Bf 110s, two Ju 88s, one Hs 126, one He 111 and one Do 17. In March he withdrawal of units of VIII *Fliegerkorps* from the central sector of the front for rest and refitting began. Almost all twin-engined bombers had gone. In March, the greatest load in the central sector fell on Bf 110 *Zerstorers* and night fighters, which suffered the heaviest losses. Fifteen Bf 110s of ZG 26, II./ZG 1, I./NJG 4, I./NJG 3 and StG 2 were shot down by fighters and anti-aircraft artillery or crashed due to weather conditions or technical problems. Another twelve suffered damage between 25 per cent and 65 per cent on the German scale.

The Last Raid of the 'Death's Heads'

In April, the spring thaw began in Russia. Russian offensive operations were exhausted, and the pressure on the Germans was relieved. After fierce fighting and numerous fruitless sorties, Russian aviation was also weakened. The number of fighters in the 6th IAK PVO decreased to 377, of which only 200 were in good condition as of 5 April. Thirteen squadrons only had between two and eight serviceable aircraft available. At that time, the Russian aircraft factories could not quickly replace lost equipment. Only a third of the Hurricanes were serviceable.

Fighter Aircraft in the 6th IAK PVO on 5 April 1942

Type	Number	Serviceable
MiG-3	159	94
Hurricane	97	29
I-16	44	36
Yak-1	27	21
I-153	19	12
LaGG-3	19	3
P-40	12	5
Total	377	200

In the Moscow area the first few days of April were peaceful and there was no air combat. Then on 6 April an element of Yak-1s of the 562th IAP, carrying out a patrol mission over the railway, was suddenly attacked near Batyushkovo by four Bf 109s that shot down the fighter of Lieutenant

Samsonov. According to German data, the only Yak-1 downed in this sector of the front on this day is credited to Feldwebel Richard Kwante of 6./JG 51.

The Luftwaffe took advantage of a 'window' of good weather and on the same day suddenly carried out an air raid on Moscow. A pair of Ju 88 A-4 dive bombers of II./KG 54 'Totenkopf' dropped seven high-explosive bombs on the city. On Bolshaya Polyanka Street in Moskvoretsky district, the building of the district Council was destroyed by a direct hit, while in the Leningradsky district a water main and water tower were hit. Five people were killed and ten injured. The bombers with 'pirate symbols' – skull and crossbones on the fuselage – arrived over Moscow without having been spotted and no air alarm was sounded.

After this, air raids on the 'Red Stronghold' stopped, which was a surprise to the command of the Russian air defences and the residents of Moscow. Air raids were not resumed in the summer and autumn of 1942. The Russians thought it was thanks to their air defences, the anti-aircraft artillery and fighters. They thought that the Germans were 'afraid of Russian defence' and 'had to give up this idea' . . .

But from April 1942 the Luftwaffe halted heavy air raids on Russian cities behind the front line in Army Group Centre's sector. Even important industrial and transport centres such as Gorky, Yaroslavl, Rybinsk, Stalinogorsk and Ryazan lived quietly and safely in this period. There were sporadic air attacks on them, but without heavy damage and casualties. Air raids against major Russian cities were resumed only in June 1943, on the direct orders of the Luftwaffe High Command (OKL).

The reason for the 'humane' attitude to Russian cities in this sector of the front (in the northern and southern sectors cities were bombed mercilessly) lies in the identity of the commander of the Luftwaffe in the area. In early April, after the stabilization of the situation at the front, the commander of VIII *Fliegerkorps*, Generaloberst von Richthofen, was sent on leave, and later Hitler ordered him to go to the Crimea and to support the Eleventh Army under Manstein. The aggressive and bloodthirsty Richthofen did not hide his pleasure at fires, large-scale destruction and murder (he wrote about it in his diary). He was an active supporter of the destruction of enemy cities. In 1942 Richthofen consistently 'burned' Kerch and Sevastopol, then Voronezh, Rostov-on-Don, Stalingrad, Astrakhan, Grozny, Ordzhonikidze and others.

Luftkommando Ost was formed in the central sector of the front. Its commander was Generaloberst Robert von Greim. He was the opposite of Richthofen: cautious, gentle to subordinates and kind in nature. Greim had no hatred of the Russians and other 'non-Aryan' peoples. In addition, he protected his subordinates. He was not a supporter of terror attacks on cities.

In the first half of April, Luftwaffe got a break. Because of the *rasputitsa*, the airfields were buried in mud, while wet and rainy weather and low clouds prevented flying.

The Luftwaffe Vanish into the Clouds . . .

The clouds cleared on 15 April. On this day, the 6th IAK PVO carried out 143 sorties. For the first time American P-39 Airacobra fighters appeared over the Eastern Front. Deliveries of these aircraft to the Soviet Union under the Lend-Lease programme had begun in March 1942. Training pilots to fly on the P-39 took place in the small town of Kineshma (located on the Volga 300km [186 miles] north-east of Moscow). The first regiment which mastered the Airacobra was the 28th IAP of 6th IAK PVO. All the best equipment was sent to protect Stalin's residence as a priority!

Russian fighters had almost no encounters with the Luftwaffe. I-16s of the 178th IAP, Hurricanes of the 488th IAP and I-153s of the 565th IAP made several sorties to intercept German planes in the Orekhovo-Zuyevo, Serpukhov and Kolomna areas. But all they ended inconclusively. The target, which the Russian hunters were trying to catch, was reconnaissance aircraft Ju 88 D-1 W. Nr. 1419 of 1.(F)/Ob.d.L. But all of them failed. However, when the Ju 88 D flew west to its base in Orsha, it was intercepted by a pair of MiG-3s of the 34th IAP in the Gzhatsk area. The pilots were guided to the plane by radio and shot it down. The crew was listed as missing.

In the days that followed Russian pilots in the Moscow area suffered setbacks. On 17 April, a pair of Hurricanes of 488th IAP attacked a single Ju 88 in Detchino district. But it was able to get away from the fighters. Lieutenant Kudinov pursued the scout to the German territory, where he was shot down by anti-aircraft artillery.

On 18 April, the 6th IAK PVO carried out 157 sorties, 59 of them to intercept German planes. But only Sergeant Major Nikolai Dudnik from the 178th IAP intercepted an He 111 in the Serpukhov district. His I-16 carried out one attack, then pursued the German plane towards the west. But soon Dudnik ran low on fuel, and broke off the pursuit.

The command of the 6th IAK PVO stated:

> Of the three aircraft during the day, flying in the area of fighters of the 6th IAK, only one reconnaissance aircraft

was intercepted by fighters. The reasons that hinder the implementation of guidance and interception are:

1. The lack of a clear organization of guidance at the Klin airbase.
2. Erroneous data from ground observation posts about the height and course of the enemy aircraft.
3. Insufficient attention by pilots.
4. Dispatch of aircraft without radios to intercept the enemy (565th IAP).
5. Lack of communication between the 6th IAK headquarters and many guidance posts.

On 20 April, Lieutenant Kostenko of the 27th IAP, who took off to intercept an enemy aircraft, found it in the Teryaeva Sloboda area, but could not intercept it because of the mistakenly determined altitude of the target by the controllers at Klin. In the Tikhonova Pustyn area, a pair of I-153s of the 565th IAP attacked an He 111 at an altitude of 3,800m (12,467ft), but it used its superior speed to simply leave the slow-moving biplanes behind, heading straight back to the west. A pair of Kittihawks of the 126th IAP had an inconclusive dogfight in the Kaluga district with a Ju 88, which disappeared into the clouds.

On 21 April, the 6th IAK PVO carried out 221 sorties, including 30 to intercept German aircraft in the Solnechnogorsk, Dmitrov, Krasnogorsk, Naro-Fominsk, Pereslavl-Zalessky and Alexandrov areas (90–100km [56–62 miles] north-east of Moscow). The MiG-3 of Lieutenant Eremenko of the 34th IAP attacked four Ju 88s in the Naro-Fominsk district, which (according to the testimony of the pilot) jettisoned their bombs and fled to the west. In the Tikhonova Pustyn area a pair of I-153s of the 564th IAP encountered three Ju 88s (probably the same ones) and unsuccessfully tried to attack them. Two P-40s of the 126th IAP conducted an unsuccessful air battle with an 'Me 110' in the Detchino area. Probably it was in fact a Do 17 P reconnaissance aircraft, as during this period there were no Bf 110s serving in *Luftkommando Ost*.

At this time on the Eastern Front, the weather became calm and sunny, the temperature rising to 15° Celsius. Fed up of the exhausting winter battles, the men were basking in the sun.

On 22 April, the air defence pilots had completed 175 sorties, including 91 fordefence of railway transportation, 41 to cover road transport, 18 in

Wreckage Bf 109 F

defence of airfields, 12 for interception, 9 to cover the river crossing at Nara and 4 to escort PS-84 transport aircraft on the Moscow–Yaroslavl routes. Patrol sorties over the highway and railways were carried out by pairs of fighters in a 20–40km (12–25 mile) area at altitudes of 2,000–5,000m (6,562–16,404ft). The change of patrols took place in the air. Interception

213

Thawed after winter the wreckage of the Russian fighter in the winter camouflage

of single targets was carried out with the help of British MRU-105 radar stations at Vnukovo, Lyubertsy and Khimki and the RUS-2 radar at Klin. But on this day there were no successful interceptions. A pair of fighters of the 27th IAP was intercepted by two Bf 109 Fs near Klin, which in a sudden attack out of the sun shot down the MiG-3 of Lieutenant Zhuravlev. The pilot bailed out safely.

On 23 April a pair of MiG-3s of the 12th Guards IAP in the area of Medyn attacked two Ju 88s at an altitude of 1,500m (4,921ft) and shot down one of them. The victory was credited to Lieutenant Sergey Rubtsov. Another pair of pilots from the 34th IAP reported another Ju 88 downed in the Yukhnov area. But neither of these victories are confirmed by German sources.

On 24 April the 6th IAK PVO carried out 135 sorties and fought two aerial combats. Captain Mikhail Naidenko of the 34th IAP intercepted a Ju 88 with the help of radio guidance in the Uvarovo area, flying at an altitude of 3,000m (9,843ft). According to the pilot's report, 'the enemy plane, with an engine on fire and losing altitude, crossed the front line'. In the same area, Lieutenants Bikov and Georgi Urvachev of the 34th IAP attacked a Ju 88. The target disappeared into the clouds, also 'with an engine on fire'.

At the end of the month the weather in the Moscow area deteriorated. The rains began and the airfields were put out of action. Then there was a sudden cold snap and in places it even snowed again. On 25 April no Russian aircraft took off, and the next day only twenty-three sorties were carried out. On 27 April, a pair of MiG-3s of the 27th IAP took off to intercept a Ju 88 in the Taldom area and at an altitude of 7,000m (22,966ft) attacked it. But then both fighters' armament jammed completely and they had to return to base. As it turned out, the technicians had mixed up the varieties of oil and had lubricated the guns with the wrong composition.

Statistics for April

The 6th IAK PVO carried out 3,512 sorties, just over 2,000 less than in March. Of these, 2,255 were to cover railway facilities and transportation, 403 for interceptions and 140 to protect troops.

Russian ground observation posts and radar stations recorded 438 flights of German aircraft in the Moscow area. But this information contained a lot of errors. Sixty-nine targets were not identified, and ten were identified as Do 215s.

In April, four victories were scored only by pilots of the 12th Guards IAP and the 34th IAP. Only one of these is confirmed. Their losses were three fighters (one Yak-1, on MiG-3 and one Hurricane).

Conclusion

In April 1942, the battle for Moscow came to an end. The Wehrmacht was now 150–200km (93–124 miles) from the Soviet capital, but held its positions on the distant approaches to the city. Later, there were fierce battles for Rzhev and Vyazma, which lasted until the spring of 1943.

The Luftwaffe air raids on Moscow were not 'an air battle unprecedented in scale', as according to Russian historians and 'patriots'. Only the first three raids in July 1941 involved more than 100 bombers, the rest were carried out by small groups and single aircraft. The damage to the city and the casualties among the population were proportionate to the number of bombers. The losses suffered by German bomber aircraft from anti-aircraft artillery and Russian fighters over Moscow were minimal. The air defences of the main 'Red stronghold' were much weaker than those of London and other British cities.

This book describes only the first part of the air battle for Moscow. Between 1942 and 1944, many interesting events took place in this region: numerous pursuits of Russian fighters of Luftwaffe long-range reconnaissance aircraft, flights of high-level Ju 86 P/R aircraft, night reconnaissance aircraft, secret Ar 232s, Go 145 and He 46 light night bombers and others. But that is the subject for another book.

Appendices

1. Aircraft in the 6th IAK PVO in June–December 1941 by Type

	30 Jun	31 Jul	31 Aug	30 Sep	31 Oct	30 Nov	31 Dec
I-15	–	–	2	–	–	–	–
I-153	63	67	100	43	31	28	13
I-16	149	168	146	154	140	94	95
MiG-3	93	127	148	177	220	212	191
YaK-1	82	91	45	36	24	60	55
LaGG-3	–	37	38	29	23	33	73
Pe-3	–	–	–	20	25	31	27
P-40	–	–	–	–	12	11	20
Hurricane	–	–	–	–	–	10	19
Total	387	495	479	459	475	479	493

2. Losses of Aircraft by I./KG 28 in the Moscow Air Defence Zone, July–December 1941

Aircraft	Squadron	Date	Cause of Loss
He 111 H-5 W. Nr. 3800	2	22/23 Jul	Damaged by flak, crash-landing in own territory
He 111 H-5 W. Nr. 3680 '1T+LL'	3	29/30 Sep	Damaged by flak, crash-landing in Soviet territory
He 111 H-5 W. Nr. 3986 '1T+EL'	3	2 Oct	Shot down by a fighter

Aircraft	Squadron	Date	Cause of Loss
He 111 H-5 W. Nr. 3643 '1T+DK'	2	3 Oct	?
He 111 H-6 W. Nr. 4230 '1T+CK'	2	4/5 Oct	?
He 111 H-6 W. Nr. 4445 '1T+LK'	2	4/5 Oct	?
He 111 H-6 W. Nr. 4482	2	5 Oct	The damaged aircraft made an emergency landing in own territory
He 111 H-6 W. Nr. 4438 '1T+NL'	3	9 Oct	?
He 111 H-6 W. Nr. 4409 '1T+?K'	2	11 Nov	Missing
He 111 H-6 W. Nr. 4543	?	13 Nov	Crashed on landing
He 111 H-4 W. Nr. 6966	?	18 Nov	Probably shot down by a fighter near Serpukhov
He 111 H-6 W. Nr. 4400 '1T+FK'	2	21 Nov	Shot down near Kashira
He 111 H-5 W. Nr. 3960 '1T+GK'	2	27 Nov	Shot down by a fighter North-West of Moscow
He 111 H-6 W. Nr. 4403 '1T+DK'	2	29 Nov	Missing in the Kashira area
He 111 H-6 W. Nr. 4479 '1T+KK'	2	4 Dec	Shot down by a fighter
He 111 H-5 W. Nr. 3815 '1T+CL'	3	10 Dec	Missing
He 111 H-6 W. Nr. 4573 '1T+LL'	3	13 Dec	Missing
He 111 H-6 W. Nr. 4412 '1T+HK'	2	15 Dec	Missing
He 111 H-6 W. Nr. 4575 '1T+MK'	2	15 Dec	Missing
He 111 H-6 W. Nr. 4408 '1T+FL'	3	16 Dec	Shot down by ground fire
He 111P-2 W. Nr. 2623	Stab.	17 Dev	Accident due to weather conditions
He 111 H-6 W. Nr. 4557	?	18 Dec	Shot down
Total: 22			

3. Losses of Aircraft by KGr. 100 'Wiking' in the Moscow Air Defence Zone, July–December 1941

Aircraft	Squadron	Date	Cause of Loss
He 111 H-3 W. Nr. 2029 '6N+MH'	1	10/11 Aug	Collision with a balloon
He 111 H-6 W. Nr. 4441 '6N+FH'	1	28 Sep	Damaged by fighter (ram), emergency landing in own territory
He 111 H-3 W. Nr. 3172 '6N+FL'	2	5/6 Oct	?
He 111 H-3 W. Nr. 4403	?	7 Oct	Shot down by ground fire
He 111 H-3 W. Nr. 6879	?	7 Oct	Shot down by ground fire
He 111 H-3 W. Nr. 6929	?	10/11 Oct	Damaged by air defences, emergency landing
He 111 H-3 W. Nr. 3207	3	11 Nov	Damaged by ground fire, destroyed in an emergency landing
Total: 6			

4. Losses of Aircraft by KG 3 'Blitz' in the Moscow Air Defence Zone, July 1941–January 1942

Aircraft	Squadron	Date	Cause of Loss
Do 17 Z-2 W. Nr. 3371 '5K+HT'	9	13 Jul	Shot down by a fighter
Do 17 Z-2 W. Nr. 3367 '5K+ET'	9	21/22 Jul	Shot down by a fighter
Ju 88 A-5 W. Nr. 5282	6	21/22 Jul	Damaged by air defences, crashed during an emergency landing
Ju 88 A-5	5	25/26 Jul	Damaged by anti-aircraft artillery, emergency landing
Ju 88 A-5 W. Nr. 6461	4	9/10 Aug	Missing
Ju 88 A-5 W. Nr. 3469	St.I	9/10 Aug	Crashed while returning to base

Aircraft	Squadron	Date	Cause of Loss
Ju 88 A-5 W. Nr. 6295	1	16/17 Aug	Damaged by air defences, crashed during an emergency landing
Do 17 Z W. Nr. 4231	9	31 Aug	Shot down by a fighter
Ju 88 A-4 W. Nr. 1200	4	9 Sep	Shot down by a fighter
Do 17 Z-2	9	2 Oct	Shot down
Do 17 Z-2	9	2 Oct	Shot down
Ju 88 A-4 W. Nr.1316	5	7 Oct	Shot down by air defences
Ju 88 A-5 W. Nr. 3409	3	15 Oct	Shot down by a fighter
Do 17 Z-2 W. Nr. 2627	8	22 Oct	Shot down
Ju 88 A-4 W. Nr. 1252	2	22 Oct	Shot down
Ju 88 A-4 W. Nr. 3574 '5K+CB'	St.I	23 Oct	?
Ju 88 A-4 W. Nr. 2563	I	23 Oct	?
Ju 88 A-5	II	6 Nov	Shot down by a fighter
Ju 88 A-4 W. Nr. 2566 '5K+BB'	St.II	25 Nov	Shot down by a fighter
Do 17 Z-2 W. Nr. 1200	10. (Croat)	1 Dec	Missing
Do 17 Z-2 W. Nr. 2666	10. (Croat)	1 Dec	Missing
Ju 88 A-4 W. Nr. 3578	5	1 Dec	Missing
Do 17 Z-2 W. Nr. 2904	9	2 Dec	Shot down by a fighter
Ju 88 A-4 W. Nr. 1368	St	9 Dec	Missing
Do 17 Z-3 W. Nr. 2633	9	10 Dec	Shot down by anti-aircraft artillery
Ju 88 A-4 W. Nr. 2605	4	14 Dec	Missing
Ju 88 A-4 W. Nr.1360 '5K+AC'	St.II	21 Dec	Missing
Ju 88 A-4 W. Nr. 1466	St.II	23 Dec	Missing
Do 17 Z-2 W. Nr. 2700	10. (Croat)	4 Jan	The damaged aircraft made an emergency landing in own territory
Ju 88 A-4 W. Nr. 2562 '5K+KP	5	16 Jan	Missing

Aircraft	Squadron	Date	Cause of Loss
Ju 88 A-4 W. Nr. 3564 '5K+CH'	5	16 Jan	Missing
Do 17 Z-3 W. Nr. 2529 '5K+BT'	10. (Croat)	19 Jan	Shot down by a fighter
Ju 88 A-4	?	30 Jan	?
Ju 88 A-4	?	30 Jan	?
Total: 33			

5. Losses of Luftwaffe Long-range Reconnaissance Aircraft in the Moscow Air Defence Zone, July 1941–April 1942

Aircraft	Squadron	Date	Cause of Loss
Ju 88 A-5(F) W. Nr. 0453 'F6+AO'	Erganzungstaffel (F)/122	25 Jul	Shot down by a fighter
Ju 88 A-5(F) W. Nr. 0285 'F6+AK'	2.(F)/122	25 Jul	Shot down by a fighter
Do 215 B-1 W. Nr. 0018 'L2+HS'	1.(F)/Ob.d.L.	7 Aug	Engine damage, emergency landing
Do 215 B-2 W. Nr. 0069 'T5+BC'	1.(F)/Ob.d.L.	7 Aug	Shot down by a fighter
Do 215 B-2 W. Nr. 0075 'T5+LC'	1.(F)/Ob.d.L.	11 August	Brought down by a fighter (ram)
Ju 88 A-5(F) W. Nr. 0309 'F6+FK'	2.(F)/122	16 Aug	Shot down by a fighter
Bf 110 C-5 W. Nr. 2447 '8M+CK'	2.(F)/33	20 Aug	Shot down by a fighter
Ju 88 D-1 W. Nr. 0587 '6M+DM'	4.(F)/11	9 Sep	Brought by a fighter (ram)
Ju 88 A-4 W. Nr. 1271 '8H+GH'	1.(F)/33	14 Sep	Brought by a fighter(ram)
Bf 110 E-2 W. Nr. 3810 'F6+PK'	2.(F)/122	24 Sep	Shot down by a fighter
Ju 88 D-2 W. Nr. 0826	1.(F)/22	29 Oct	Shot down by a fighter
Do 17 P W. Nr. 3591	2.(F)/11	21 Dec	Missing

Aircraft	Squadron	Date	Cause of Loss
Ju 88 D-1 W. Nr. 1133 '5F+BM'	4.(F)/14	6 Jan	Shot down by anti-aircraft artillery
Ju 88 D-1 W. Nr. 1485 '8H+GL'	4.(F)/11	16 Jan	Missing
Ju 88 E-1 W. Nr. 1239 '6M+AM'	4.(F)/14	17 Jan	Shot down by a fighter
Ju 88 D-1 W. Nr. 1199 '5F+FM'	4.(F)/14	28 Jan	Shot down by a fighter
Ju 88 D-1	4.(F)/11	30 Jan	Missing
Ju 88 D-5 W. Nr. 1719	4.(F)/14	8 Mar	The damaged fighter, and emergency
Do 17 M W. Nr. 2306	2.(F)/Nacht.	31 Mar	The damaged fighter, and emergency
Ju 88 D-1 W. Nr. 1419	1.(F)/Ob.d.L.	15 Apr	Shot down by a fighter
Total: 20			

6. Ivan Klimov-commander of the 6th IAK PVO

Klimov was born in 1904 in a peasant family. Before the Bolshevik revolution of 1917, this origin guaranteed a poor and difficult life for all. However, under the Soviet regime, the situation changed to the diametrically opposite. Children of peasants and workers had privileges.

In 1920 – 1926 Klimov worked as a Telegraph operator at the railway station Tula. At the age of 22, he began his service in the Red Army, deciding to become a pilot. After graduating from two aviation schools in 1938, Ivan Klimov was promoted to commander of the elite 27th IAP. Aviation regiment was based at the airport Klin and defended Moscow. During Stalin's repressions in the army and aviation many vacancies were released 'out of turn', they were filled by young fanatical Stalinists. In the air defense of Moscow gathered the best pilots with impeccable proletarian origin.

Stalin loved young pilots, perceived them as 'sons' and personally promoted through the ranks. 'Father' gave them titles and awards. However, mentally unstable pathological sadist could easily 'fall out of love' and execute his recent favorites for the slightest disobedience. Ivan Klimov was one of the fanatics who never objected to Stalin and worshipped him as a God. In February 1941, Klimov was appointed commander of the 24th aviation division, in June it was transformed into the 6th fighter air defense corps (6th air defense IAK). This unit was the first to receive fighters of 'new types' (Yak-1, LaGG-3 and MiG-3).

Despite the fanaticism and a large number of aircraft, the 6th IAK could not provide serious resistance to experienced Luftwaffe. German reconnaissance aircraft flew freely over Moscow, and the bombers caused her great destruction. But Klimov skillfully falsified documents and reports, telling Stalin about the continuous victories of 'Stalin's falcons' over the city. Klimov's headquarters reported on hundreds and thousands of enemy aircraft moving to Moscow, and always repeatedly overestimated the numbers of air victories. Despite the great destruction in the capital, Stalin believed Klimov's reports. In November 1941 he was appointed head of the entire air defense Department. Until the end of the war Klimov held high positions. August 21, 1944 he was awarded the title of Colonel general aviation (corresponds to Generaloberst in Luftwaffe).

False and fabricated reports signed by Klimov, and in modern times mislead Russian historians.

7. Portrait of a typical 'Stalin's Falcon'. Viktor Talalikhin

Talalikhin is the most famous air defense pilot in Moscow. He was born in 1918 in a family of workers, in his youth he worked at the Moscow meat processing plant. In that era, thousands of teenagers saw planes in the sky and dreamed of being in their cabins. The pilots were the main characters and ideals to follow. Victor quickly realized that his purpose-to be a pilot. In the USSR, it was the only social Elevator that allowed people from peasant and working families to make a successful career and become famous

throughout the country. To succeed in the plant required many years of hard work, and the peasants under Stalin were slaves without passports and rights.

Talalikhin's dream came true. In 1937, at the age of 19, he entered the Borisogleb military aviation school of pilots, where he received the rank of Junior lieutenant. During the Soviet-Finnish war Talalikhin has completed 47 sorties, on account of his group had 4 air victories. He was awarded the order 'Red Star'. During the war with Germany Victor Talalikhin served of the 177 IAP, defending Moscow. When the Luftwaffe air attacks began, the pilot flew many times on the job, but did not succeed. Russian 'night fighters' were different from 'daytime' only because fly by night. Devices, radar and radio stations on them were not. The pilots relied on the sharp eyes, the bright moon and the searchlight beams, and it does not always guarantee success.

On the night of August 7, Talalikhin suddenly saw the silhouette of a bomber and decided that such a chance should not be missed. After a short attack and exchange shots with side shooter He 111, 'Stalin's Falcon' has rammed the enemy. Bomber He 111 H-5 '1H+NR' of 7./KG 26 fell near the village of Kusnechiki. I-16 Talalikhina fell into the forest, and he landed on a parachute in the river Severka. It was the first incident of ramming at night on the Eastern front. The next day, the pilot was urgently awarded the title of Hero of the Soviet Union. Soviet propaganda took maximum advantage of Talalikhin's ramming exploit. 'The fascist vulture was struck by Stalin's Falcon,' the press wrote. In the first month of the war the Russian command didn't encourage ramming, believing that Russian aircraft are the best in the world. But after she suffered huge losses was the slogan 'bring down the enemy at any cost.' Talalikhin became a model of the red fanatic and one of the most famous heroes. On August 17, he made a speech to the residents of Moscow and vowed to protect the city from Luftwaffe.

After that, Talalikhin won another 4 air victories, but they are not confirmed by German information. October 27, the pilot died in the air battle West of Moscow. His I-16 was shot down in combat with the German Bf 109.

8. 6th IAK PVO

The 6th Fighter Aviation Corps was formed three days after the start of Operation 'Barbarossa'. It was intended specifically for the air defense of the Russian capital - Moscow. During the Second World War, it was the largest compound of Russian aviation. The 6th IAK was a  priority for the supply of fighter aircraft of the 'new types': LaGG-3, MiG-3 and YaK-1. Most of the pilots were members of the Bolshevik Party, that is the real 'Stalin's Falcons'. In the fall of 1941, the 6th IAK was the first in Russian aviation to start fighting on British and American aircraft — the Hurricane and the P-40 Tomahawk. In July 1941, there were about 400 fighters in the corps, and this number remained stable even during crises and defeats on other fronts. When the Wehrmacht approached Moscow, the situation of the Soviet Union was so desperate that the 6th IAK air defense fighters began to be used for strikes against ground targets and German tanks. And then air defense pilots collided with German fighters Bf 109 and Bf 110.

9. Hans Bätcher, the typical bomber pilot

Hans Georg Bätcher was born on January 13, 1913 in Fistenwalde to the family of an engineer. In childhood, he was fond of horse riding and technical creativity, during school holidays he worked as a turner at the factory. In his youth, Bätcher began to build models of aircraft, and then he had a dream – to become a pilot. In that era when planes conquered the sky, millions of young men had such a dream. And Bätcher was one of them. In 1935, he enrolled in the Luftwaffe and began training at a bomber school. Batcher's first flights were on a Do 23 bomber, on which most future *Kampfgeschwader* pilots were trained in air attacks.

During the Polish campaign in September 1939, Hans Bätcher flew in with I./KG 27 'Boelcke', using He 111 bombers. June 5, 1940, his plane was shot down over France by a Moran fighter. Bätcher was captured by a French, but after France capitulated he was released. He made no further operational flights until the summer of 1941, and on 1 July 1941 the 27-year-old pilot took part in a raid in a raid on England with KGr. 100. Soon his *Kampfgruppe* was transferred to the Eastern Front, where he was noted for his courage and composure, and his ability to get out of the most difficult situations. Batcher's first operation was with 'Clara Zetkin' – air raids on Moscow. Taking part in many raids on the city, Bätcher acted both as part of his group and alone, dropping high calibre bombs on important targets.

After the Moscow campaign, Bätcher participated in the battles for Sevastopol, Stalingrad, the Caucasus, and Operation Citadel. In 1942 - 1944, the pilot was many times involved in getting supplies through to German troops encircled by the Russians. During Operation 'Barbarossa', Hans Bätcher was the commander of the 1st *Staffel* KGr. 100 'Wiking'. In 1943, he became the commander of I./KG 100, then commanded I./KG 4 and III./KG 76. During the war, Bätcher undertook 658 sorties, the majority on the Eastern Front. In 1945, he made several air attacks in an Ar 234 B jet bomber.

10. KGr. 100 'Wiking'

Kampfgruppe 100 'Wiking' was activated in 1940. It was the first group of pathfinders (*Zielfinder*) in the Luftwaffe. The task of these aircraft was to create conditions for accurate night bombing. To do this, the bombers were fitted with the secret X-Geraet equipment. The pathfinders could receive radio signals sent by ground radio transmitters towards a target, enabling the pathfinders to accurately reach the target, even in zero visibility conditions, by following the intersection of the radio beams. Upon arrival at the target area, the pathfinders would illuminate the target with flares and incendiary bombs, so that when the rest of the bombers arrived they could readily identify where they were to drop their bombs.

During Operation 'Clara Zetkin' KGr. 100 functioned in accordance with its purpose, as pathfinders. But in many aerial attacks, the group performed the duties of ordinary bombers, dropping powerful high-explosive bombs on

strategic objects and important targets on Russian territory. The 'Wikings' were the elite of the Luftwaffe, only the best pilots fought in this division. Their losses in air battles were minimal, but the damage they caused to the Russians were is enormous.

11. MiG-3

The MiG-3 fighter was created in 1940. In Soviet aviation, it was considered a high-altitude interceptor and was intended for air combat at an altitude of 5,000 to 9,000 metres. The aircraft was equipped with a high-altitude engine AM-35A with a capacity of 1200 PS. The armament of the fighter included a 12.7mm machine gun Berezin UB mounted on the engine and two 7.62mm machine gun ShKAS. In 1941, the MiG-3 was actively used on different parts of the front. However, air battles on the Eastern Front often took place at altitudes from 300 to 1000 metres, in conditions of bad weather. Under these conditions, the MiG-3 was ineffective. The main drawback of the aircraft was its very small range. It could fly for only 45 - 50 minutes, so many pilots did not have enough fuel for the return flight which often led to disasters. Despite these shortcomings, the Russians actively used the MiG-3 in air defence. It was

the only aircraft capable of intercepting Luftwaffe reconnaissance aircraft at high altitude.

12. Wolfram von Richthofen – The Führer's 'Nazgûl'

Baron Wolfram von Richthofen (born 10 October 1895 at Gut-Berzdorf in Silesia, died 12 July, 1945, bad Ischl, Austria) – German warlord Generalfeldmarschall der Luftwaffe, General-field Marshal of aviation (1943).

The combination of innate aggressiveness and the influence of the social environment of Prussian officers made young Wolfram an ardent fanatic, ready to faithfully serve any regime that would give him an opportunity to realize the only passion in his life – the desire to fight and destroy. This obsession was clearly demonstrated from the beginning of his career in the Great War. Interest in advanced military technology led him out of the cavalry to the newest branch of the military. Starting to serve in aviation under the direction of his famous relative Manfred (the 'Red Baron'), he showed phenomenal courage and willingness to sacrifice himself for victory over the enemies, of which the Germans always had many.

The most severe test in the life of Richthofen was the demilitarization of Germany as a result of defeat in the war. But he compensated for dismissal from the army by diligent study. In 1920-1923 he was educated at the higher technical school in Hannover; on 10 May 1924 he received an engineering

diploma engineer, and since 1929 awarded a doctorate of engineering. The efforts of the young fanatic were appreciated, and he was returned to military service.

The coming to power of the Nazis gave Richthofen unlimited opportunities for the implementation of his characteristic bloodthirsty inclinations. He is obsessed with a single idea – to kill as many enemies with the latest and technically advanced weapons – aviation. His fanaticism literally had no boundaries, which ads one to suspect a psychopathic personality disorder.

To achieve his goals, Richthofen was ready for anything. His zeal and fanaticism were received favourably by Hitler, who made him a likeness of 'Nazgûl' (Ghost king, adjutant Lord of Darkness); a devoted servant in his implementation of the bloody Nazi plans. Richthofen fully lived up to the expectations of his ruthless patron, causing death and total destruction in all sectors. Ascetic in everyday life, he employed all his strength and the forces entrusted to him in the Luftwaffe to cause maximum damage to the 'enemies of Germany'. In just 10 years, Richthofen rose from an unknown major in the Reichswehr to generalfeldmarschall of the Luftwaffe. At 47, he was the youngest of Hitler's generalfeldmarschalls but looked much older. It can be said that von Runstedt, though 20 years his senior, looked cheerful and polished in comparison.

During the battle of Moscow, Richthofen commanded Luftkorps VIII and tried his best to provide massive support to the advancing troops. He directed terrorist raids on Moscow but due to the general weakening of the Luftwaffe he was unable to fully realize his bloodthirsty tendencies. During the Russian counteroffensive Richthofen tried to squeeze all opportunities out of the entrusted units; even light aircraft, such as Fi 156 Storch, were used as bombers on his orders. However, the task was not fully accomplished, and the Luftwaffe suffered serious losses.

By the end of Richthofen's military service and the end of the Second World War, dozens of towns and cities, along with hundreds of villages, had been wiped out. Thousands of civilians had been killed. Hundreds of young German pilots, deceived by Richthofen and abandoned for the slaughter, had either found their graves or gone missing on various fronts of the bloody world war, including his only son. Richthofen himself went insane and died from progressive brain disease in captivity in July 1945.

13. He 111 H-5

The Heinkel bomber He 111 was introduced in 1936 as a civil aircraft. The plane officially so designated under the pressure of the Treaty of Versailles, which forbade Germany to have combat aircraft. When the masks were dropped, the He 111 turned into a deadly fighter that destroyed cities, railroads, factories and plants. The aircraft was actively used to support the offensive during the blitzkrieg. Towards the of 1940, the He 111 ad become the main force with which Hitler tried to break the resistance of Britain.

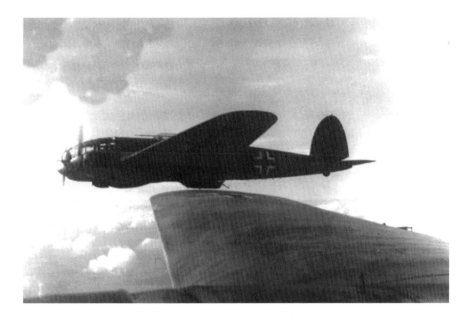

This bomber as updated many times, and his combat power gradually increased. During operation 'Clara Zetkin' most *Kampfgeschwaderen* were equipped with a modification He 111 H-5. The main feature of the design was the Jumo 211 D-1 with a capacity of 1200 PS and no internal compartments for bombs. All bombs were suspended under the fuselage and wings. He 111 H-5 could deliver 2500kg of bombs over a distance of 1000 kilometres. The plane had good protection from fighters: 4 MG 15 machine guns and 1 MG / FF gun.

Sources

Archives

Central Archives of the Ministry of Defence of the Russian Federation (TSAMO RF).

TSAMO RF Foundation 20530. Inventory 1. Case 21.
TSAMO RF Foundation 20530. Inventory 1. Case 96.
TSAMO RF Foundation 20530. Inventory 1. Case 98.
TSAMO RF Foundation 20530. Inventory 1. Case 68.
TSAMO RF Foundation 13609. Inventory 20354. Case 519.
TSAMO RF Foundation 13608. Inventory 20395. Case 59.
TSAMO RF Foundation 13609. Inventory 20354. Case 474.
TSAMO RF Foundation 13609. Inventory 20354. Case 509.
TSAMO RF Foundation 13609. Inventory 20354. Case 307.
TSAMO RF Foundation 13608. Inventory 20395. Case 59.
TSAMO RF Foundation 13609. Inventory 20354. Case 236.
TSAMO RF Foundation 13790. Inventory 0020191. Case 0006.
TSAMO RF Foundation 13731. Inventory 0020134. Case 0007.
TSAMO RF Foundation 13731. Inventory 0020134. Case 0009.
TSAMO RF Foundation 13609. Inventory 20354. Case 628.
TSAMO RF Foundation 16. Inventory 1071ss. Case 3545.
TSAMO RF Foundation 500. Inventory 12462. Case 548.
TSAMO RF Foundation 13609. Inventory 20354. Case 21.

Published Sources

Aders, G., and Held, W., *Jagdgeschwader 51 'Molders'. Eine Chronik. Berichte. Erlebnisse. Dokumente* (Stuttgart: Motorbuch Verlag, 1993).
Balke, U., *KG 100. History* (Stuttgart: Motorbuch Verlag, 1981).

SOURCES

Battle of Moscow. Chronicle, facts, people: in two books (Moscow: OLMA-press, 2002).

Bykov, M. Yu., *Aces of the Great Patriotic War. The Most Successful Pilots 1941 – 1945: a Handbook* (Moscow: Yauza, 2007).

Dierich, W., *Kampfgeschwader 55 'Greif'* (Stuttgart: Motorbuch Verlag, 1994).

Gundelach, K., *Kampfgeschwader 'General Wever' 4* (Stuttgart: Motorbuch Verlag, 1978).

Khazanov, D.B., *Unknown Battle in the Skies of Moscow. 1941 – 1944* (Moscow: Technique of Youth, 2006).

Khazanov, D.B., Air Defence Forces for the Defence of Moscow. 1941–1945; the 75th anniversary of the Soviet counteroffensive (Moscow: 'Fifth Rome', 2017).

Kiehl, H., *Kampfgeschwader 'Legion Condor' 53* (Stuttgart: Motorbuch Verlag, 1996).

War. People. Victory, 1941-1945. Articles. Essays. Memories: Vol. 1 (Moscow: Politizdat, 1984).

Nauroth, H., *Stukageschwader 2 'Immelmann'* (Preussich Oldendorf: Verlag K.W. Schutz, 1988).

Index